FDI
&
Corporate Governance

FDI
&
Corporate Governance

Dr. N.N. Sharma

Gaurav Book Centre Pvt. Ltd.

Published by
Gaurav Book Centre Pvt. Ltd.
4832/2, Prahlad Lane, S-207
Ansari Road, Daryaganj, New Delhi-110 002
Mob. 09873096176
Email.gauravbookcentre@gmail.com

ISBN: 978-93-83316-30-4

First Edition: **2019**

Price: 1295/-

Laser Typesetting:
JEE-VEE Graphics # 09911902109

Printed by:
Balaji Printers, Delhi

"Dedicated
To
*my loving **FATHER**"*

Preface

Foreign investment plays an important role in the long-term economic development of a country by augmenting availability of capital, enhancing competitiveness of the domestic economy through transfer of technology, strengthening infrastructure, raising productivity, generating new employment opportunities and boosting exports. Foreign investment, therefore, is a strategic instrument of development policy.

In the wake of economic liberalisation policy initiated in 1991, the Government of India has taken several measures to encourage foreign investment, both direct and portfolio, in almost all sectors of the economy. However, the emphasis has been on foreign direct investment (FDI) inflows in the development of infrastructure, technological upgradation of industry and setting up Special Economic Zones (SEZs).

India has consistently been classified as one of the most attractive investment destinations by reputed international rating organisations. With a vast reservoir of skilled and cost-effective manpower, India offers immense opportunities for business process outsourcing (BPO), knowledge process outsourcing (KPO) and engineering process outsourcing (EPO).

In spite of the fact that India is strategically located with access to a vast domestic and South Asian market, its share in world's total flow of direct/portfolio investment to developing countries is dismally low. China, with GDP size 2.2 times of India, is able to attract 20 times the FDI inflow to India. Similarly, Singapore, Indonesia, Philippines, and Thailand also attract greater amounts of foreign investment than India. The current world scenario calls for further liberalisation of norms for foreign investment in India.

The present book deals with almost all aspects of foreign investment in India. It particularly focuses on current policies and procedures for foreign direct investment as well as foreign portfolio investment. Foreign investment policies of other countries have also been highlighted to make suitable comparisons with India's policies in order to underscore the measures that are needed to attract higher levels of foreign capital and technology

Foreign direct investment (FDI) has grown dramatically as a major form of international capital transfer over the past decade. Between 1980 and 1990, world flows of FDI-defined as cross-border expenditures to acquire or expand corporate control of productive assets-have approximately tripled. FDI has become a major form of net international borrowing for Japan and the United States (the world's largest international lender and borrower, respectively).

Foreign Direct investment has grown even more rapidly of late within Europe. To what extent is this sudden worldwide surge in FDI explained by traditional theories? These theories predict the scale and scope of multinational enterprises by looking to differences in competitive advantage, across firms or countries, that might lead to the extension of corporate control across borders.

Traditional theories are very useful for explaining basic long-term patterns of FDI. For example, they help understand the behavior of U.S. firms during the post-World War I1 period (the experience on which these theories were honed). At that time, advanced U.S. firms were superior in technology and well established in foreign markets. U.S. firms tended to move overseas to retain competitive access (or to preempt competitors' access) to those markets and, in the process, met with relatively little competition. These theories also help us understand why the tide of U.S. FDI flows has slowly turned. The evolution of the United States from a home for domestically.

Corporate governance is part of an economy's system which has today become the most important mechanism for resource allocation. It is affected by capital market, block holders, institutional investors, proxy wars, company law and capital market regulations, and many other macro-economic as well as political factors. Historical evolution of corporate governance naturally has a bearing on current developments. This book is an attempt to weave these factors together coherently.

Much of the concerned literature revolves around the agency problem, while in developing countries expropriation of small shareholders is the governance problem. However, shareholder activism is not likely to resolve the issue. Many more measures, from audit committees of the board, rigorous disclosures, exercise of voting rights by institutional investors, strict monitoring by capital market regulator to takeover bids are required to ensure corporate accountability.

The term 'corporate governance'raises a debate: is it an analogy or just a metaphor? Could it be considered a discipline on its own or is it a part of business ethics? This is a question of etymology rather than of corporate Iegal ease. Pundits of different disciplines, like economics, management, law and political science, considered the corporate a social mechanism necessary to carry out the day-to-day activities of life. However, the statement might not be

accepted by traditionalists who consider the corporate simply as a vehicle of investment. Vlfl Gossett, Vice—President in General Council of the Ford Motor Company, once said 'The modern corporation is a social and economic institution that touches every aspect of our lives; in many ways it is an institutionalized expression of our way of life. During the past 50 years industry in corporate form has moved from the periphery to the very centre of our social and economic existence. Indeed it is not inaccurate to say that we live in a corporate society'. This book, aims to provide the reader with a quick overview of the subject. It explains the need for corporate governance. The book records the perceptions of different authors across the country with the aim of giving the reader as comprehensive a picture as possible.

Corporate governance is part of an economy's system which has today become the most important mechanism for resource allocation. It is affected by capital market, block holders, institutional investors, proxy wars, company law and capital market regulations, and many other macro-economic as well as political factors. Historical evolution of corporate governance naturally has a bearing on current developments.

This book is an attempt to weave these factors together coherently. Much of the concerned literature revolves around the agency problem, while in developing countries expropriation of small shareholders is the governance problem. Editors are feeling very happy to bring this book on the occasion of 'ICSSR sponsored National Seminar on Economic reforms in India' at Dharamshala, Himachal Pradesh.

This book is a collection of assorted researchers that addresses a large vista of FDI & Corporate governance related issues. The research articles are all, in their own part, notable scholary contributions documenting diverse aspects and studies related to the FDI & Corporate Governance. This book offers an inclusive glance into issues related with the status of FDI & Corporate Governance. The FDI & Corporate Governance is well on its way to becoming one of the most powerful growth engines in coming time, thus these research studies are relevant for a number of stakeholders like Governments, students etc. This book seeks to fulfil the needs of planning for the Industry.

Editor acknowledge the valuable research of the contributors and believe that this publication is a significant contribution towards future development and planning purposes. Editors sincerely believe in the standards of academic integrity and highest levels of scholastic conduct, thus declare that the respective author would be responsible for any kind of plagiarism found in his contribution.

Dr. N.N. Sharma

Dean

Himachal Pradesh Technical University

Contents

Impact of Multi Brand FDI in Retail Sector of India

Prof. (Dr.) Kulwant Singh Pathania

Prof. (Dr.) Kulwant Singh Pathania, Faculty of Commerce and Management Studies H.P University, Shimla -171005.

Dharmender Kumar

Dharmender Kumar, Research Scholar, Faculty of Commerce and Management Studies, H.P University, Shimla-171005.

Abstract

This paper discussed impact of Multi Brand FDI in Retail sector in India. India as a booming economy has always had a mystic luring effect on the foreigners. India has been placed at first position in the category of countries with the best opportunity for investment in the Retail Sector by a survey of A.T. Kearney's 2005 on Global Retail Development. The increasing disposable incomes among the Indian middle class and increasing young population have been cited as the main reasons for such attractive optimism. Foreign investors are also very enthusiastic to invest in India's Retail Sector. At present India has allowed FDI in multi-brand retail up to 51 percent and in single brand retail up to 100 percent. This paper examines consumers' attitudes and perceptions towards FDI in multi-brand retailing in India. For measuring the response of consumers' towards FDI in multi brand retailing in India, a questionnaire has been developed and a survey was conducted of 100 respondents of state capital region of Himachal Pradesh across a variety of consumers and rewarded their response towards the incoming of FDI in multi-brand retail. A number of statistical tools and techniques namely Likert scale, cross tab analysis and Chi-square test has been used to analyze the response obtained and to arrive at a meaningful conclusion. The overall results signifies that a majority of the population believes that FDI in multi brand retailing in India will bring numerous benefits for consumers, farmers and help generating employment opportunities. At the same times consumers perceives several threats of multi brand retailing including loss of business of small vendors. Therefore it has been found that people are apprehensive about whether the overall economy would be benefitted after the coming of FDI in multi brand retail in India. This Research Paper focuses on whether this policy will be beneficial for the Indian Economy as a whole or not.

Introduction

Foreign Direct Investment plays an important role in the development process of a country's economy. India has been able to attract significant amount of Foreign Direct Investment, especially after the liberalization and is still continuing to explore opportunities in FDI inflows. This has gradually led to the advent of FDI in the retail sector in India which has positively impacted the retail and ancillary industries such as supply chain, manufacturing and agriculture. The recent liberalization of the FDI retail policy has come as a major advantage to foreign retailers for those who are looking to set up or expand operations in the country. India has further decided to relax sourcing and investment rules for the retail sector in a renewed attempt to attract foreign supermarket chains such as Wal-Mart Stores and Tesco. Amidst lot of political controversies, the government decided to permit 51 percent FDI in multi-brand retail trade and raised foreign direct investment (FDI) in single-brand to 100 per cent in September 2012 subject to approvals by the states. Opening up of FDI in multi brand is expected to bring benefits like employment opportunities, organized retail stores, availability of quality products at a better price etc. There are various viewpoints regarding the impacts it will have on the retail sector in specific and the Indian economy in general, but the decision is a big step in the direction of strengthening organized retail in the country.

This policy can take India's consumerism to a new growth route as it is likely to result in increase in investments and growth in Indian retail sector, which is ranked amongst the top retail destinations in the world. It is also expected that FDI in multi brand retail will address the concerns of the foreign investors who have till date tried to understand the nuances of the FDI policy related to multi brand retail. Different stakeholders have different opinions based on their perception of the likely impact of FDI in MBRT in India on their interests. Though foreign players are already operating in the Indian market as cash and carry and single brand retail formats, present controversy centers on outcome of FDI in multi-brand retailing. Against this background, it becomes very important to examine the highly debated decision that has allowed foreign capital in multi-brand retailing and its likely impact on the sensitive issues that might have an implication on the different stakeholders of the society. As it has been widely acknowledged by many parties that consumers will be benefited by price reduction and treated with wide choice of products under one roof which in turn can lead to greater output and domestic consumption, the study aims to examine the perception of consumers with regard to Impact FDI in Multi Brand Retailing in India as they are the ones who will be affected or benefited by this decision.

Numerous studies have been carried out to analyse the impact and benefits of FDI in Multi brand Retailing. Joshi Deepak (2012) carried out an exploratory research to find out the perception of the unorganized retailers in business capital of Uttarakhand with respect to FDI in MBRT and has found out that correlation of the various responses led to a conclusion that the source of information was also a factor of voicing against the FDI and the influence of Education level was quite evident.

Baskaran Kamala Devi (2012) in her study "FDI in India's Multi Brand Retail -Boon or Bane" explores the myths and realities of the global giants' entry to India and studies the status of organized food retailing in India with SWOT Analysis and highlights on farmer's issues towards FDI in multi brand retailing.

Khan A.Q. and Siddiqui Ahmad Taufeeque (2011) studied the impact of FDI on Indian economy and a comparison with China & USA.

The paper has set strategies to deal with the issues & problems in attracting FDI for promotion & growth of international trade. The double log model has been used to find elasticity between different factors in this paper. They also highlight the impact of FDI on employment. As a common consensus cannot be reached from the above review of past studies, it becomes vital to study this topic and this study aims to bring more light to the topic under investigation.

Objectives of the Study

- To find out the status of Multi Brand FDI in Retail Sector of India.
- To evaluate the policy that opened up Foreign Direct Investment (FDI) in Multi-Brand Retail Trade (MBRT) in India.
- To analyse the implications and consequences emerged with the introduction of FDI in Multi-Brand Retailing in India.
- To examine the perceptions of consumers about the impact of FDI into Multi- Brand Retailing on the basis of education background.

Hypotheses of the Study

- Ho- The Null Hypothesis assumes that there is no significant relationship between Education Levels and the Consumers' perceived value towards FDI in Multi-Brand Retailing in India.
- Ha- The Alternative Hypothesis accepts that there is significant relationship between Education Levels and the Consumers' perceived value towards FDI in Multi- Brand Retailing in India.

Materials and Methods

This study aims to examine the current FDI policy with regard to Foreign Direct Investment (FDI) in Multi-Brand Retailing in India and also to analyse the perceived value of consumers with respect to various factors. The methodology of the study is Convenient sampling method was adopted for administering the questionnaires to measure the perceptions of 100 consumers among the age groups (20-30, 30- 40 and 40&above) was collected from Shimla City state capital region of Himachal Pradesh. However, the data was gathered only from consumers who had awareness about the concept of FDI in Multi brand retailing in India as the aim of the study was not to explore the awareness of FDI but to measure the perception of the consumers with regard to the same.

This study has been carried out with the help of both secondary and primary sources of data in order to conduct a quantitative analysis. The secondary data pertaining to the study has been gathered from various secondary sources including peer reviewed journals, magazines, news papers, government reports and other published data to understand the policy, its impact and likely benefits.

The primary data has been gathered with the help of a survey from State capital region of Himachal Pradesh. A chi-square analysis has been made to analyze the data collected and to determine the extent of relationship among the variables. Then the Cramer's Value has been computed to find out the strength of association among the levels of the row and column variables.

Results and Discussions.

Status of FDI in Multi Brand Retail

Foreign direct investment (FDI) or foreign investment refers to long term participation by country A into country B. It usually involves participation in management, joint-venture, transfer of technology and expertise. FDI is a result of receptive attitude of governments to investment inflows, the process of privatization, and the growing interdependence of the world economy. Investing in general is beneficial for countries; foreign direct investment allows companies to expand their reach across the globe. FDI can be done in two ways they are inward foreign direct investment and outward foreign direct investment. Inward FDI is when a foreign country invests in another country, while outward FDI deals with a company buying shares in a foreign country. These terms are usually used depending on the country in which the FDI is either entering or exiting. We have to discussed argument in favour and against Foreign direct investment as a form of investment has need to be understood very carefully. Following are some points which are in the favor of FDI are:

- Help in economic development of the country in which invested.
- Help in creating jobs and increases employment.
- Resource transfer, countries are able to learn newer forms of technologies and skills.
- Increase in productivity due to newer equipment.

When one country is investing in another country they have need to understand the laws which apply to foreign direct investment, following are some argument which are against of FDI:

- Exchange rates increasing in one and reducing in the other.
- Capital intensive from the investor's point of view.
- FDI rules might harm the investing country, at times the percentage of investment rate might be less.
- Investment in certain areas is banned in foreign markets.

Company's must understand the market it is entering, at times it might be beneficial and times risky, the merits and demerits need to be kept in mind while entering a foreign market. Companies must understand the laws of the country before investing.

FDI norms in Multi Brand Retail Trade (MBRT)

FDI in Multi Brand retail implies that a retail store with a foreign investment can sell multiple brands under one roof. When the government decided to allow 51 per cent FDI in multi-brand retailing and 100 per cent FDI in single-brand retailing, though subject to certain conditions, this was considered as a long-awaited advantage to large international retailers who had been eagerly waiting to tap into the estimated US$ 750 Indian retail market. Almost year later, no global retailer has moved so far to file applications with the Foreign Investment Promotion Board (FIPB). No foreign investment has taken place in the sector so far. This attitude of the foreign retailers is also largely the result of earlier policy confusions and global retailers like Walmart, Tesco and Carrefour demanded further clarifications in the policy. So the government clarified the policy and took safer measures by allowing FDI in multi-brand retail only in those Indian cities with a population of one million or more as per the 2011 census, covering an area of 10 kms around the limits of that city. This automatically restricts the number of cities to 53 where it can be implemented. Only 10 states and UTs have so far conveyed to the Centre their agreement to open FDI in the multi-brand retail. The retail trading in any form by means of e-commerce has been made non-permissible for companies with FDI in multi-brand retailing.

The policy also ensures that there should be a minimum investment of US $ 100 million by the foreign investor and 50 per cent investment shall be allowed through the government route and they need to invest half of the funds in back-end infrastructure development within three years, where back-end infrastructure will include capital expenditure on all activities, excluding that on front-end units. FDI in multi-brand retail must also domestically outsource 30 per cent of the finished products sold in the market. This procurement clause ensures that domestic industry is not adversely impacted by the FDI inflows but stand to benefit from sales. If we look at the domestic front with regard to the above policy framework, lot of debate has been going on. According to the majority of the opponents; some of the likely impacts of the policy are as follows:

- The policy will affect the small retailers (Kirana shops).
- Millions of jobs will be lost.

Implications and Consequences emerged with the introduction of FDI in Multi-Brand Retailing in India: entities like Walmart, with deep pockets, will take over large segments of the retail sector. In our investigation about the likely impact, we have come to the conclusion that the issues that are feared to emerge with the introduction of FDI in MBRT are only a misconception. The policy is only an enabling policy and it is up to the State Governments to take their own decisions with regard to implementation of the policy. Retail is a booming sector and as indicated in the policy, it can be seen that FDI in multi-brand retail can be set up in those Indian cities that has a population of one million or more as per the census 2011, covering an area of 10 kms around the limits of that city. Again, if we take the example of Shimla, there is no possibility of big foreign entity being hilly set up of state and there is no land easily approachable and due to high price and lack of enough availability of land. Hence it would become an uneconomical venture. There is also no empirical data to suggest that small retail stores would vanish. The second proposition which claims millions will be out of a job, is equally baseless. In fact, more jobs will be created as it is mandatory in the FDI policy 2013, that 50 per cent of any investment over a $100 million would be in the backend infrastructure. So investments will be made at the back-end of retail and more supply chains will be established. This will also eliminate agents who survive merely on trading and pave way for more jobs. Lastly, the argument that it would destroy the retail sector as it will take over our retail is not accepted because it is Indian retail which is going to tie up with FDI in multi-brand retail. The local retailers who already are aware of the fine distinctions of our market conditions will have enough domestic demand to cater to consumers` needs. From the above discussion, it is evident that the consequences that are feared to emerge are only a falsehood.

Perception of Consumers about the Impact of FDI on Multi Brand Retail.

Table 1.1 shows the cumulative percentages of the responses on a five point likert scale for the seven statements that were administered on the respondents. As the aim of the study is also to test the association between education and perceptions of the respondents, it becomes imperative to find out the education levels of the respondents.

The detailed descriptive figures of table 1 which breaks down the figures in to our two participant categories based on education level (Below graduation and Graduation and above Graduation) along with the cumulative percentages of the respective statement's level of agreement, disagreement and neither agreement nor disagreement respondents felt towards each statement that was posed. The study was carried out on a sample of 100 respondents out of which 59 were male respondents and 41 were female respondents. Next for analysis purpose, the cumulative percentages of the responses as shown in 2.1, the degree of agreement and disagreement were collapsed by combining the upper and lower categories into a 3 level "Agree/Neither/Disagree" breakdown. The collapsed cumulative percentages are presented below.

Table 1: Cumulative percentages of Consumers' Perceptions

Sr. No.	IVs*	Statements	% of Disagreement	% of Neither Agree nor Disagree	% of Agreement
1	X1	I am not in favour of FDI in multi brand retail in India	49	30	21
2	X2	FDI in Multi brand retailing will give rise to big arrogant international retailers.	32	42	26
3	X3	FDI in Multi brand retailing will offer wide choice of products under one roof	9	18	73
4	X4	Customers will be forced to buy products at high rates	33	46	21
5	X5	FDI in multi brand retailing would create lot of job opportunities	15	22	63
6	X6	Average.expenditure of the customers would decrease because of big retailers	27	56	17
7	X7	FDI in Multi brand retailing would be a threat to small retailers	35	29	36

Source: Compiled from Primary Data

*IVs-Independent Variable Factors

Table 1 given above, shows that respondents bend forward either positively or negatively in terms of agreement towards statement no 1, 3 & 5 and majority of the respondents neither agreed nor disagreed for statements 2, 4 &6. It can also be observed from the results presented above that the highest degree of agreement was for statement 3.This indicates that majority of the respondents (53 per cent) feel that FDI in Multi brand retailing will offer wide choice of products under one roof. This also reflects their level of awareness. Availability of wide variety of products could also possibly be one important reason why 49 per cent of respondents have favored FDI in multi-brand retail in India. Almost 30 per cent of respondents have remained neutral in this regard. It can also be seen that 42 per cent of the respondents have neither agreed nor disagreed for statement 2 which says that FDI in Multi brand retailing will give rise to big arrogant international retailers. This is an important finding for the policy makers and the retailers, because these groups of customers are watching the strategies adopted by the players. Almost 46 per cent of respondents have neither agreed nor disagreed for the statement

'Customers will be forced to buy products at high rates'. This indicates that majority of respondents feel that big retailers can't assure the customers of products at lower prices. This could be due to the high establishment costs and recurring expenditure. It can also be interpreted that as Indian consumers are quite price-sensitive, they will continue to shop in traditional outlets. Majority of the respondents (63 per cent) are of the opinion that FDI in multi brand retailing would create lot of job opportunities. This is an important observation because this issue has been one of the most feared consequences of this policy and the primary data result proves that the consumers feel that it will only create more job opportunities. When an attempt was made to find out whether average expenditure of the customers would decrease because of big retailers, majority of the respondents (56 per cent) remained neutral. This reflects clearly that they were actually not sure about this or may be not willing to comment about the said statement. The fear that the emergence of multi brand retailing will be a threat to small retailers is not fully founded in my survey. There is no empirical evidence to prove that the entry of big multinational retailers would affect the small retailers as 29 per cent of the respondents chose to be neutral in this regard. This also indicates the respondents are still not clear about FDI in MBR's impact on small retailers and they are divided in their opinions.

Table 2: Consumers' Perceived Effects of Education level against FDI in Multi brand Retailing

Sr. No.	IVs*	Statements	% of Disagreement		% of Neither Agree nor Disagree		% of Agreement	
			BG ***	G & A **	BG ***	G & A **	BG ***	G & A **
1	X1	I am not in favour of FDI in multi brand retail in India	11	38	8	22	13	8
2	X2	FDI in Multi brand retailing will give rise to big arrogant international retailers.	3	29	8	34	21	5
3	X3	FDI in Multi brand retailing will offer wide choice of products under one roof	7	2	5	13	20	53
4	X4	Customers will be forced to buy products at high rates	7	26	9	37	16	5
5	X5	FDI in multi brand retailing would create lot of job opportunities	14	1	13	9	5	58
6	X6	Average expenditure of the customers would decrease because of big retailers	14	13	13	43	5	12
7	X7	FDI in Multi brand retailing would be a threat to small retailers	1	34	3	26	28	8

Source: Compiled from Primary Data

*IVs-Independent Variable Factors

*** Indicate - Below Graduate & ** Indicate - Graduate and above.

The results shows that 32 per cent of the respondents were below the graduation level and 68 per cent were above the graduation level. Further, the observations that were made clearly shows that majority of the respondents whose educational level is below graduation have inclined negatively towards opening up of FDI in Multi brand retailing in India. A majority of below graduate of 14 respondents out of the total 32 respondents are of the opinion that FDI in multi brand retailing would not create lot of job opportunities. This could be due to fear of loss of jobs. They also felt that the average expenditure of the customers would not decrease because of big retailers. A majority of the respondents who have not graduated have expressed similar view points for statements 2, 3 & 4. They have also expressed their fear by strongly agreeing (28 out of 32) that FDI in Multi brand retailing would be a threat to small retailers. In difference, the educated category has positively of a mind towards FDI (53 out of 68) due to availability of wide variety of products under one roof. The reasons could be convenience, time factor and quality products. This group is also of the opinion (58 out of 62) that there is a possibility of lot of job opportunity. Thus the results indicate clearly that the educated respondents have of a mind positively and the respondents below graduation level have tending negatively towards FDI in multi brand retailing in India.

Statistical Results of Perceived effects of Education level against favoring of FDI in Multi brand Retailing

Table 3: Computation of Chi Square

S. No.	Education Level	Below Graduation	Graduation and Above
1	% of Disagreement	11	38
2	% of Neither Agree nor Disagree	8	32
3	% of Disagreement	13	8
Chi-Square	Df	P	
11.08	2	5.991	
Cramer's Value	0.3329		

Source: Field Survey 2014.

In order to statistically test the hypothesis and to find out the relationship between education levels and perceptions of consumers with reference to the statement, 'I am not in favour of FDI in multi-brand retail in India', agree, strongly agree and disagree, strongly disagree were collapsed as agree and disagree as discussed earlier. Next, 3x5 cross tabulations were computed between educational level variable and the perceived value of the factor under consideration. Then a Chi-square statistics was used to analyze the data collected and to determine the extent of relationship among the variables. The computed value of Chi-square statistics is 11.08.Since the computed value of 11.08 is greater than the table value of 5.991, so that there is significant relationship between Education Levels and the Consumers' perceived value towards FDI in Multi-Brand Retailing in India. The computed value of Cramer's V, which is 0.3329, also indicates a strong association among the levels of the row and column variables. This further proves the relationship between the dependent and the independent variables.

Conclusions and Suggestions

The decision to liberalize FDI norms in multi brand retailing comes in the backdrop of the country's economic growth. The intentions look admirable but its impacts are widely debatable. Arguments like destruction of Kirana stores, loss of employment to millions of people etc. have been cited as the negative impact of FDI in Multi brand Retail. So, this study made an attempt to examine the policy related to FDI in Multi brand retailing in India and also to investigate the issues that are feared to emerge with the policy. After very carefully examining the policies and the likely impacts of the policy, this study concludes that, the government has introduced the policy only as an enabling policy and sufficient safe measures for each clause has been adopted.

There is also no empirical evidence to prove that the small retailers will be affected or millions would be out of job. So all the propositions placed by the critics against the policy is only a misconception. The study which also attempted to find out the perception of consumers with regard to the policy has found out that there is significant relationship between Education Levels and the Consumers' perceived value towards FDI in Multi-Brand Retailing in India.

The results of the survey clearly shows that consumers who are educated are positively of a mind and the consumers who are not educated are negatively of a mind towards FDI in Multi-Brand Retailing in India. These research findings have important implications for the policy makers and the government needs to focus more on, educating small and unorganized retailers for future course of action to excel in their business and to create awareness about the benefits of the policy in the minds of the uneducated consumers.

From the survey, it has been found that 53 per cent of respondents feel that FDI in Multi brand retailing will offer wide choice of products under one roof. Out of the total respondents, 42 per cent of the respondents have neither agreed nor disagreed when asked FDI in Multi brand retailing will give rise to big arrogant International retailers. The respondents who are of the opinion that FDI in multi brand retailing would create lot of job opportunities have been found out to be 63 per cent.

Out of the total respondents surveyed, 32 per cent of the respondents were below the graduation level and they have inclined negatively towards opening up of FDI in Multi brand retailing in India.

Out of the total respondents surveyed, 68 per cent of the respondents were above the graduation level and they have inclined positively towards opening up of FDI in Multi brand retailing in India. Finally, the study concludes that with the opening up of FDI in multi brand retail, the sector is expected to bring in adequate infrastructure creation, better quality product offerings to the consumers and create numerous job opportunities directly as well as indirectly but the apprehensions of the different stake holders need to be resolved immediately to generate wider acceptance of this policy.

Recommendations

- The Government should play a vital role to increase the level of awareness of FDI in Multi brand retailing trade in India and its implications in the minds of the stake holders so as to build a positive environment.
- Government should lookout against the risk of foreign retailers becoming monopolistic and charging high prices by allowing them in restrictive manner.
- It is also important for Indian policymakers to learn lessons from FDI in multi brand experiences of other countries like China and adopt a cautious approach.
- The government must strengthen the Competition Commission's role for enforcing rules against predatory pricing.
- In order to increase the credit facilities to Indian farmers, monetary transactions should be done through Indian Banks only.
- First priority should be given to the Indian goods and products produced by Indian in corporate for consumption purpose.

Thus it can be seen that FDI in Multi brand retailing can play a significant role for economic growth and development through its strengthening of domestic capital, productivity and employment creation by integrating its economy with that of the global economy.

Reference

- Bahree, M. "India unlocks door for global retailers", Wall Street Journal, Nov 24, 2011.
- Baskaran, Kamala Devi, "FDI in India's Multi Brand Retail - Boon or Bane", Universal Journal of Management and Social Sciences, Vol. 2, No.1, January 2012.
- Basu, R., Sengupta, K., & Guin, K. K. "Format perception of Indian apparel shoppers: Case of single and multi-brand stores" IUP Journal of Marketing Management, 2012, 11(3), 25-37.

- Bisaria, G. "Foreign Direct Investment in Retail in India" Journal of Marketing Management, 2(1), 31-36.
- Choudhury, S., & MAMGAIN, P.,"Government may allow 100% FDI in single-brand retail retailing", The Economic Times, 2012. Retrieved from http://search.proquest.com
- FDI in retail and aviation sectors set to become a reality now policy. The Economic Times, Sep 22, 2012 (Online). Retrieved from http://search.proquest.com.
- FDI in retail: It's time for states to ensure FDI in multi-brand retail policy, The Economic Times, 2011, Nov 26 (Online), Retrieved from http://search.proquest.com.
- FDI in retail: Won't step back on retail FDI, says PM Manmohan Singh, The Economic Times, Nov 2011. Retrieved from http://search.proquest.com
- Government of India 2012. "Ministry of Commerce & Industry"-Press Note No.5, 2012. Series- Review of the policy on Foreign Direct Investment- allowing FDI in Multi-Brand Retail Trading.
- Government panel decides not to make any suggestion for FDI in multi Multi-brand FDI to hit Kirana shops: Metro cash & carry retailing, The Economic Times, July 2013. Retrieved from http://search.proquest.com.
- Jain M. and Sukhlecha M. L. "FDI in Multi Brand Retail: Is it the need of the hour?" Zenith International Journal of Multidisciplinary Research, 2(6), 108 -131.
- Khan.A.Q&Siddiqui Ahmad, Taufeeque, 'Impact of FDI on Indian Economy: A Comparison with China & USA', International Journal of Business & Information technology, vol-1 no 1: 2011.
- OECD (2001).Global Forum on International Investment New Horizons and Policy Challenges for Foreign Direct Investment In the 21st Century. Mexico City, 26-27 November 2001.
- Sen., A. "States opposing FDI in multi-brand retail have constitutional right to do so", The Economic Times, June 30, 2012.
- www.businessstandard.com.
- www.epwrf.res.in
- www.equitymaster.com
- www.indiaretailnews.com.
- www.metro.co.in
- www.wikipedia.com.

FDI in Multi-Brand Retailing

Dr. Sultan Singh Jaswal
Associate Professor, Department of Commerce
Govt. College Dhaliara, Kangra (H.P.) Pin;- 177103
E-mail: ssj_64@rediffmail.com

Abstract

The economy of India is one of the fastest growing economies in the world. Since its independence in the year 1947, a number of economic policies have been taken which have led to the gradual economic development of the country. On a broader scale, India economic reforms has been a blend of both social democratic and liberalization policies. The economic liberalization in India refers to ongoing economic reforms in India that started on 24 July 1991. FDI is one of the result of economic liberalization. Foreign Direct Investment (FDI) is the outcome of the mutual interest of multinational firms and host countries. Foreign Direct Investment or FDI means to allow foreign companies to enter in to Indian market and open and control their own companies. Foreign companies will come, invest money, and work independently without any joint venture in India. While Multi-Brand retail means selling many products under one roof by a single company. The best examples of Multi Brand stores in India are Reliance Fresh, Big Bazar, Value Bazar, Vishal Mega Mart ,Walmart and many more such stores. In these stores many different products are sold but under their banner. Multi-Brand retail is one of the burning issues to discuss in India. As the retail industry in India is the 2nd largest source of employment after agriculture, so policies related to retail sector should be well managed. Retailing in India is one of the pillars of its economy and accounts for 14 to 15 percent of its GDP. The Indian retail market is estimated to be US$ 450 billion and one of the top five retail markets in the world by economic value. India is one of the fastest growing retail markets in the world, with 1.2 billion people. On 7 December 2012, the Federal Government of India allowed 51% FDI in multi-brand retail in India. The current debatable issue in India is whether to permit FDI in Multi Brand Retail (MBR)100%. This paper attempts to study of various aspects of FDI in Multi- Brand Retail. The paper examines the present set up of retail sector in India. Further it focuses on the benefits of FDI which are expected in terms of better quality, better technology, better customer services and infrastructural development of India and how to protect the interest of small retailers? Keeping in view the employment opportunities. Thus, FDI is also considered as a good step towards the economic reforms in India.

Keywords: Foreign Direct Investment (FDI), Multi Brand Retail(MBR), Economic Liberalization in India, Economic reforms, Stakeholders.

Introduction

Foreign Direct Investment or FDI means to allow foreign companies to enter in to Indian market and open and control their own companies. Foreign companies will come, invest money, and work independently without any joint venture in India. The government has also not defined the term Multi Brand. FDI in Multi Brand retail implies that a retail store with a foreign investment can sell multiple brands under one roof. The best examples of Multi Brand stores in India are Reliance Fresh, Big Bazar, Value Bazar, Vishal Mega Mart, Walmart and many more such stores. In these stores many different products are sold but under their banner. Retailing industry in India is one of the main pillars of the economy and accounts for about15 percent of its GDP. The value of Indian retail market is estimated to be 450 billion US$ and is rated as one of the top five retail markets in the world. Indian Retail is growing at a faster rate backed by a huge population of 1.2 billion people. Indian retail industry comprises sole proprietary small units which are in the form of small shops and business establishments meeting the needs of people around their locality. It is estimated that in India chain stores ,larger departmental stores and supermarkets are situated in metropolitan cities and other urban centers and account for about 4 percent of the industry. India's retail industry employs about 40 million people (3.3% of Indian population). Retail market in India is spread over in two major sectors:-

1) Organised and 2) Unorganised Retailing

Organised retailing refers to trading activities undertaken by licensed retailers, that is, those who are registered for sales tax, income tax, etc. These include the corporate-backed hypermarkets and retail chains, and also the privately owned large retail businesses.

Unorganised retailing, on the other hand, refers to the traditional formats of low-cost retailing, for example, the local kirana shops, owner manned general stores, paan/beedi shops, convenience stores, hand cart and pavement vendors, etc.

The Indian retail sector is highly fragmented with 97 per cent of its business being run by the unorganized retailers. The organized retail however is at a very nascent stage. The sector is the largest source of employment after agriculture, and has deep penetration into rural India generating more than 10 per cent of India's GDP.

There are two spheres in retail market. Viz Single- Brand Retail Market and Multi- Brand Retail Market. On 14 September 2012, the government of India announced the opening of FDI in multi brand retail, subject to approvals by individual states. This decision has been welcomed by economists and the markets, but has caused protests among general public and opposition parties. On 20 September 2012, the Government of India formally notified the FDI reforms for single and multi brand retail, thereby making it effective under Indian law.

The announcement of opening of FDI in multi-brand retail market for international operators with 51% equity holding has evoked mixed reactions from individuals and organizations across the country. There are two views expressed in this context:

Supporter of FDI in multi-brand retail argue that:--

1. The decision would benefit stakeholders across the entire span of the supply chain. Farmers stand to benefit from the significant reduction in post-harvest losses, expected to result from the strengthening of the backend infrastructure and enable the farmers to obtain a remunerative price for their produce.
2. Small manufacturers will benefit from the conditionality requiring at least 30% procurement from Indian small industries, as this would enable them to get integrated with global retail chains. This, in turn, will enhance their capacity to export products from India.
3. As far as small retailers are concerned, it is evident that organized retail already co-exists with small traders and the unorganized retail sector.
4. The young people joining the workforce will benefit from the creation of employment opportunities.
5. Consumers stand to gain the most, firstly, from the lowering of prices that would result from supply chain efficiencies and secondly, through improvement in product quality, which would come about as a combined result of technological up gradation; efficient grading, sorting and packaging; testing and quality control and product standardization.
6. Implementation of the policy will facilitate greater FDI inflows, additional and quality employment, global best

practices and benefit consumers and farmers in the long run, in terms of quality, price, greater supply chain efficiencies in the agricultural sector and development of critical backend infrastructure.

Against the FDI in multi-brand retail argue that:-

1. It is observed that FDI eliminates small producers from international and national level competition, as they operate with old fashioned traditional infrastructure.
2. Foreign companies always try to achieve quick and large returns on their capital. They take interest only in profit oriented ventures and neglect domestic and traditional business while investing.
3. Due to open-minded business policy of India, the problem of surplus FDI will create hurdles in the economic growth of India.
4. Problem of unemployment in rural area is not adequately solved
5. FDI favors only urban regions for the investment and neglect rural & backward regions.

Objectives of The Study:

1. To study the sector wise distribution of the FDI in Indian Multi Brand Retail Market.
2. To examine the risk factors associated and legal framework formulated by the Government of India, to encourage FDI in Indian Multi Brand Retail Market.
3. To study various strategies and instruments of entry and exit used by the Multi-National Companies (MNCs) investing in FDI in Indian Multi Brand Retail Market.

Methodology:

The present study is based on the secondary data published by various agencies and organizations. The present study makes use of data and information provided by RBI bulletins, Department of Industrial Policy and Promotion, Ministry of Commerce and Industries, Newspapers, Magazines, Books, Economic journals and Internet etc.

Background of FDI in Retail Sector: As part of the economic liberalization process set in place by the Industrial Policy of 1991, the Indian government has opened the retail sector to FDI slowly through a series of steps:1995 : World Trade Organisation's (WTO) General Agreement on Trade in Services, which includes both wholesale and retailing services, came into effect.1997 : FDI in cash and carry (wholesale) with 100% rights allowed under the government approval route;2006 : FDI in cash and carry (wholesale) was brought under automatic approval route; Upto 51% investment in single brand retail outlet permitted, subject to Press Note 3 (2006 series)2011 : 100% FDI in Single Brand Retail allowed'2012 : On Sept. 13, Government approved the allowance of 51 percent foreign investment in multi-brand retail, [It also relaxed FDI norms for civil aviation and broadcasting sectors]'

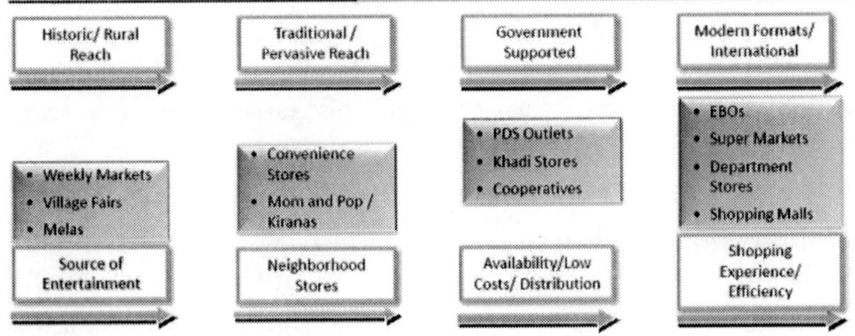

Retailing is the interface between the producer and the individual consumer buying for personal consumption. As such, retailing is the last link that connects the individual consumer with manufacturing and distribution chain. Indian Government has announced 51 per cent foreign direct investment (FDI) in multi-brand retail & left it to the States to decide. The decision is met with both praise and criticism as some likely to gain and other will lose substantially.

Advantages of FDI in multi-brand retail sector:—

General consumers are the biggest gainers as they will receive world class services at competitive price, better quality products and they will be better informed about the product content.

•Real estate agents and developers: The slow down real estate industry will benefit immensely due to increase in demand. Developers were finding difficult to find buyer for their unutilized space so perhaps this is the best news for them as it will help them to fill their vacant space in their shopping malls. •Banking sector will also grow consequently with the real estate sector growth as money is added. • Economy on the whole will gain momentum as foreign investment along with the required skills is coming into the country, consumers are benefiting, supply chain system will improve, better logistics and warehousing facilities in the country, quality food, jobs to the middle class and it can be expected that farmers will get good price and contract farming concept may develop in India.

•A foreign retailer needs to invest minimum $100million dollars of which 50% must be on backhand infrastructure which is great as India needs trillions of dollars to improve infrastructure problems and reduce the wastage of farm produce and improve the life of farmers.

Disadvantages of FDI in multi-brand retail sector:—

•Majority of the Indian small-scale industries or manufacturers will be forced to shut down and Indian manufacturing jobs will be lost as MNC retail brand in order to compete would prefer to source 2/3rd of their products cheaper from outside the country such as China. • Majority of small traders and shopkeepers will end up closing their shops, stores and lower middle class workers would end up losing their jobs as the Illiteracy level among them is very high. •Contrary to the most people belief, International brands such as Wal-Mart won't be able to make any profits out of it for at least in the next 5 to 10 years they would only see the losses considering the low purchasing power and transaction value, uncertainty in the Indian political scenario, unrealistic rental and real estate pricing and heterogeneous consumer consumption in south,north east and western states in India

Statement on Sector-Wise FDI equity inflows from April, 2000 to July, 2013

Table-1

S. No	Sector	Amount of FDI Inflows		
		(In Rs crore)	(In US$ million)	%age with total FDI Inflows (+)
1	SERVICES SECTOR*	178,045.57	38,255.23	19.10
2	CONSTRUCTION DEVELOPMENT: Townships, housing, built-up infrastructure and construction-development projects	103,140.99	22,439.24	11.20
3	TELECOMMUNICATIONS	58,797.85	12,867.85	6.42
4	COMPUTER SOFTWARE & HARDWARE	54,018.53	11,906.02	5.94
5	DRUGS & PHARMACEUTICALS	54,332.65	11,320.16	5.65
6	CHEMICALS (OTHER THAN FERTILIZERS)	42,564.54	9,235.07	4.61
7	AUTOMOBILE INDUSTRY	42,745.67	8,932.26	4.46
8	POWER	37,335.68	8,042.64	4.01
9	METALLURGICAL INDUSTRIES	35,904.43	7,697.07	3.84
10	HOTEL & TOURISM	33,954.46	6,754.49	3.37
11	PETROLEUM & NATURAL GAS	24,950.25	5,406.70	2.70
12	TRADING	19,415.74	4,092.59	2.04
13	INFORMATION & BROADCASTING (INCLUDING PRINT MEDIA)	16,925.66	3,533.62	1.76
14	ELECTRICAL EQUIPMENTS	14,945.81	3,231.38	1.61
15	NON-CONVENTIONAL ENERGY	14,090.99	2,795.01	1.40
16	CEMENT AND GYPSUM PRODUCTS	11,941.58	2,656.29	1.33
17	INDUSTRIAL MACHINERY	12,193.97	2,503.40	1.25
18	MISCELLANEOUS MECHANICAL & ENGINEERING INDUSTRIES	11,458.29	2,481.50	1.24

S. No	Sector	Amount of FDI Inflows		
		(In Rs crore)	**(In US$ million)**	**%age with total FDI Inflows (+)**
19	CONSTRUCTION (INFRASTRUCTURE) ACTIVITIES	10,338.55	2,199.70	1.10
20	CONSULTANCY-SERVICES	9,978.08	2,144.66	1.07
21	HOSPITAL & DIAGNOSTIC CENTRES	9,731.83	2,008.40	1.00
22	FOOD PROCESSING INDUSTRIES	9,569.07	1,970.09	0.98
23	PORTS	6,717.38	1,635.08	0.82
24	AGRICULTURE SERVICES	7,917.19	1,629.09	0.81
25	ELECTRONICS	5,986.66	1,292.51	0.65
26	TEXTILES (INCLUDING DYED,PRINTED)	5,875.42	1,259.55	0.63
27	SEA TRANSPORT	5,504.57	1,196.64	0.60
28	RUBBER GOODS	6,038.32	1,170.31	0.58
29	FERMENTATION INDUSTRIES	5,266.38	1,163.94	0.58
30	MINING	4,386.25	1,001.54	0.50
31	EDUCATION	4,483.06	883.52	0.44
32	PAPER AND PULP (INCLUDING PAPER PRODUCTS)	4,110.15	875.16	0.44
33	PRIME MOVER (OTHER THAN ELECTRICAL GENERATORS)	4,196.03	860.24	0.43
34	MEDICAL AND SURGICAL APPLIANCES	3,477.04	702.30	0.35
35	SOAPS, COSMETICS & TOILET PREPARATIONS	3,395.11	679.17	0.34
36	MACHINE TOOLS	3,064.65	639.70	0.32
37	CERAMICS	2,907.82	632.85	0.32
38	AIR TRANSPORT (INCLUDING AIR FREIGHT)	2,066.22	456.84	0.23
39	GLASS	2,122.17	420.35	0.21
40	DIAMOND,GOLD ORNAMENTS	1,968.54	417.90	0.21
41	VEGETABLE OILS AND VANASPATI	1,921.45	389.63	0.19
42	RAILWAY RELATED COMPONENTS	1,698.33	351.26	0.18
43	AGRICULTURAL MACHINERY	1,660.07	337.35	0.17
44	FERTILIZERS	1,536.11	318.24	0.16

S. No	Sector	Amount of FDI Inflows		
		(In Rs crore)	(In US$ million)	%age with total FDI Inflows (+)
45	PRINTING OF BOOKS (INCLUDING LITHO PRINTING INDUSTRY)	1,407.84	297.65	0.15
46	COMMERCIAL, OFFICE & HOUSEHOLD EQUIPMENTS	1,198.20	257.60	0.13
47	EARTH-MOVING MACHINERY	770.82	175.25	0.09
48	LEATHER,LEATHER GOODS AND PICKERS	554.92	112.35	0.06
49	TEA AND COFFEE (PROCESSING & WAREHOUSING COFFEE & RUBBER)	476.63	104.97	0.05
50	SCIENTIFIC INSTRUMENTS	534.30	101.51	0.05
51	RETAIL TRADING (SINGLE BRAND)	468.37	96.96	0.05
52	TIMBER PRODUCTS	433.45	85.23	0.04
53	INDUSTRIAL INSTRUMENTS	310.56	67.06	0.03
54	PHOTOGRAPHIC RAW FILM AND PAPER	269.26	66.54	0.03
55	BOILERS AND STEAM GENERATING PLANTS	306.75	62.00	0.03
56	SUGAR	242.32	51.82	0.03
57	COAL PRODUCTION	119.19	27.73	0.01
58	DYE-STUFFS	87.32	19.50	0.01
59	GLUE AND GELATIN	71.31	14.69	0.01
60	MATHEMATICAL,SURVEYING AND DRAWING INSTRUMENTS	39.80	7.98	0.00
61	DEFENCE INDUSTRIES	24.36	4.94	0.00
62	COIR	10.37	2.17	0.00
63	MISCELLANEOUS INDUSTRIES	36,306.27	7,992.75	3.99
SUB-TOTAL	936,311.11	200,335.24		100.00
64	RBI'S- NRI SCHEMES (2000-2002)	533.06	121.33	-
GRAND TOTAL	936,844.17	200,456.57		

Services sector includes Financial, Banking, Insurance, Non-Financial / Business, Outsourcing, R&D, Courier, Tech. Testing and Analysis

FDI inflows data re-classified, as per segregation of data from April 2000 onwards.

„+Percentage of inflows worked out in terms of US$ & the above amount of inflows received through FIPB/SIA route RBI's automatic route & acquisition of existing shares only.

• FDI Sectoral data has been revalidated / reconciled in line with the RBI, which reflects minor changes in the FDI figures (increase/decrease) as compared to the earlier published sectoral data.

Foreign direct investment (FDI) in India has played a crucial role in the development of the Indian economy. It has enabled the country to achieve a certain degree of financial stability, growth and development. This money has allowed India to focus on the areas that may have needed economic attention, and address the various problems that continue to challenge the country.Table-1 the Sector wise Analysis of FDI Inflow in India reveals that maximum investment in India has come for the service sector including the telecommunication, information technology, travel and many others. The service sector is followed by the manufacturing sector in terms of FDI. High volumes of investment take place in electronics and hardware, automobiles, pharmaceuticals, cement, metallurgical and other manufacturing industries.

Personal View

All in all, from whatever articles be in newspapers, or on Internet, that I have read, I can take out that overall FDI in Retail would be beneficial for India. Regarding statements that

many local shopkeepers would be forced to shut their stores, I can say that if big stores like Big Bazaar, Spencer's , Easy Day, More etc could not shut them, Walmart, Tesco etc also won't. Moreover, we have the regulatory body Competition Council of India(CCI), and Monopolistic and Restrictive Trade Practices Act(MRTP) to keep these retailers in check.

- Many people in bigger cities and metros are already buying from big stores. Yet, they still go to Kirana stores since they cannot make a trip each time to big stores for all their needs.
- In smaller cities and towns, many people buy goods on credit(not credit card!), and pay after they get the money

with them. I do not think that stores like Big Bazaar etc have any such practice? So, these people are highly unlikely to think about Walmart, or other new comerstoIndia.

- Many small scale traders have formed big unions and try to control prices and supply of goods. They influence and fund political parties and oppose the entry of more big retailers. Themselves, they never give bills, and even opposed a move by Delhi government a few years of ago of mandating giving bills to the consumers. So, do they have the moral right of misinforming public about the entry of the bigger retail stores. Why not reform their own practices?
- The government and the regulatory agencies will have to be careful that the big players like Walmart do not use their power and reach to exploit the Indian market. This is easier said than done. Yet, this might be required if they do start such acts.

Main Findings

Most Countries of the world which embarked on the road to economic development had to depend on foreign capital to some extent. The most important channel through which foreign Capital flows into the Country is FDI. FDI in multi-brand retail will give a boost to the organized retail sector, which positively impacts several stakeholders including producers, workers, employees, consumers, the government, and hence, the overall economy in spite of many disadvantages associated with that. China's example indicates clearly that FDI in retailing does not necessitate the complete closure of local retailers. China is the world's largest FDI recipient and it started with an FDI investment of $ 19 billion and at present that figure has been increased many times. Carrefour from France, Tesco from England, Metro from Germany, and Wal-Mart from US have entered the Chinese retail sector and has uplifted the country economy. Initially during 1992, china allowed FDI only in a few selected cities and also restricted the ownership by26 percent. Later, only in 2004 did china finally permit 100 percent FDI and local Chinese grocery stores have since grown from 1.9 million to more than 2.5 million. In India, opening up of FDI, can increase organized retail market size to $ 260 billion by 2020. However, the rationale for allowing FDI in multi-brand retail trade may be set out as follows:

- Allowing FDI in multi –brand retail trade will benefit consumers and farmers, and will also aim at bringing down inflation. Farmers, in this case, may be protected from the domination of intermediaries who dominate the interface between the manufacturers or producers and consumers in most cases and major part of the share of profit is eaten by those middlemen causing loss to the farmers. Further, consumers will get variety of products at cheaper prices and will have more choice to get international brands at one place.
- Allowing international retailer such as Wal-Mart and Carrefour, which have already set up whole sale operations in the country, to set up multi-brand retail stores will assist in keeping commodity prices under control, will cut waste, as big players will build backend infrastructure.
- Public Distribution System is expected to be improved through allowing FDI in retail trade.
- FDI in retail trade, if permitted, then more foreign companies will come and new infrastructure will build. Banking Sector will grow consequently as money required to build infrastructure would be provided by banks.
- Lack of infrastructure (e.g., cold storages) in the retailing chain has been one of the big issues for years which have led the process to an incompetent market mechanism. FDI might help India over come such issues by channelizing the resources in the right manner.
- Permitting FDI in retail trade will open huge job opportunities. Estimate says it will touch not less than 80 lakh Jobs.

- Allowing FDI in multi-brand retail will contribute to foreign currency reserve and narrow the current account deficit as well .Further, Competition within the host country sector is a critical driver of improvements in sector performance as a result of FDI. FDI's potential for impact can be greater because of the combination of scale, capital, and global capabilities which allow MNCs to close existing large productivity gaps more aggressively. FDI can be a powerful catalyst to spur competition in industries characterized by low competition and poor productivity such as retail industry due to the current scenario of low competition and poor productivity.

Conclusion

In one hand, it is clear that foreign companies will have ample scope to go for FDI in Indian retail sector as it is promising one and allowing FDI in multi -brand retail trade of India is expected to open many opportunities to the Indian people, as mentioned earlier. On the other, there is a big question whether it will benefit to one section of people at the cost of others. At this

point, it is very difficult to ensure these two view points through a particular study. However, the Present study attempts to highlight some of the important issues that may be taken care of before taking any decision with respect to such strategic issue.

At first, it is very important to match the benefits that can be derived out of such foreign investment with the losses that will cause to any section of people in the country, if any. Second, deciding the percentage of stake that will be allowed to foreign companies if they invest in Indian multi-brand retail outlet. In this case, they may be allowed minority stake that is to say,less than 50 percent.

Third, foreign investors may be imposed number of conditions while allowing them to operate in India.

Fourth, foreign investors may be allowed to invest in Indian retail sector if it is not backed by political interests of one Country.

Finally, the paper concludes by saying that FDI in multi-brand retail can be permitted as long the

interests of farmers and small traders are protected. There will be no job losses. Further, it will

not impose any condition on the present economic structure. When the Indian multi brand stores started, people had same fear that these stores will lead to closing of small shops. Shop keepers opposed the government's decision at that time but the truth is, now both these retail giants and small shops co-exist and are flourishing. Rather they have improved the economy of the nation and provided employment to large number of people. Similarly, I feel that there will be no major negative consequence of allowing 100% FDI in multi brand retail. All the opposition is just a political move to increase the vote bank of crores of retailers.

References:

1. Ministry of Finance, Report of the economic
2. RBI Bulletin October 2013
3. DIPP's Fact Sheet 2013
4. India's Economic Policy Preparing for the Twenty-First Century. Bimal Jalan
5. Tax Policy and FDI Influence of Transfer Pricing. Ganapati Bhat

Impact of FDI on Nutritional Knowledge: A Comparative Study Between Males of Organized and Unorganized Sector

Kalyani Singh

Kalyani Singh, Assistant Professor, Department of Home Science (Foods and Nutrition) MCMDAV College, Chandigarh

E-mail: singh.kalyani26@yahoo.com

Tanvi

Tanvi, Assistant Professor, University Institute of Hotel Management and Tourism, Panjab University and Doctorate student, DTHM, KUK

E-mail: tanubeniwal@yahoo.com

Monica Malik

Monica Malik, Associate Professor, Department of Foods and Nutrition, Government Home Science College, Chandigarh

E-mail: malikmonica@hotmail.com

Arti

M.Sc. Student, Department of foods and Nutrition, Government Home Science College, Chandigarh

Abstract

Foreign Direct Investment (FDI) is a key mechanism shaping the market for highly processed foods in developing countries as it had made processed foods available to one and all, increasing sales and consumption. Increased incomes, reduced time for preparation has led to consumption of such foods in today's time of rapid urbanization. A change in dietary habits and practices and with rising consumption of energy-dense, nutrient-poor foods high in fats, sugars and salt has taken place leading to global concern and towards a trend known as 'Nutrition Transition'. A person's nutritional knowledge has great potential to help dietary behavior changes become permanent fixtures in one's life. Thus, this study was undertaken to evaluate the impact of nutritional knowledge, by assessing and comparing age, socioeconomic status, and education factors among male employees of organized and unorganized sectors of Chandigarh.450 male employees were assessed using a self-designed questionnaire for collecting the data for the above stated demographic information. It was observed that all respondents were literate. The nutritional knowledge scores were higher in the organized sector (21.1±3.4) as compared to unorganized sector (20.4±3.0). Higher nutritional knowledge scores were seen among respondents who had received higher education. Mean scores of respondents with respect to their nutritional knowledge were higher in the lower middle (22.2±2.6) socioeconomic group in organized sector whereas in unorganized sector, nutritional knowledge scores were higher in upper lower socio-economic group (21.52±3.8). Thus, it was observed that the respondents had nutritional knowledge and were aware of ill effects of wrong dietary practices, but minor efforts were made by them to follow correct pathways for a healthier lifestyle.

Key words: Foreign Direct Investment (FDI), Demographic Information, Nutrition Transition

Introduction

The Indian Retail Industry is the 5th largest retail destination and the second most attractive market for investment in the globe after Vietnam as reported by AT Kearney's seventh annual Globe Retail Development Index (GRDI), in 2008.The growing popularity of Indian Retail sector has resulted in growing awareness of quality products and brands. Indian retail sector specially organized retail is growing rapidly, with customer spending growing in unprecedented manner. The retail industry is divided into organized and unorganized sectors. Organized retailing refers to trading activities undertaken by licensed retailers, that is, those who are registered for sales tax, income tax, etc. These include the corporate-backed hypermarkets and retail chains, and also the privately owned large retail businesses. Unorganized retailing, on the other hand, refers to the traditional formats of low-cost retailing.(1)

India is fast emerging as a key destination for Foreign Direct Investment. According to the FDI Confidence Index prepared by A T Kearney, India ranks third in Foreign Direct Investment attractiveness ranking, the first being China.(2)

Foreign Direct Investment (FDI) is a key mechanism shaping the market for organized and unorganized sector (retail sector (3).

The changes in dietary practices, physical activity levels associated with rising affluence induced by developmental transition mentioned above contribute to the increasing prevalence of overweight/ obesity. (4)

Chandigarh ranks first in India in the Human Development Index, quality of life and e-readiness. Chandigarh has been rated as the "Wealthiest Town" of India. In terms of family wealth, it was rated as the sixth most prosperous city. According to the latest census report (2011) and NFHS-3 findings, Chandigarh is the 8th most literate state in India with highest literacy rate the literacy rate in Chandigarh has been 86.43% with male literacy rate of 90.54% and female literacy rate of 81.38 %, as compared with Punjab, Haryana and all India statistics, The Per Capita Income (Rs.) (at current prices) has been noted to be 67370 Rs. /- averagely, which is highest in All India. Gross Domestic Product (GDP) is growing at 16.06% in the year 2004-05 against all India Growth of 8.2 %. (5)

The Socio-Economic Status of an individual can predict overall health status and mortality. The impact of Socio-Economic Status on nutritional intake can directly impact a person's body weight.(6)

According to National Family Health Survey -3 (2005-2006) findings, Shown in the following table,

Population that was covered under NFHS-3	Men		Women	
	% Underweight (U) U- % Abnormally Thin	% Obese (O) O- % Overweight / Obese	% Underweight (U) U- % Abnormally Thin	% Obese (O) O- % Overweight / Obese
Urban (%)	27	16	25	24
Rural (%)	38	6	41	7
Total (%)	34	9	36	13

(Table 1.1: Source – NATIONAL FAMILY HEALTH SURVEY -3 (2005-2006), by MINISTRY OF HEALTH AND FAMILY WELFARE GOVERNMENT OF INDIA)

Review of Literature

The multinationals with 51% opening of Foreign Direct Investment in single brand retail has led to direct entrance of companies like Nike, Reebok, Metro, McDonald's etc. or through joint ventures like Wal-mart with Bharti, Tata with Tesco etc. (8)

FDI (Foreign Direct Investment) as defined in Dictionary of Economics is investment in a foreign country through the acquisition of a local company or the establishment there of an operation on a new (Greenfield) site. To put in simple words, Foreign Direct Investment refers to capital inflows from abroad that is invested in or to enhance the production capacity of the economy. (9)

High income and growing urbanization have also contributed to a shift in the traditional Indian food habits. High-income urban dwellers are seeking variety in their choice of foods and are willing to spend more in the international cuisine, including fast foods. Consequently, a growing number of domestic fast food outlets, home delivery, take-away restaurants, and American restaurant chains, such as Kentucky Fried Chicken (KFC), TGI Friday's, Domino's Pizza, Pizza Hut, McDonald's and Baskin Robbins, have opened in the last few years. (10)

Rapid economic growth, urbanization and globalization have resulted in dietary shifts in Asia, away from staples and increasingly towards livestock and dairy products, fruits and vegetables, and fats and oils. Besides, current consumption patterns seem to be converging towards a western diet. (11)

In an analytic study carried out by, Gearheart, RF., Gruber, DM., and Vanata.DF., in 2008, which was conducted to examine the reasoning for burgeoning obesity in lower Socioeconomic Status populations and suggest possible methods of intervention. Obesity has been shown to be associated with low socioeconomic status (SES) in industrialized, developed nations. Lower socioeconomic status has been associated with less health consciousness (thinking about things to do to keep healthy) and lower life expectancies. Three factors associated with risk for obesity and socioeconomic status is physical activity, nutrition and certain psychosocial factors (Self esteem, body image, depression etc.). Education is linked to income, which in turn can influence food options, meal preparation, or food security issues, as well as one's potential exercise habits. Therefore, incorporating school-based interventions increases the likelihood of success in lifelong management of body composition. (6)

Wang, Y., Beydoun, MA., in 2007 based on national data, in the United States , provided a review of the prevalence of obesity based on, comprehensive description of the current situation, time trends, and disparities across gender, age, socioeconomic status, racial/ethnic groups, and geographic regions in studies published between 1990 and 2006. Among adults, obesity prevalence increased from 13% to 32% between the 1960s and 2004. Minority and low-socioeconomic-status groups were disproportionately affected at all ages. It was estimated that, by 2015, 75% of adults will be overweight or obese, and 41% will be obese. (12)

Mahroos, FA., Roomi, Al-KH., surveyed 2013 Bahraini subjects aged 40-69 years [males (40-59 years) and females (50-69 years)], in a cross-sectional national epidemiological community survey, to determine prevalence and risk factors for the overweight and obese in the native adult Bahraini population.(13)

In a cross-sectional study, carried out by Sidhu, S., Sandhu. KH., in 2004, the data from 1,000 adult males of age 30-50 years of Amritsar city of Punjab, was collected belonged to upper middle class of Punjabi origin (well-to-do officers, professors, doctors and businessmen), with income ranging from Rs. 10,000 to Rs. 20,000 per month. The pre-tested interview regarding age, education, occupation, and income and health status. For the assessment of obesity, the value of BMI was calculated for each Subject with reference to, Critical limits of BMI by WHO/IOTF (2000). (14,15) The findings revealed that, a comparative picture of the prevalence of overweight and obesity in various populations showed that, there was higher prevalence of overweight (298 people) and obesity (148 people in obesity grade I, and 69 in obesity grade II) in Punjabi adult males as compared to other populations of India (16). In India, Urban upper middle class of Punjab has achieved a socioeconomic status similar to that of the developed countries, especially with respect to living conditions and nutritional intake and physical activity levels contributing to the problem of overweight and obesity. (17,18)

Objective

This study was undertaken to evaluate the impact of Nutritional Knowledge by assessing and comparing age, educational qualifications and socioeconomic status among male employees of organized and unorganized sectors of Chandigarh.

Research Methodology

The present study was conducted on a sample of 450 Male employees. (225 Organized and 225 unorganized) working in the retail stores of Organized and Unorganized sector of Chandigarh. The 225 organized sector employees were working in Café Coffee day, Mc Donald's, Subway, More refresh, Gopal Sweets, Unisex saloons like Matrix, Oleega, and Hair Raiserz. The other 225 employees were working in unorganized local retail shops, departmental stores in different sector markets of Chandigarh city.

The purposive sample collection technique was used on male employees in various unorganized and organized retail stores of Chandigarh in the age group of 19 yrs to 60 yrs.

The self-designed questionnaire was used to gather information. The questionnaires were pretested on a sample of 20 males. This was done in order to check if the questions were properly understood and elicited desirable changes. Questionnaire include questions related to:

- Age, educational qualification, socioeconomic status

"Kuppuswamy's Socioeconomic Status Scale (2010)" was used to assess Income group division such as low, middle, upper-middle, & higher income group.

- Nutritional Knowledge

The Nutrition knowledge scale included five subjects: 1) 10 items on the relationship between diet and disease; 2) 10 items on the comparison of foods in terms of specific nutrient content; 3) 6 items on the daily serving requirements of different food groups; and 4) 5 items on weight and weight loss.

Scoring: The scale was in multiple choice formats with one point awarded for correct answers, and zero otherwise.

Results and Discussion

The present study was conducted on a sample of 450 working men 225 each in organized and unorganized sector of Chandigarh.

Table 1

GROUP	MEAN SCORES	Nutritional Knowledge total score
Organized sector (N=225)	Mean±SD	21.1±3.4
	N	225
Unorganized sector (N=225)	Mean±SD	20.4±3.0
	N	225
Total	Mean±SD	20.75±3.2
	N	450

The mean scores of nutritional knowledge was higher in the respondents of organized sector as compared to unorganized sector.

Table 2

Distribution of the Respondents on the Basis of Nutritional Knowledge, Scores According to Their Age

GROUP	MEAN SCORES	AGE	N	Mean ± SD	p-value
Organized Sector (N=225)	Nutritional Knowledge total score	19-26	26	21.7±3.6	0.750 NS
		27-34	85	21.2±3.1	
		35-42	55	20.9±3.5	
		43-50	39	20.6±3.6	
		51-60	20	21±3.9	
Unorganized sector (N=225)	Nutritional Knowledge total score	19-26	19	18.7±2.7	0.088 NS
		27-34	86	20.5±2.8	
		35-42	51	21.1±3.3	
		43-50	44	20.2±3.3	
		51-60	25	20.5±3	

NS-Non-significant

*Significant at 0.05 level

It was found that mean scores of nutritional knowledge were almost similar in all age groups however; it was seen to be maximum in the age group of 19-26 years in the organized sector as compared to the scores in the unorganized sector which were observed to be higher in the age group of 35-42 years. Mean total scores of nutritional knowledge of the respondents were higher in organized sector as compared to the respondents of unorganized sector. There was no statistical significance found in the subjects on the basis of their mean scores of nutritional knowledge.

Table 3

Distribution of the Respondents on the Basis of Educational Qualification and its Relation to Their Nutritional Knowledge

Group	Mean Total Scores	Education	Mean±SD	p-value
Organized Sector (N=225)	Nutrition Knowledge total score	8	-	.242 NS
		10	18.2±2.8	
		12	21.1±3.4	
		Graduates	21±3.5	
		Post graduates	21.9±3.3	
Unorganized sector (N=225)	Nutrition Knowledge total score	8	20.17±2.8	.054 NS
		10	21.3±2.9	
		12	19.8±3.0	
		Graduates	20.2±3.6	
		Post graduates	19.9±3.6	

NS-Non-significant

*Significant at 0.05 level

Table 3 revealed that the mean scores of nutritional knowledge in the organized sector were higher in respondents who were qualified upto post graduation. Thus.as increase in the mean scores of Nutritional knowledge was observed as the educational qualification of the respondents increased. Whereas, in unorganized sector the nutritional knowledge scores were higher in the respondents qualified upto 10th standard.

Thus in the unorganized sector, it was observed that the nutritional knowledge scores followed an unsteady pattern, raised with some age groups and declined with the other.

No statistical significance was found to be in the mean nutritional knowledge scores.

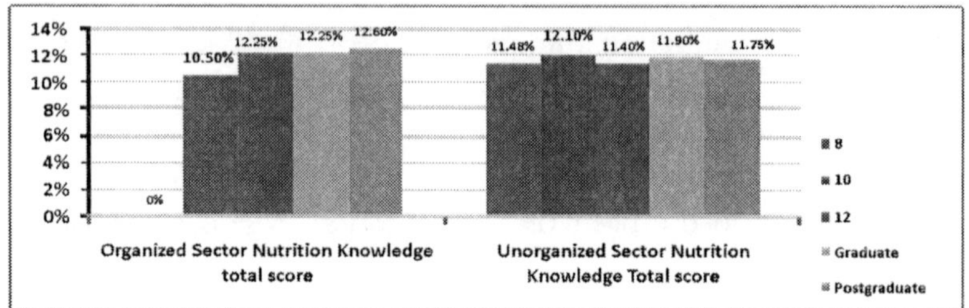

Figure 1: Distribution of the respondents on the basis of educational qualification and its relation to their nutritional knowledge

Table 4

Distribution of the respondents on the basis of socioeconomic status and its relation to their Nutritional Knowledge

Group	Mean Total Scores	Socioeconomic Status	Mean±SD	p-value
Organized Sector (N=225)	Nutrition Knowledge total score	Upper Lower	17.5±3.5	0.027*
		Lower Middle	22.2±2.6	
		Upper Middle	21.05±3.4	
		Upper	16±2.8	
Unorganized Sector (N=225)	Nutrition Knowledge total score	Upper Lower	21.52±3.8	0.008**
		Lower Middle	20.3±2.86	
		Upper Middle	20.32±2.86	
		Upper	20.6±3.0	

*Significant at 0.05 level

**Highly Significant at 0.01 level

Table 4 explained the distribution of the respondents on the basis of their socio-economic status and its relation to their mean scores of knowledge. It illustrated that, mean scores of respondents with respect to their nutritional knowledge were higher in the lower middle socioeconomic group in organized sector whereas in unorganized sector, nutritional knowledge scores of the respondents were higher in upper lower socio-economic group. Nutritional knowledge scores and socio-economic status scores of organized sector and unorganized sector were found to be statistically significant and highly significant respectively.

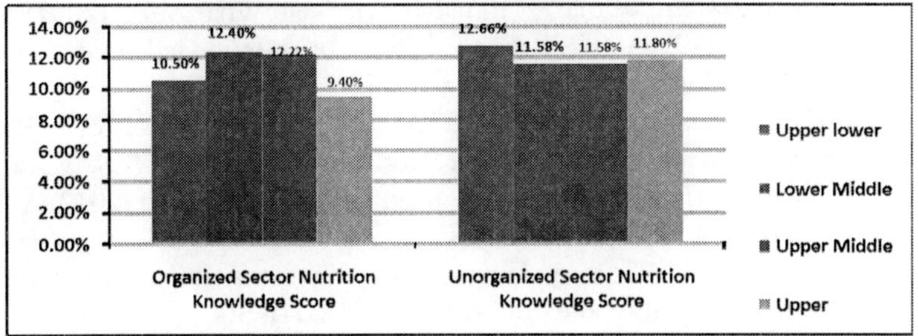

Figure 2 Distribution of the respondents on the basis of socioeconomic status and its relation to their nutritional knowledge

Conclusion

In the study conducted, it was observed that all respondents of organized and unorganized sector were literate. The nutritional knowledge scores were higher in the organized sector (21.1±3.4) as compared to unorganized sector (20.4±3.0). Higher nutritional knowledge scores were seen among respondents who had received higher education. Mean scores of respondents with respect to their nutritional knowledge were higher in the lower middle (22.2±2.6) socioeconomic group in organized sector whereas in unorganized sector, nutritional knowledge scores were higher in upper lower socio-economic group (21.52±3.8). Mean total scores of nutritional knowledge of the respondents were higher in organized sector as compared to the respondents of unorganized sector. The FDI has led to a shift in eating pattern from traditional practices. Thus, it was observed that despite knowledge and low socioeconomic status, the Foreign Direct Investment has affected the style of dietary patterns of respondents. The FDI has been a boost to the economy of Indian GDP, hospitality and tourism, and despite knowing the ill effects of wrong dietary practices, minor efforts were made by them to follow correct pathways for a healthier lifestyle.

References

1. Purushothaman, R., Does Urban Development Drive Rural Growth in India?; IndiaKnowledge@Wharton; (2007);p. (212);221-9595-407. Retrieved from, http://knowledge.wharton.upenn.edu/india/article.cfm?articleid=4224
2. Kesari, R., Srivastava, AK., RETAILING IN RURAL INDIA:AN OVERVIEW OF MARKETS & OPPORTUNITIES. South Asian Journal of Marketing & Management Research; (2012); vol 12, issue 4 ; ISSN 2249-877X.
3. Howkes. C., The role of foreign direct investment in the nutrition transition. Public Health Nutrition; (2004); 8(4), 357-365.
4. Gopalan. C., Obesity in the Urban 'Middle Class'. Bulletin of Nutrition Foundation of India; (1998); Vol 19: 1-5.
5. http://chandigarh.nic.in/knowchd_redfinechd.htm CHANDIGARH the City Beautiful, The official website of the Chandigarh Administration.
6. Gearheart.RF., Gruber.DM., Vanata.DF., Obesity in the lower socio-economic status segments of American society. Forum on Public policy; (2008);1-20\
7. National family health survey 3 (NFHS-3) 2005-2006 by ministry of health & family welfare government of India. http://www.measuredhs.com/pubs/pdf/SR 128/SR 128.pd Ministry of Health.
8. Dash, K., McDONALD'S IN INDIA; Thunderbird, The Garvin School of International Management; (2005); p (1-25); A-07-05-2015.
9. Gupta. R., FDI IN INDIAN RETAIL SECTOR: ANALYSIS OF COMPETITION IN AGRI-FOOD SECTOR. Competition Commission of India; (2012); 1-57.
10. Foresight Project on Global Food and Farming Futures. January 2011. The Government Office for Science. URN: 11/593. Retrieved from, http://www.bis.gov.uk/Foresight.
11. Labour_in_India.htm. Wikipedia.
12. Reddy, BN., Body Mass Index and Its Association with Socioeconomic and Behavioral Variables among Socioeconomically Heterogeneous Populations of Andhra Pradesh, India. Human Biology ; (1998) : Vol 70, no.5: pp. 901-917
13. Singh, A., Purohit, B., Evaluation of Global Physical Activity Questionnaire (GPAQ) among Healthy and Obese Health

Professionals in Central India. Baltic Journal of Health & Physical Activity; (2011); Vol-3, No 1, 34-43. DOI: 10.2478/v10131-011-0004-6

14. Yang, FY., Wahlqvist, ML., & Lee, MS., et al. Body mass index (BMI) as a major factor in the incidence of the metabolic syndrome and its constituents in unaffected Taiwanese from 1998 to 2002. Asia Pac J Clin Nutr;(2008); 17(2):339-351.
15. Wanga, Z., Rowley, K., Wanga, Z., et al. Anthropometric indices and their relationship with diabetes, hypertension and dyslipidemia in Australian Aboriginal people and Torres Strait Islanders. European Journal of Preventive Cardiology; (2007) vol. 14 no. 2 172-178.
16. Shetty, P., Obesity: an emerging public health problem in Asia. Bull NFI;(2003) 24: 6-8.
17. Weiner, J.S. & Lourie, J.A. (1981) Practical human biology. New York: Academic Press, Inc.
18. WHO/IOTF. (2000) The Asia-Pacific perspective: redefining obesity and its treatment. WHO Regional Office, Western Pacific Region, 56.

Foreign Direct Investment in India-A Critical Analysis of Retail Sector

Dr Yudhvir Singh
Associate Professor
Department of Commerce,
Government College Hamirpur (HP)
yvsapc@gmail.com

Abstract

India was one of the founder members of the GATT. Following the GATT and WTO many countries reduced investment barriers. India Govt. too has reduced the barriers of investment and allowed more than 51% in certain sectors and up to 49% almost in all the sectors. India being a signatory to WTO's General Agreement on Trade in Services (GATS) which includes whole sale and retailing services had to open up the retail sector to foreign investment. The Indian Govt. in series of moves opened up retail sector slowly to foreign investment. In 1997 FDI in cash and carry (wholesale) with 100% ownership was allowed under the Govt. approval route. Then 51% investment in single brand retail was permitted in 2006. In December 2011 the Indian Govt. removed the 51% cap on FDI into single- brand outlets and thus opened the market fully to foreign investors by permitting 100% foreign investment in this area. In September 2012 the Govt. approved to allow 51% foreign investment in multi- brand retail. In this backdrop the paper tries to analyze the structure/trends of retail sector in India and tries to find out how the FDI impact on various parties related to the retail sector.

Keywords-Foreign Direct Investment, Multi-brand retail, Tariffs and Trade, World Trade Organization

Introduction

FDI (Foreign Direct Investment) is a process which enables the residents of one country to directly invest in their funds in another country and acquire ownership of assets and exercise control over the investment in terms of production, management, distribution, effective decision making, employment etc. "FDI is an international financial flow with the intention of controlling or participating in the management of an enterprise in a foreign country."Foreign investment is a means of making foreign resources available to a developing country. Such investment can take place for many reasons, including to take advantage of cheaper wages, special investment privileges (e.g. tax exemption) offered by the country. OECD has defined FDI as investment by a foreign investor in at least 10% or more of the voting stock or ordinary share of the investee company.

There are two main types of foreign investment:

1. Portfolio investments-Portfolio investments are investments in purely financial assets such as, stocks denominated in national currency. Portfolio or financial investment take place primarily through institution such as banks investment funds.
2. Direct investments-These investments are the real investments in factories, capital goods, land and inventories where both capital and management are involved and the investors retains over use of the invested capital.

Foreign Direct Investment (FDI) is investment directly into production in a country by a company located in another country, either by a company in the target country or by expanding operations of an existing business in the country.

Concept of Retailing in India

Retail sector is one of the supports to Indian economy and accounts 15 percent of its GDP. The Indian retails estimated to be US$ 450 billion and one of the top ten retail sectors in the world by terms of economic value. India is one of the fastest emerging retail sectors in the world, with 1.2 billion people.

In simple words retailing is making the final product directly available to the consumers of the product or a sale to the ultimate consumer. Retail can also be defined as a link or interface between bulk producers and individual consumers who purchase for final consumption. Retail is the last step in the distribution of merchandise.

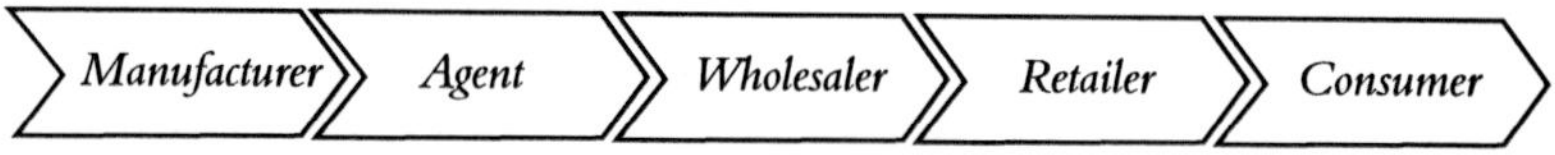

Manufacturer → *Agent* → *Wholesaler* → *Retailer* → *Consumer*

Classification of Indian Retail Sector:

Modern Format Retailers	Traditional Format Retailers	Large Indian Retailers
Super Markets (Food World)	★ kiranas: Traditional mom and pop stores ★	
	★ Hypermarkets	
Hypermarkets (Big Bazaar)	★ Street markets	★ Big Bazaar
Departmental Stores (Shoppers' stop)	★ Exclusive/Multiple Brand outlets	★ Giants
Specialty Chains (IKEA)		★ Departmental Stores
Company owned / Company operated Stores		★ Lifestyle
		★ Shoppers Stop
		★ Trent

Division of Retail Sector:

The retail sector is mainly divided into:

1) Organized Retail Sector

2) Unorganized Retail Sector

Organized retailing refers to trading activities undertaken by licensed retailers, that is, those who are registered for sales tax, income tax, etc. These include the corporate- backed hyper markets and retail chains, and also the privately owned large retail businesses. It covers only 3% of retail business.

Unorganized retailing refers to the traditional formats of low-cost retailing, e.g. local kirana shops, owner manned general stores, paan/ biddi shops, convenience stores, hand cart (street sellers) and pavement vendors etc. and covers almost 97% of the retail business. The sector is the largest source of employment after agriculture, and has deep penetration into rural India generating more than 12% of India's GDP.

Evolution of FDI in Retail Sector in India:

1997 ⋆ 100%FDI in cash and carry (wholesale) allowed under govt. approval.

2006 ⋆ 100% FDI in cash and carry (wholesale) brought under the automatic route.

2006 ⋆ FDI up to 51% in single- brand retail trading allowed under govt. approval route.

2009 ⋆ Guidelines for cash and carry (wholesale) prescribed.

2012 ⋆ 100%FDI allowed in single- brand product trading under govt. approval route subject to certain conditions.

2012 ⋆ 51% FDI allowed in multi- brand retail trading under the govt. approval route subject to certain conditions.

FDI Policy in India

Foreign Investment in India is governed by the FDI policy announced by the Govt. of India and the Foreign Exchange Management Act (FEMA) 1999. The Reserve Bank Of India (RBI) in this regard had issued a notification, which contains the Foreign Exchange(Transfer or issue of security by a person resident outside India) regulation 2000.This notification has been amended from time to time.

Department of Industrial Policy and Promotion (DIPP) under the Ministry of Commerce and Industry, Govt. of India is the nodal agency for monitoring and reviewing the FDI policy on continued basis and changes in sectoral policy/ sectoral equity cap which goes from 26% to 100% at present.

The foreign investors are free to invest in India, except few sectors/activities, where prior approval of the RBI or Foreign Investment Promotion Board (FIPB) would be required. FDI is allowed under Automatic and Govt. route. FDI in retail sector is allowed through Govt. route only.

FDI Policy with Regard to Single-Brand Retail in India

Foreign Investment in single brand product retail trading (100% govt. route) is aimed at attracting investments in production and marketing, improving the availability of such goods for the consumer, encouraging increased sourcing of goods from India, and enhancing competitiveness of Indian enterprises through access to global designs, technologies and management practices.

FDI in single- brand product retail trading would be subject to the following conditions:

a) Product to be sold should be of a 'Single Brand' only.

b) Products should be sold under the same brand internationally.

c) 'Single Brand' product-retail trading would cover only products which are branded during manufacturing.

d) Only one non- resident entity, whether owner of the brand or otherwise, shall be permitted to undertake single brand product retail trading in the country, for the specific brand ,through a legally tenable agreement, with the brand owner for undertaking single brand product retail trading in respect of specific brand for which approval is being sought.

e) In respect of proposals involving FDI beyond 51%, sourcing of 30% of the value of goods purchased will be done from

India, preferably from MSME, village and cottage industries, artisans and craftsmen, in all sectors.

f) Retail trading, in any form, by mean of e-commerce, would not be permissible, for companies with FDI engaged in the activity of single-brand retail trading. Application seeking permission of the Govt. for FDI in retail trade of 'single Brand' product would be made to the Secretariat for Industrial Assistance (SIA) in the Department of Industrial Policy & Promotion.

FDI Policy with Regard to Multi-Brand Retail in India

The government has also not defined the world Multi- Brand. 51% FDI in Multi-Brand retail implies that a retail store with a foreign investment can sell multiple brands under one roof with following conditions:

(a) Minimum amount to be brought in, as FDI, by foreign investor, would be US$ 100 million.

(b) At least 50% of total FDI brought in, shall be invested in 'back- end infrastructure' within three years of the first tranche of FDI, where back-end infrastructure will include capital expenditure on all activities, excluding that on front-end units; for instance, back-end infrastructure will include investment made towards processing, manufacturing, distribution, design improvement, quality control, packaging, logistic, storage, warehouse, agriculture market produce.

(c) Infrastructure etc Expenditure on land cost and rental, if any, will not be counted for purposes of back- end infrastructure.

(d) At least 30% of the value of procurement of manufactured processed products purchased shall be sourced from Indian 'small industries' which have total investment of plant& machinery not exceeding US$1.00 million.

(e) This valuation refers to the value at the time of installation, without providing for depreciation. Further, if at any point of time, this valuation exceeded, the industry shall not qualify as 'small industry' for this purpose. This procurement requirement would not have to be met, in the first instance, as an average of five years of total value of the manufactured, processed products purchased, beginning 1st April of the year during which the first tranche of FDI is received.

(f) Thereafter, it would have to be met on an annual basis.

(g) Self-certification by the company, to ensure compliance of the conditions at serial nos. (b), (C) and (d) above, which could be cross-checked, as and when required. Accordingly, the investors shall maintain accounts, duly certified by statutory auditors.

(h) Retail sales outlets may be set up only in cities with a population of more than 10 lakh as per 2011 census and may also cover an area of 10 kms around the municipal/urban agglomeration limits of such cities. In States /UT's not having cities with population of more than 10 lakh as 2011 census , retail outlets may be set up in the cities of their choice, preferably the largest city and may also cover an area of 10 kms around the municipal/urban agglomeration limits of such cities. The location of such outlets will be restricted to conforming areas, as per the Master/Zonal plans of the concerned cities and provision will be made for requisite facilities such as Transport connectivity and parking.

Major Players Expected to Enter Indian Retail Sector

- WAL-MART STORES INC
- CARREFOUR
- TESCO PLC
- METRO AG
- IKEA

Objectives of The Study and Methodology of The Study

The objectives of the study are to study the trends in FDI in different sectors in India and analyze the impact of FDI in retail sector in India. The analysis will be done with help of secondary data (from internet site and journals). The data is collected mainly from website, annual reports, World Bank reports, already conducted survey analysis, data base available etc.

The Reasons for Investing Retail Sector in India

AT Kearney (a globally famous international management consultancy) recognized India as second most alluring and thriving retail destination of the world, among thirty growing and emerging markets. At present, other profitable retail destinations of the world are China and Dubai of Asia. Diverse FDI in Indian retail is greatly cherished by most of the major and leading retailers of USA and European countries, including Wal-Mart (USA),Tesco (UK) Metro(Germany) and Carrefour(France). Liberalization of trade policy and loosening of barriers and restrictions to the foreign investment in the retail sector of India, have collectively made the FDI in retail sector quite easy and smooth. Our services are economically available for the following ways of FDI in Indian retail.

The retail sector of India is vast, and has huge potential for growth and development, as the majority of its constituents are unorganized. The retail sector of India handles about US $250 billion every year, and is expected by veteran economists to reach to US $660 billion by year 2015. The business in organized retail sector of India, is to grow most and faster at the rate of 15-20 per cent every year, and can reach the level of US $100 billion by the year 2015.Here, it is noteworthy that the retail sector of India contributes about 15% to the national GDP, and employs a massive workforce of it, after the agriculture sector. India's growing economy with a rate of approximately 8% per year makes its retail highly fertile and profitable to the foreign investors of all sectors of economy of all over the world.

Table-1 Share of organised retail in selected countries

Country	Per Capita Retail Sale Rs. p.a.	Share of Organized Retail %
United States	353295	80
France	320580	80
Germany	229905	80
USA	448785	85
Japan	416205	66
Korea South	186480	15
Czech Republic	148545	30
Poland	141750	20
Hungry	106920	30
Russia	87300	33
Brazil	68400	36
Argentina	61155	40
Malaysia	56880	55
Thailand	46935	40
Indonesia	29925	30
China	26955	20
Philippines	26595	35
Vietnam	13905	42
India	12915	4

Source: India Retail Report 2009

Based on the facts given in the Table-1 (above), it clear that developed countries in the world have got major share of organized retailing. Organized retailing is one of the benchmark of development. Consumerism is also is also very high comparatively in developed countries, per capita retail sale are also very high because of purchasing power and disposable income. Per capita retail sales are very low in developing countries due to again the purchasing power and disposable income. India has got a very low share of organized retailing, even comparatively in other developing countries. India has almost lowest share of organized retailing. As far as the per capita retail sales are concerned, India comes at the last among all selected developed countries. It is very clear from the data that it is just a beginning of organized retailing in India and potential is very high.

Table-2 FDI inflows in different sectors in india

Sl. No.	Sector	FDI Inflows 2000-12 August in US $	%
01	Services Sector	158252	19
02	Construction	97028	12
03	Telecommunications	57188	7
04	Computer Software and Hardware	511149	6
05	Drugs and Pharmaceuticals	45440	5
06	Chemicals	39468	5
07	Power	34936	4
08	Automobile Industries	34201	4
09	Metallurgical Industries	30142	4
10	Petroleum and Natural Gas	24783	3

Source: DIPP, Federal Ministry of Commerce& Industry, Govt. of India

Table-2 clearly indicates the FDI inflows in different sector for the period of 2000-Agust 2012.Most of the foreign countries were liked to invest their amount in Service sector, Construction industry, Telecommunications and Computer software and Hardware, because these sectors earn more profit compared to others.

Table-3 FDI in flows in India

Sl. No.	Year (April-March)	Amount of FDI Inflows		%
		IN Rs. Crore	IN US$ Million	
1	2000-01	10733	2463	
2	2001-02	18654	4065	+65
3	2002-03	12871	2705	-33
4	2003-04	10064	2188	-19
5	2004-05	14653	3219	+47
6	2005-06	24584	5540	+72

Sl. No.	Year (April-March)	Amount of FDI Inflows		%
		IN Rs. Crore	IN US$ Million	
7	2006-07	56390	12492	+125
8	2007-08	98642	24575	+97
9	2008-09	142829	31396	+28
10	2009-10	123120	25834	-18
11	2010-11	88520	19427	-25
12	2011-12(April-Jan. 2012)	122307	26192	+35
Cumulative Total (from April 2000 to Jan. 2013)		723367	160096	-

Source: DIPP Federal Ministry of Commerce &Industry, Govt. of India.

Table-3 reveals the FDI inflows in India for the period of 2000-01 to 2011-12. The inflows of FDI are increased year by year due to various reasons, such as Heavy Demand of Indian Consumers, Liberalized Government Policy, Communications facilities, etc.

Table-4 Share of Top Ten Investing Countries FDI Inflows in India

Sl . No.	Country	Cumulative FDI Inflows (2000-2012 Aug)	% of Total inflows US$	Rank
1	Mauritius	303262	37	1
2	Singapore	82867	10	2
3	U.K.	77694	10	3
4	Japan	64297	8	4
5	U.S.A.	49126	6	5
6	Netherlands	37319	4	6
7	Cyprus	31148	4	7
8	Germany	23031	3	8
9	France	13871	2	9
10	U.A.E.	10823	1	10

Source: DIPP, Federal Ministry of Commerce & Industry, Govt. of India.

Table-4 Shows that top ten countries investing in India. Out of this Mauritius plays major role in FDI inflow in India. The main reason for higher level of investment from Mauritius was that the fact that the India entered into a Double Taxations Avoidance Agreement (DTTA) with Mauritius were protected from taxations in India. Singapore and U.K. equally invest (10 per cent) in India during the study period. Japan and U.S.A following countries 8 per cent and 6 per cent respectively.

Impact of FDI in Retail Sector in India

On the backdrop of permission of FDI in retail (single as well as multi-brand) the scenario of Indian retail industry going to change drastically. It is likely to impact not only unorganized sector but also the domestic organized sector considerably. The entry of foreign companies into Indian retailing will not only create many employment opportunities but, will also ensure quality in them. Inflow of FDI will ensure quality jobs and improve the standard of living and life style. The retail will be more expanded creating large of additional jobs. It will vary from ordinary workers to top level management. Such retails will make professional approach and salary will be more lucrative than domestic retailer. A study by Bhaskhar (2005) finds that, entry of big giant retailer like Wal-Mart increases retail employment in the year of entry. While contrasting evidence indicates that each Wal-Mart worker replaces approx. 1.4 retail workers representing a 2.7% reduction in average retail employment (Neumark ,2008) The opening of Wal-Mart may reduce the average earning of retail workers(Dube, 2007).

The Indian consumer will have the luxury of world class opportunity of shopping to meet the requirement of daily life. Retailing in organize sector with computerized billing system will also yield more revenue by collection of service tax and VAT by the government. On other hand Indian retailer will have the opportunity to make partnership with the global firm.

FDI in retail sector would be beneficial to agriculture and its allied activities. It will enable to increase their production capacity with better reward in terms of supplying to organized retailers. Due to the high purchasing power of foreign retailer, the small farmers will be more benefitted as compared to sales in local mandi. This system will also remove the composition of middle men in the market.

FDI in multi-brand retail would either displace various wholesale markets or the size of such markets would shrink. Such local markets are run on capitals which floating in nature. But with coming of multi brand retail stores this floating capital would freeze and small retailers and vendors will be evicted from the market (Chahal, 2013). Kalhan (2007) highlights how small shops in Mumbai are adversely affected, in terms of falling sales, by the growing influence of shopping malls in the city.

Conclusions

A large number of changes that were introduced in the country's regulatory economic policies heralded the liberalization era of FDI policy regime in India and brought about a structural break through the volume of the inflows into the economy maintained a fluctuating and unsteady trend during the study period .It might be interesting to note that more than 50% of the total FDI inflows received by India came from Mauritius, Singapore and the U.K. The main reason for higher levels of investment from Mauritius was that the fact India entered into a double taxation avoidance agreement (DTAA) with Mauritius were protected from taxation in India. Among the different sectors, the service sector had received the larger proportion followed by computer software and hardware sector and telecommunication sector. The impact of FDI can be beneficial to the home country, if it is properly manage. In the Indian context, the government considers FDI as the remedy to solve the economic problem, but it should not influence into functioning of traditional local business. It is also important to consider possible consequences of FDI to the large scale exit of incumbent domestic retail sector, especially the small family owned business. Participation into global market should be designed with compromising the value of indigenous retailers. Therefore, adequate care has to be taken to safeguard the advantage of FDI in retail sector are not overtaken by the disadvantages.

It can be said that the advantage of allowing unrestrained FDI in the retail sector evidently overweigh the disadvantages attached to it and same can be deduced from the example of successful experiments in countries like Thailand and China where too the issue of allowing FDI in retail sector was first met with incessant protest, but later turned out to be one of the most promising political and economical decisions of their governments and led not only to the commendable rise in the level of emolument but also led to enormous development of their country's GDP.

References:

Websites:

1. www.legalserviceindia.com
2. www, retail guru.com
3. www.dipp.nic.in
4. www.rbi.org.in

Reports and Government Notifications

1. Revised FDI Policy issued in 2011 &2012
2. FDI Policy in" Multi Brand Retail" Care Research, Ministry of Commerce, GOI

Research Papers & Journals

1. Preeti Jain, Foreign Direct Investment in Indian Retail Sector, International Journal of Advance Research in Computer Science and Management Studies. Vol.1, issue 4, September 2013.
2. R.Renuka, Impact of FDI in Indian Economy with special reference to Retail Sector in India, Global Research Analysis vol.2 issue 1 Jan. 2013.
3. N.V. Shah & M.A. Shinde, FDI in Indian Retail Sector: A Critical Analysis, Tactful Management Research Journal vol.1, issue 5 Feb. 2013.
4. Kh. Dhiren Meetei, Impact of FDI in Retail Sector in India, Indian Journal of Research, vol.2 issue 7, July 2013
5. K. R. Kausik, Foreign Direct Investment in Indian Retail Sector Pros and Cons, International journal of Emerging Research in Management & Technology.

Impact of FDI in Multi Brand Retailing in India

Ms. Cheshta Kapuria
Research Associate, K.R.Mangalam, Institute of Higher Studies, New Delhi
Mr. Rambir
Research Scholar, Central University of Himachal Pradesh, Himachal Pradesh
Ms.Noor-ul-ain-Rizvi
Student, Delhi School of Economics, New Delhi

Abstract

India is a land of retail democracy. The India Retail Industry is gradually inching its way towards becoming the next boom industry. National Economic Policy, 1991 "Structural Adjustment Program" apart from bringing about changes in fiscal industrial policy and changes in other important economic policies involved a major change in FDI as it was not possible to continue its restrictive economic policies, so it became a possibility to liberalize the economy implemented LPG (Liberalization, Privatization, Globalization) which involves free operations of international market forces. This sector has not been able to achieve success because of the heavy initial investments that are required to break even with other companies and compete with them.

As of now FDI in multi brand retailing is allowed up to 51% but local investors were not able to bridge the gap between the need and actual investment.

India is one of top five most attractive hot spot for foreign investor. It is interpreted that inward FDI can intensify competition and accelerate the process of innovation in the local Retail Sector. This paper evaluates the need of the community to invite FDI in multi brand retailing. The final decision in this respect is yet to be taken by the government of India. To evaluate the future prospects towards the phase of FDI initiated at Multi Retail sector, roles of FDI in multi brand retail sector and its positive impact on Indian economy.

It also offers suggestions in FDI policy about FDI inflow in multi brand retail sector. This paper also makes an understanding about the challenges and opportunities faced by FDI Inflow and the future outlook towards FDI in multi brand retail Sector

Introduction

The India Retail Industry is the largest among all the industries, accounting for over 10 per cent of the country's GDP and around 8 per cent of the employment. India is a land of retail democracy. Economy has Thousands of weekly Haats, Bazaars which are people's owned self organizational capacities and interests. There are estimated to be 11 shops per 1000 people and around 15 millions, gives India the highest retail shop density in the world.

Since independence India had severe scarcity of capital resources; however that initiated foreign capital investment in the country since second five year plan 1956-1961 more emphasis was given to industrialization which leads to the development of local industries.

Certain restrictive measures were adopted towards FDI in the late 1960's; however it was liberalized in 1980's due to industrial policy measures. It was in 1991 National Economic Policy "The year 1991 was marked with severe balance of payments deficits. Foreign exchange reserves went down to US$ 1.1 billion June 1991 – less than sufficient for two weeks of import requirements" (Misra, S.K.2000)

At that time India was on the verge of default and it got financial assistance from IMF on certain terms and conditions. This involved "Structural Adjustment Program (SAP)"by India. These "SAP" apart from bringing about changes in fiscal industrial policy and changes in other important economic policies involved a major change in FDI as it was not possible to continue its restrictive economic policies ,so it became a possibility to liberalize the economy. Moreover due to these LPG (Liberalisation, Privatisation, Globalisation) involves free operations of international market forces. This also had lead to India being one of top five most attractive hot spot for foreign investor.

Driving Force towards expansion of Retail Sector

It employs more than 40 million people as on July 2012 (businessmapsofIndia.com) and it contributes more than 33 percent to GDP of India in last few years (survey report of cci.in)

This sector has not been able to achieve success because of the heavy initial investments that are required to break even with other companies and compete with them.

As of now FDI in multi brand retailing is allowed up to 51% but local investors were not able to bridge the gap between the need and actual investment.

Objectives of the Study

To evaluate the need of opening up of FDI in multi brand retail.

To review the problems faced by FDI in Multi Brand Retail Sector in India recently

To study the future trends towards the phase of FDI initiated at Multi Retail sector.

The roles of FDI in multi brand retail sector and its positive impact on Indian economy.

To offer suggestive measures in FDI policy about FDI inflow in multi brand retail sector.

Determinants like large young working population nuclear families in urban areas, increasing working women population and emerging opportunities in the services sector the key factors in the growth of the organized Retail in India.

In India the vast middle class and its almost untapped retail sector are the powerful attractive forces for global retail giants wanting to enter into newer markets, which in turn will help the India Retail Industry to grow faster. Indian retail is expected to grow 25 per cent annually.

- Modern retail in India could be worth US$ 175-200 billion by 2016.
- The Food Retail Industry in India dominates the shopping basket.
- The Mobile phone Retail Industry in India is already a US$ 16.7 billion business, growing at over 20 per cent per year.

The future of the Indian Retail Industry shows potential with the growing of the market, with the government policies becoming more positive and the emerging technologies facilitating operations.

Scope of the Study

The study will highlight the current position of the FDI inflows in India. It is concerned with FDI in multi brand retail sector and discusses the relevant reforms to formulate, create and force regulatory and legal reforms in this sector and achieve its aim of economic growth. This study reviews accessible studies conducted by the Government and other entities on this topic examines, it's possible impact on farmers, employment, consumers and retailers.

Foreign Direct Investment: Current Scenario

Presently FDI is allowed in India in almost all the sectors; except in the areas of strategic concerns. It is Restricted in sectors not opened to private sector investment including Atomic Energy and Railway Transport, Multi-Brand Retail Trading, Lottery Business including Government and private lottery, online Lottery, Real Estate Business or Construction of Farm Houses. Gambling and Betting including casinos, Manufacturing of Cigars, cheroots, cigarillos and cigarettes, or of tobacco substitutes, Business of chit fund, Nidhi company and Trading in Transferable Development Rights (TDRs).

In all the other sectors it is permitted with different equity limits ranging from 26 percent to 100 percent matter to certain terms and conditions what so ever are applicable

FDI is allowed in India through two ways the Automatic Route and the Government Route. Under the Automatic Route, the non-resident investor or the Indian company does not have need of any approval from the RBI or Government of India for the investment. Under the Government Route, first approval of the Government of India through Foreign Investment Promotion Board (FIPB) is required. Proposals for foreign investment under Government route as laid down in the FDI policy from time to time are considered by the Foreign Investment Promotion Board (FIPB) in Department of Economic Affairs (DEA), Ministry of Finance (DIPP).

Services remain the attraction of highest equity inflows of 20.93% for the April 2000 to June 2010 .Since 1992 to 2000 the growth of FDI most of the years has been optimistic. Table 2 highlights the fact that there has been positive growth in FDI inflows over most of the years for the 2000-01 to 2010-11.During 2002 -04, 2009-10 and 2010-11 a harmful growth rate was found in the FDI inflow due to the economic meltdown in the world.

Foreign Direct Investment in Retail Sector

FDI in multi brand retail sector is 51 % allowed in India. In 1997 India allowed FDI through government approval route with 100 percent equity in Cash and Carry wholesale trading .In 2006 it was permitted under automatic route up to 51 percent in single brand retail, multi-brand retailing was proscribed in India. Afterwards in 2012 FDI was increased 100% in single-brand retail while creating a path for FDI in multi-brand retail to the tune of 51%.

The concept of shopping changed in terms of format and consumer buying behavior, revoulationalising shopping in India. This has lead to large scale investments in the real estate sector with major national and global players investing in developing the infrastructure The trends that are driving the growth of the retail sector in India are Low share of organized retailing, Falling real estate prices, Increase in disposable income and customer aspiration, Increase in expenditure for luxury items.

Lastly, it is to be noted that the Indian Council of Research in International Economic Relations (ICRIER), economic think tank of the country, appointed to look into the impact of BIG capital in the retail sector, has estimated the worth of Indian retail sector to reach $496 billion by 2011-2012, concluding that investment of 'big' money (large corporate and FDI) in the retail sector would not harm the interests of small, traditional retailers in the long run perspective.

FDI in Multi Brand Retailing

India is being seen as a potential goldmine for retail investors across the world and latest research and developments has rated India as the top destination for retailers for an attractive emerging retail market. It is already home to several organized retailers such as Food Bazaar, Reliance, Pantaloon and Shoppers Stop, which have been lucratively working in the country Industry has seen parallel growth for the last 15 years. And there are estimates that organized retailing will rise due to various factors and will grow beyond 10% soon This is the post liberalization era, because of which many Multinationals turn up in India, created numerous job opportunities at various strata levels and helped India develop. The size of the middle class population has been towering since then. People have higher disposable incomes, which changed the mindset and lifestyle also the conversion from being unorganised to being organised in nearly all sectors. Shortage of investment in the logistics of the retail chain, leads to an inefficient market mechanism. Lack of Storage has been one of the most alarming of these infrastructure gaps.

The unorganized retail sector covers largely over 94% of India's total retail sector. It consists of over 13 million kirana stores and presently employs about 40 million people. With this as

the backdrop, the new entrants for sure will face tough competition from local organized as well as unorganized retailers, i.e., the kirana shops, Even though India has well over 5 million retail outlets, the country mainly lacks ingredients that can resemble a retailing industry in the modern sense of the term. The organized retail sector is expected to grow stronger than GDP growth in the next five years driven by changing lifestyles, escalating income and positive demographic outline. This presents international retailing specialists with a great opportunity.

FDI will be a powerful catalyst to the required growth in the retail industry and, in long term, will be valuable to all the major stakeholders. The new policy can benefit both foreign retailers and their Indian partners. The settlement to foreign players will be access to local market knowledge and an augmented consumer base, while Indian companies will benefit by global best management practices and technological know-how. There will be investment in storage and transportation infrastructure, technology and supply chain operations.

With advancement comes the problems and in spite of a bright future for organised retail in India some facts have to be considered to optimistically begin the retail momentum and ensure its persistent growth. The increased flow of capital, if used efficiently, will promote both the farmers and the consumers.

Farmers will earn profit from the better price indexing and direct selling to the retailer. The consumer, in addition to having a better shopping experience, will encourage the competition and the resultant reduced prices. The real estate retail industry will benefit immensely due to increase in demand and enlarged investor confidence. We can also expect better transparency in the retail real estate sector. Additionally, the country will thrive in terms of quality standards and consumer expectations, since the inflow of FDI into the retail sector is bound to pull up the quality standards and cost-competitiveness of Indian producers in all the segments.

Global Retail Development Index (GRDI)

This index is based on more than 25 macro-economic and retail –specific variables for example, the country risk includes parameters like political risk, economic risk, performance risk, financial risk and business risk. The market magnetism covers retail sales per capita, urban population, laws and regulations and business efficiency. India is ranked second in Global Retail Development Index of 30 developing countries drawn up by AT Kearney.

FDI in Multi Brand Retail Sector: Prospects and Challenges

Consumption pattern has drastically changed with urbanization With emergence of a large middle & upper middle class ,substantial increase in income of the people rising nuclear families there has been a radical change in the consumption as well as buying behavior of the Indian consumers. Apart from that the economic position of Indian middle class favors the opening of retail giants. According to Euro monitor Retail Survey Indian consumer sector is undergoing higher growth rate As the young population of India is more fashion conscious is ready to pay more money for good quality and branded products. People are spending on lifestyle improvement. Entertainment, leisure, food and shopping are highly welcomed. All this makes India an lucrative destination for foreign investors. Out of The 500 Fortune companies 100 are already investing in India, which is already generating various employment opportunities, income, technology transfer and economic stability. India is targeting on maximizing political and social stability with a regulatory environment.

On the other hand, it is by no means clear that FDI generates more payback than costs for host countries, as if often implicit. As a key part of the modification package, most developing countries have a dismantle the limitations and regulations which were in place on FDI ,and are now welcoming Transitional corporations (TNC's) and competing to be a focus for them.

The Department of Industrial Policy and Promotion has issued a discussion paper on the topic relating with permitting FDI inflows in Multi Retail Sector. It is significant to point out that technological development is always needed for a developing country like India and therefore it is a benefit that MNC'S are concerned to bring their highly developed and innovative technology and high end products to India. In sort to build back-end infrastructure it is essential to develop high end infrastructure. FDI in multi brand needs to be stated as creditable. It is anticipated to benefit not only the retail traders but even the interest of people of other sections including farming, cooperative, service sector in non corporate enterprises and consumers as well. The best standards and the utmost quality of the goods for which these global retailers are if brought, will change the structure of retailing in India.

Very high stamp duties on transfer of property affect the industry. Real estate the sector also faces very high stamp duties on transfer of property, which varies from state to state (12.5% in Gujarat and 8% in Delhi). The problem is compounded by problems of clear titles to possession, while at the same time land use conversion is time overriding and complex as is the legal process for settling of property disputes. Presence of strong Pro-tenancy laws makes it difficult to remove tenants and this is posing problems. Land-use conversion is time consuming and becoming difficult for settling property disputes, it consumes lot of time. Rigid building laws makes procurement of retail space difficult. Non residents are not permissible to own property except they are of Indian origin.

Growth of the rural area in general and agriculture in particular sense depends to a large extent on the Infrastructural facilities and secure markets for the farm produce. In the lack of nearby & adequate markets for cash crops, most of the farmers remain confined to the production of wheat and other traditional crops, even though the soil conditions may not appropriate for their cultivation. Indian farmers grasp only one-third of the total prices paid by the final consumer against two-third by the farmers in nations which hit the farmers badly. This could be achieve through removal of structural deficiencies, through liberalized markets, with direct marketing and contract farming programmes, from which farmers could expand, as also more conventional farm gate prices, steadier incomes and better access to evolving consumer preferences through private investors ,especially the organized retail sector FDI in multi brand retail will create markets for cash crops and motivate farmers for farming products according to their climatic and soil conditions of that particular area. The Bharti-Wal-Mart, the joint venture between Bharti Enterprises and US-based Wal-Mart Stores, said it tactics to buy agriculture produce directly from 35,000 small and medium farmers in India by the end of 2015. The retail joint venture proposes to fetch in the best farm management practices and groom farmers to grow additional with less resources and optimum use of fertilizers and pesticides. Wal-Mart Stores Inc chief executive Mike Duke said, "We are confident that these initiatives would result in a 20 percent increase in the income of farmers and have a multiplier effect to benefit one million farmers and other workers associated with agriculture" (Economic

Times 2010), investment in infrastructure like storage, transport, food processing etc will help in reducing the intermediaries and it will help in reducing the bridge between prices paid by the consumers and prices received by the farmers. Investment in back end infrastructure will reduce the expenditure of farmer produce, time and quality worsening. If these facilities are shared with farmers on logical prices would help in increase income for the farmers and will bring "farm to Folk"

Thomas Verghese, MD and CEO , Aditya Birla Retail , and Chairman, Confederation of Indian Industry (CII) National Committee on Retail ,said, "There is a clear case that modern retail is good for country presenting employment opportunities, and stimulating business for the small and medium enterprises (SMEs) and the farmers in fact, in the south, modern retail has been successful achieving 20-25 per cent penetration ."

The Department of Industrial Policy and Promotion discussion paper discussion of strategic investment and not financial investment which is in fact, the need of the hour –the industry is in need of capital blend ,amply bear out by the fact that over the last few years, only the largest Indian corporate with deep pockets like Tatas, Birlas and Reliance have met with any success. The reason is that these companies can take in losses for 8-10 years, the typical gestation period till pay back commence.

Retail giant houses such as Wal-Mart, Carrefour, Ahold, JC Penny can bring their better managerial practices and IT-friendly techniques to reduce wastage and set up incorporated supply chains to gradually replace the presented disorganized and split retail market. India wastes nearly Rs 50,000 crores in the food chain itself. These international retail outlets can help extend the food processing industry which requires $28 billion of modern technology and infrastructure .Lack of latest technical expertise , is a major handicap for Indian business houses .Foreign direct investment can only pave the want for prosper and professional entrepreneurship for retail value chain.

FDI in retail sector will generate one million jobs in three years. Export would be high especially in agriculture sector. It will reduce depletion, number of distribution channels and will reduce the transportation costs .Consumer will be benefited by paying low prices for quality produce will get more services and will have greater choices of product.FDI will integrate Global economy with the Indian economy.FDI in retail would reduce the intermediate cost and cost of production by integrating supply chains and will give producers a better prices for their products.FDI will develop infrastructure and technological up gradation would be there.

Retailing also helps small scale units to have easy entrance market. They provide a platform for small scale unit's goods. 4 lakh plus medium handcraft manufacturers are supported by this Industry, leading to development of small scale units.

FDI can contribute immensely to the growth of the economy. It has an essential impact on country's trade balance, increasing labor standards and skills, transfer of technology and innovative ideas, skills and the general business climate. Window of opportunity for technological transfer and up gradation, access to global managerial skills and practices ,optimal utilization of human capabilities and natural resources, making industry internationally competiteve,opening up export markets,aceess to international quality goods and services and augmenting employment opportunities open up. Technological advancement lowers the prices but indirectly it would lower the margin of unorganized players consequently the unorganized market will be affected.

While there are statistics of international retailers like Tesco, Carrefour analyzing business opportunities in India; Reliance, the largest Indian corporation is investing $3.4 billion to become its largest modern retailer.

British high street retailer, Marks and Spencer (M&S) plans to hike its retail presence in India, targeting 50 stores in the next three years. M&S which presently operates 17 stores in Venture

(JV) with Reliance Retail. Spain's Inditex, Europe's largest clothing retailer started the first store of its Zara brand in India in June 2010. It further plans to open a total of five Zara outlets in India.

Estimates on reports of investments for Hypercity Retail by K.Raheja Group to establish 55 hypermarkets by 2015. These factors will contribute in taking Indian retail business to unexpected growth based on the consumer preference for shopping in pleasant environment.

Conclusion:

There is very huge scope for the growth of organized Retailing in India. By following some of the strategies it can increase tremendously and can reach each and every nock and corner. A trade must be maintained between brand building and promotion. Non-marketing factors like gas prices, weather etc. should be avoided and new friendly schemes should constantly be launched.

Even though organized retail sector in India is at the infant stage, India today has become a up-and-coming target for FDI. Most persuasive investment opportunity for mass merchants and food retailers looks to be enlarge overseas as Indian economy is expanding at a rapid pace with consumers having high purchasing power. With a vigorous economy experiencing insistent growth, India has exerted a pull and an irresistible inducement to companies looking to extend their scope of operations. FDI is a powerful source for the strengthening of retailing and will create massive opportunities for innovation in retail sector in India but at the same time it is quite probable that a section of the domestic retailing industry will be severely impair due to the entry of foreign retailers. In this paper researchers have tried to emphasize both the thoughts in detail and concluded the most constructive viewpoint on FDI in Indian Multi Brand Retailing.

Consumers are always eager for trendy ways of shopping. Indian retail sector is Mounting fast and its employment potential is growing fast. The retail scene is changing rapidly.

Retailers are rethinking and redeveloping their approaches towards the suppliers so that they can get the best pricing strategies There is no surprise why from Malaya to Mittal,Godrej to Birla, Tata to Ambani, everybody is ready with their plans to kick start retail revolution in India. Apart from above, retail sector in India is also catalyst for the enlargement of tactics of below the line marketing used by major retail players Like Spencer, big bazaar, reliance fresh etc.

FDI in multi brand retail can fetch about Supply Chain Improvement, Investment in Technology,

Manpower and Skill development, Tourism Development, Greater Sourcing from India, Development of modern ways in Agriculture, Efficient Small and Medium Scale Industries.

References:

1. Bhardwaj,R.K. and Urvashi Makkar."Recent Practices in Retail in India", 2009. p.p 21-29
2. Chaturvedi, Ila."Role of FDI in Economic Development of India: Sectoral Analysis", http://www.trikal.org/ictbm11/pdf/globalization/d1314-done.pdf, 2011.
3. The Hindu, Business review, "Lofty Ambitious rekindle interest in Retailing" , June 2010.
4. Philip Kotler, 2004 "marketing Management", Pearson Education, New Delhi p.p544-545
5. Babu, S. Harish." SWOT Analysis for opening of FDI in Indian Retailing", http://www.iiste.org/Journals/index.php/EJBM/article/view/1047/967, 2012.
6. Dua, P. and A.I. Rasheed. "Foreign Direct Investment and Economic Activity in India", Indian Economic Review, 33, 1998. pp. 153-168.
7. Batra, Hemant. "Retailing Sector in India Pros Cons", http://www.Legallyindia.com/1468-fdi-in-retailing-sector-in-india-pros-cons-by-hemant-batra,Nov 30, 2010.

8. Jain Dr. Mamta, Meenal and Sukhlecha." FDI in Multi Brand Retail: Is It The Need of The Hour".
9. Nair, Suja."Retail Management", Himalaya Publishing House, 2006. p.p401-429.
10. Economic Times ."FDI in multi-brand retail set to get 100% backing", May 2010.
11. Foreign Direct Investment Policy. Department of Industrial policy and promotion, Ministry of Commerce and Industry, Government of India. 2006.

FDI in Multi-Brand Retail: Issues and Implications on Indian Economy

Akhil Gautam
Assistant Professor, Department of MBA
Govt. P.G.College, Dharamshala (176215)
E-Mail: akhil_gautam5@yahoo.com

Abstract

Retail Sector is one of the most important pillars of Indian economy and it is growing at a phenomenal pace. Foreign Direct Investment (FDI) in retail sector plays an integral role in the economic growth. FDI in Multi-brand retail can be seen as an important reform to revive the economy and to ease supply side pressures especially in unorganized sectors. In this context the present study attempts to discuss the issues and implications of FDI in Multi-brand Retail on Indian Economy. To revive the Indian economy, FDI policy in multi-brand retail is an important reform that would ease supply side pressures and mitigate inflation. Implications of FDI in multi-brand retail sector discussed outweigh the issues related to the new FDI policy reforms.FDI in multi-brand retail can go a long way in improving the efficiency of supply chain, infrastructure facilities, technological advancement and other relevant areas of growth in retail sector. The FDI policy on multi-brand retail creates opportunities for the Micro, Small and Medium Enterprises (MSMEs) to reach out the International markets. Farmers and consumers would benefit from the new entry of organized retailers in multi-brand and would help tame food inflation by improving agri-commodity management.

Keywords: Foreign Direct Investment; Organized Retail, Unorganized Retail, Multi- brand Retail Sector, Economic Growth.

Introduction

India has the highest retail density in the world, with 12 million small shops catering to 209 million households. India has a high potential market with accelerated retail growth of 15-20% expected over the next five years. However, a significant decrease of 60% (amounting to $24.2 billion) of FDI was noticed in 2010, when compared to 2009. This appeared to be mainly because most the Indian rural and small towns' retail markets are unorganized (Moghe, 2012). The Indian retail sector is highly fragmented and weighted towards unorganized retailers which is 93% of the market and only 7% by organized retailers but is quickly growing and organized retail market is expected to reach 20% by 2020 (Kearney Report, 2011). According to A.T. Kearney Global Retail Development Index (GRDI) 2012, India ranks fifth after Brazil, Chile, China and Uruguay. India is treated as a high potential market with accelerated retail market growth of 15 to 20 percent expected in the coming 5 years, supported by a GDP growth of 6 to 7 percent, which will considerably increase disposable income and rapid urbanization. The changing FDI climate has provided an interesting dynamic international retailers' entry and expansion plans in India (Kearney Report, 2012).

Unorganized retail operates at low cost and small size format. These include the local kirana shops, owner manned general stores, paan/beedi shops, the local mom and pop store convenience stores, hand cart and pavement vendors, etc. In the last 10 years there has been significant development from small unorganized family owned retail formats to organized retailing. This effect of branded retailing can already be seen with the Bharti-Wal-Mart collaboration, which has joined forces with state governments to open training and development centers in Amritsar, Delhi and Bangalore, preparing local youth for jobs in retail (Federation of Indian Chambers of Commerce and Industry Report, 2010). In November 2011, India's Central Government announced retail reforms for both Multi-brand stores and single brand stores and this however suggest that this may be about to change global market chain stores such as Wal-Mart (United states), Carrefour (France), Marks & Spenser and TESCO (United Kingdom) and Shoprite (South Africa) may finally be allowed to set up in India. The organized retail sector includes licensed retailers, that is, those registered for sales tax, income tax, etc. It also includes corporate-backed hyper- markets and retail chains and the privately owned large retail businesses.

FDI Trends in Indian Retail Sector

FDI policy plays a major role in the economic growth of developing countries around the world. The government of India has been considering opening up the retail business to FDI. Many other sectors have been exposed to FDI, the retail sector has had to wait for quite some time due opposition from political parties, including ally Trinamool Congress, UPA II and various trade organization. FDI will be a powerful catalyst to the growth of retail industry (The Siasat Daily, 2012). In 1995, the general agreement on trade in services with World Trade Organization (WTO)opened FDI for wholesale and retailing services. In 1997, FDI cash and carry (wholesale) with 100% rights was allowed with government approval. There had been a greater momentum in the retail sector since 2006 as the Government of India liberalized FDI policies. The FDI policy in cash and carry (wholesale) brought under the automatic route and in single-brand 51% investment was permitted. On November 24, 2011, the Government of India announced that it had approved

FDI in multi- brand retail subject to a number of conditions. FDI will be allowed at up 51 percent foreign equity subject to government approval on Multi-brand retails. A foreign company initial investment must be at least $100 million and at least 50 percent of which is required to be in back-end infrastructure like supply-chain operations. Investors will have to source 30 percent their products from "micro and small" industries with not more than $1.0 million in capital investment. Foreign direct investment will be allowed in retail stores only which operate in cities with populations of over one million.

Prospects of FDI policy for Multi-brand Retail

The new policy would benefit both foreign retailers and Indian companies. The foreign retailers' will get better local market knowledge and thus an increased consumer base, whereas Indian companies will gain advantage from global best management practices and technological know-how. The primary aim of the policy is to attract greater FDI inflows and to create a friendly business environment. Foreign investors may experience a liberalized legal and financial framework to have the potential growth in the multi-brand retail sector. Researchers (Palit and Nawani 2007; Pires, Stanton and Salavrakos 2010; Jain and Sukhlecha 2012) argued that FDI will infuse technological advancement and induce capital flow which enhances production possibilities and maintains general macroeconomic stability. To revive the Indian economy, FDI policy in multi-brand retail is an important reform that would ease supply side pressures and mitigate inflation. This would bring better prospects and higher profit margins for the small and medium enterprises as it creates greater market access.

The Government of India considers safety measures in order to calibrate FDI in multi-brand retail sector as it is concerned about the competition among the domestic retailers and the monopolization of the domestic market by International giant retailers. The safety measures like a fixed percentage of FDI in the sector is obligatory to be spent on building back-end infrastructure, logistics or agro-processing units so as to ensure that the foreign investors make a valid contribution to the development of infrastructure and logistics. The government ensures at least 50 percent of the jobs in the retail outlet are reserved for rural youth and a certain amount of farm produce is required to be procured from poor farmers. A minimum percentage of manufactured products are required to be sourced from the small and medium entrepreneur sector in India. The government has reserved the right to procure a certain amount of food grains in order to ensure that the public distribution system and the Indian food security system, is not weakened. An exclusive regulatory framework is set in order to protect the interest of small retailers and the giant retailer do not resort to predatory pricing or acquire monopolistic tendencies (Agarwal, 2011).

Issues in Allowing FDI in Multi-brand Retailing

The new FDI policy has become a key battleground in the emerging multi-brand retail markets, researchers (Henley 2004; Palit and Nawani 2007; Pires, Stanton and Salavrakos 2010; Jain and Sukhlecha 2012; Moghe have highlighted a number problems related to backend infrastructure, implementation of improved technology, improvement in supply chains, issues of real estate and human resources. It is observed deficiency of appropriate investment in logistics and storage facilities which are two alarming factors leading to an inefficient market mechanism. The technology used in Indian retail is also largely obsolete, resulting poor efficiency at the supply side economy. Overall food based inflation has been a matter of concern though it is given substantially good subsidies to farmers. Henley (2004) study shows China is in better position in attracting FDI when compared to India. India's performance is understated because of various reasons like high tariffs, poor physical infrastructure, unfriendly regulatory system etc. It concludes with a hope of liberalization which would be driven by external pressures and state level initiatives.

A.T. Kearny report (2006) by CII (Confederation of Indian Industry) indicated the best practices adopted by China and South Africa in FDI policy where infrastructure facilities were given preferences. It highlighted the role of regulatory bodies in promoting retail which is leading to the related economic benefits such as tax revenue, employment etc. The report identified the specific actions which can be taken to foster retail success and growth. Foreign Players' view is that the legal environment in India is not conducive enough to invest and many are willing to enter with 100% FDI. Inadequate data on consumer behaviour towards the retail market also is an issue for them. Some experts claim that the entry of retail giants will enable rapid expansion of Indian economy.

Palit and Nawani (2007) attempted to explain the country-wise dissimilarities in the arrangement of FDI flows in the developing Asian economies. The study refers that the location of retail markets influences FDI flows and also argues that certain countries enjoy comparative advantages in the form of superior technological capabilities and infrastructure which attracted greater volumes of FDI. Developing countries like India find the production processes becoming complex due to intensive technological development.

Joseph et.al (2008) study on organized retailing shows all segments of the Indian economy could be affected by the entry of large corporate giants in the multi-brand retail business. It has found that unorganized retailers experienced a decline in their sales and profit with the organized retailers. The liberalization of FDI for Multi- brand retail sector would affect unorganized small retailers by giving rise to monopolies of large corporate houses with respect to pricing and availability of goods.

Pires, Stanton and Salavrakos (2010) argue that the legal, technical and socio-economic problems at the macro-level interlink FDI and economic growth. The study stress on the importance of prioritizing the incentives offered to the FDI infrastructure. The entry of other players would create a competitive landscape for the e-commerce business, leading to the larger benefits for the Indian customers. The only challenge they fore see is the state approval clause. Indian government has put a clause that allows state government to opt out of the system, which would bar multi-brand retailers from opening up the physical stores in the states. They are not clear how this clause is going to affect the e-commerce. The investors would be more comfortable investing in a company that is complying with all the requirements set by the cabinet and the letter of law. From the company's perspective the investors will now be able to pursue foreign investments but have to be cautious to comply with the regulations.

Economic Survey (2011-12) for FDI in multi-brand retail states that the Inter-Ministerial Group (IMG) on inflation has recommended for leveraging FDI as it noted concerns for high rates of food inflation and low prices grasped by Indian farmers. Study (McKinsey Report,2012) states that the retail productivity in India is very less compared to other International counterparts. The over-all retail employment in India, account for about 6 of current Indian labour force, mostly unorganized, and which is about half when compared to the other emerging economies. A comprehensive expansion of retail sector in India would create more than 50 million jobs. Training and development for labour in the retail sector for a better productivity is considered to be a challenge.

Jain and Sukhlecha (2012) studied FDI in multi-brand retail and tried to establish the need of the retail community to invite FDI in multi-brand retailing. It was noticed that there are few issues to be addressed for the consumer's right to be saved, for the employment opportunities to be generated and also for the regularization of the retailers working in different areas. But it inferred that in spite of having all these problems the entry of foreign investment in retail sector is found to be the most effective for the country's development and supremacy in the world scenario.

The government's decision to allow up to 51% Foreign Direct Investment (FDI) in multi-brand retail, has been challenging for all the sectors mentioned in the various studies throughout the literature review. Additionally, more than 20 crore people are selling vegetables on footpath without a fixed shop throughout the country. There are other farmers, milkmen, fruit producers and others also make their lives through retail trading upon footpath and hand carts across the country. It is reported that the notification would hit the livelihood all these small retailers (Hindu, 2012).

In India life of a farmer is very much cheaper than their western counterparts. The current market system is not farmer supportive, as the big giants are directly dealing with agents. If the other retail players are allowed to enter over this market segment, small retailer in organic food shops will close down. The gap between farmer prices and consumer prices would be very high even with the entry of large retailers. Small retailers would be squeezed and the movement will suffer in the long run (Hindu, 2012). This movement has to be taken up more in urban cities as the people needed this most. Small retailers must be allowed to exist with their independent shops as such to enable them to have a peaceful livelihood.

New policy ensures 30 percent of the products must be obtained from small scale industries which have a total investment of not exceeding $1 million in plant and machinery. It further emphasizes that the fresh agricultural produce may be unbranded. The retail giants will have to comply with self-certification. They have to keep all documentation intact and the government will have the right to procure agricultural produce. New policy of 30% of obtaining manufactured and processed products should be secured from small industry (Department of Industrial Policy and Promotion Statistics, 2012). Experts' points out that Indian retail trade sources more than 30% from small industry currently. The FDI policy is not ensuring a concession on this matter.

Moghe (2012) critically analyzed the decision of Indian government to open retail sector for FDI in single-brand and multi-brand category and it's likely to have impact on various components of Indian economy. In addition, it was suggested to have a strong enforcement mechanism to ensure that big retailers do not dislocate small retailers by unfair means and to build a co- existence of both the arms. The high-level group which is to be constituted under the Minister of consumer affairs is expected to look into the aspects such as internal trade and recommendations on trade reforms to the government. Reforms in the internal trade will ensure distribution efficiencies and overall development to all sections of the society.

Implications of FDI in Multi-brand Retail Sector

Ozturk and Ilhan (2007) reviewed various literatures dealing with effects of FDI and observed significant effect on economic growth is through multiple channels such as capital formation, technology transfer and spillover, human capital enhancement and so on. Hence the new FDI policy on multi-brand sector emphasizes the multi-brand retailers to bring minimum of 100 million US dollars with half of the investment on back-end infrastructure facilities life cold chains, transportation, refrigeration etc. It was because the government of India wanted to minimize post-harvest losses and to provide reasonable remuneration prices to farmers with this new policy. So, now the retailers will be able get at least 30% of source for goods from small and medium sized suppliers in multi-brand and at the same time it will also enable the single-brand retail sector to get benefits out of this.

The FDI policy on multi-brand retail would create opportunities for the Micro, Small and Medium Enterprises (MSMEs) to reach out the International markets. Research studies on Indian Economy emphasizes the need for development of MSME sector, as most of them are highly unorganized. It has seen that the reason behind this is largely because their inability to get access to advanced technology and availability of limited options to improve its market interface. Mandeep (2009) in an attempt to review the advent of global retailers in India examined and evaluated that FDI brings latest technological know- how, well-integrated supply chains, standards and quality products. It not only upgrades human skills but also increases sourcing for Indian retail sectors to reach Global retailers.

The Indian logistics has always suffered due to lack of investment mainly in retail chain, due to which market mechanism failed to gain desired level of efficiency in- spite of being a second largest producer of fruits and vegetables. The limited integration in cold-chain infrastructure has always been a challenge to Indian economy. Currently there are 5386 stand-alone cold storages with total capacity of 23.6 million MT, whereas the production of fruits and vegetables amount to about 180 million MT (Prime, Subramanyam and Lin, 2012). The existing cold-chains are highly fragmented, which bring great challenges to farmers to make their perishable horticultural commodities to markets including overseas markets. The shortage of cold store not only brings heavy losses but also leads to wastage of produce both in terms of quantity and quality. With new policy on 'multi-branding' such issues may be resolved and the flow of FDI is expected to be more infrastructure development and a significant improvement can be seen in Indian agriculture. Over many years, Indian farmers suffer under the hands of intermediaries, who often flout mandi norms and dominate the value chain.

Lack of transparency in pricing has led to development of unorganized sector. Researcher (Discussion paper on FDI, 2010) have investigated that farmers receive only 1/3rd of total price paid by final consumers. The flaws of intermediaries are likely to be eliminated with the development of new FDI policy of the government, as the pricing would become more transparent and the farmers are expected to be benefited due to involvement of big retailers. The exploitation of intermediaries is mostly likely to be reduced.

There has always been a big question on the effectiveness of the public procurement and setting up of worthy Public Distribution System (PDS). Studies have shown that inflationary tendency in food pricing and absence of a 'farm-to-fork' retail supply system has always been a matter of concern to Indian government (Roy and Kumar, 2012).While developing FDI policies, the government has taken measures to resolve this issue through the new FDI policies.

The FDI in multi-brand retail sectors are likely to open doors for big supermarkets, which would tend to bring larger benefit to consumer, as they would experience lower prices with more diverse products and higher quality product than the traditional retailers. Increasing price in various sectors like food industry and other essential commodities the ultimate suffer are the consumers. Study conducted by Chari and Raghavan (2011) reveals that allowing entry to giant retailers to the Indian market may help tackle inflation especially in food prices. Moreover, it will help to enhance the technologies and distribution systems and supply chain efficiency in India. Some studies have shown that the basic foods of the urban poor are noted cheaper in supermarkets than in traditional retail shops. For example in Delhi (India) the price of rice and wheat are 15% cheaper and vegetables are 33% cheaper in supermarkets when compare to traditional retail shops. Survey (Pan-Indian survey, 2011) from ten major cities overwhelm that majority of farmers and consumers support the retail reforms, 90% of consumers said that the FDI in multi-brand retail reform would bring down the prices and would have more better choices of goods; 78% of farmers said that this will enable them to get better prices for their produce and 75% of traders claimed their sales may increase due multiple channels openings for marketing their products. Recent studies on new FDI policy reforms has claimed that consumers are tend to get the most benefit due to FDI in multi-brand retail (Suklecha, 2012). Research (Moghe, 2012) has shown that Indian Farmer's associations like Shriram Gadhve of All India Vegetable Growers Association (AIVGA) and Bharat Krishak Samaj revealed their support to FDI in multi-brand retail reforms. AIVGA strong believe the new FDI policy would help to resolve issues relating to cold storage and would minimize the exploitation of the middlemen commission agents.

Bharat Krishak Samaj supports new FDI policy because it would not only improve the wholesaler in sabzimandis (vegetables and farm produce) but a spillover effect can be found in small shopkeepers in the unorganized retail market.

Earlier research studies (Sharma, 2001) assessed FDI's contribution to India's export performance is considered to be one of the important channels which influence economic growth and development. It was observed that FDI have statistically no significant impact on export performance. However, the exiting retail firms like Spencer's, Food world Supermarkets Ltd, Nilgir's and ShopRite also support the new FDI in multi-brand retail sector as this would enable them to create opportunities for joint ventures with major global supermarkets with more scope for expansion in capital and flow of gain expertise in supply chain management. Research shows Food world Supermarkets Ltd. already tied up with Hong Kong-based Dairy Farm International and with new reforms their global relationship will get stronger (AP Retail conference, 2007).a Research (Wie, 2005; Blomström and Kokko, 2001) examines the links between FDI and human capital and it discuss the interaction between FDI and human labour is complex and non-linear. FDI has potential for spillovers of knowledge and advance technology which would lead to the development of labour skills. Balasubramanyam and Mahambare (2002) argued that FDI is very effective in promoting development activities conditioned by co-operant factors in the host economies which possess a threshold level of human capital. The new FDI reforms will help the Indian economy to bring structural change in labour markets with better work environment. Research (Wakchaure, 2011) argues that

Indian workers in small shops work without formal contracts for long hours with very low wages. Most the unorganized sector largely depends on child labour. Hence with new FDI policy these issues may be resolved as the main agenda of the new FDI reforms is to minimize unorganized sectors in India.

Thus it can be said that the rationale behind allowing FDI in multi-brand retail sectors is due to competition in retail industry and current trends of poor productivity with high level of unorganized sectors operating in India. This would bring adequate flow of capital into the Indian Economy and help the country to promote welfare to society in general and farmers and consumers in particular. Apart from this, the Indian Economy would flourish in terms of better quality standards and gain some cost-efficacy. The Indian Council for Research on International Economic Relation (ICRIER) has projected the impact of BIG capital in retail sector will reach to $496 billion by end of 2011-12 and this would not harm the interest of small, traditional, retailers (Prime, Subramanyam and Lin, 2012). FDI in multi- brand retail would lead to substantial growth in GDP and overall economic development. The new liberalized FDI policy in multi-brand retailing is favoured by the Retail Association of India (RAI), Shopping Centers Association of India (a 44 member association of Indian multi-brand retailers and shopping malls) and International retail players like Wal-Mart, Carrefour, IKEA and Tesco (Abrar, 2012).

Research studies (Baskaran, 2012; Gupta, 2012) have indicated that FDI in multi-brand retail will lead development with an increase in the sales for modern retail outlets in India. With entry of retail giants' it is likely to eliminate informal retail sectors out of business and is likely to bring market consolidation in the formal sectors. This would help the small/less capitalized retailers to maintain a sustainable price for their product. Studies argue that the informal sectors will not be displaced with big retail giants, but in turn they are likely to grow and become more organized (Moghe, 2012). Indian economy has great scope developing informal sector to formal sectors with increased favourable investments. Bhaskaran (2012) conducted a SWOT analysis of FDI towards the multi-brand retailing which brought out the significant challenges and key success factors of FDI in Indian scenario. It reviews the impact of organized retailing on the unorganized sector. Surveys specified (Joseph, 2008) some specific policy recommendations for regulating the interactions of large retailers and suppliers and for firming the good response of the unorganized retailers.

Conclusion

In view of the above, allowing FDI in multi-brand retail will lead to a significant improvement in India's GDP and overall economic development. The Policy of multi- brand retail by Indian government would bring improvements in rural infrastructure, technology, price for agricultural produce and employment opportunities. Evidences from various literature reviews indicate that the emergence of giant retailers would lead to extensive growth in the retail sector. By new policy Indian economy is likely to get additional benefits as the industries will be able to focus on intermediaries and create more jobs for skilled employees in Indian retail sector.

Prominent increase in inflation is one of the key reasons behind the move of the Indian Government towards multi-brand retail. The retailers in India will get much assistance in keeping prices under control both in food and commodity by allowing already well-established retail giants like as Wal-Mart and Carrefour. Moreover, on one hand they will build backend infrastructure that will help to cut waste and on the other hand the retail giants will also help to narrow down the current account deficit.

The present study indicates that there would no threats to kiranas (mom and pop stores). FDI would help to integrate India's economy with that of the global economy. In future the Indian retail market would be highly organized and would resolve issues of unorganized retails and provide quality products at lower prices. FDI in multi-brand retail can go a long way in improving the efficiency of supply chain and other relevant areas and the existing negative impact would weaken overtime. It indicates that farmers and consumers would benefit from the new entry of organized retailers in multi-brand. The government of India has taken safety measures for regulating the interaction of large retailers and suppliers for firming good response for unorganized retailers.

Implications of FDI in multi-brand retail sector discussed in the paper clearly outweigh all the issues attached to it. It is evident from literature that FDI plays an important role in the economic growth of India. The study examined all possible issues that could be affected with the policy for FDI multi-brand retail sector and show that FDI reforms in multi-brand would positively accelerate GDP and also improve strategic alliances with foreign investors.

References

- Agarwal, P. (2011). Foreign Direct Investment in Indian Retail Sector - An Analysis: Available from: http://www.legalindia.in/foreign-direct- investment-in-indian-retail-sector-%E2%80%93- an- analysis (Accessed on September 23, 2012).
- A.T. Kearney Report (2011). Retail Global expansion: A portfolio of opportunities, Chicago, USA Balasubramanyam, V.N and Mahambare, V. (2002).
- Foreign Direct Investment in Developing countries, Lake District, September 13th- 14th, 2002.Lancaster University Management School, Working paper-1.
- Baskaran, K. (2012). 'FDI in India's Multi Brand Retail- Boon or Bane',Universal Journal of Management and Social Sciences, 2(1), 1-16.
- Blomstorm, M. and Kokko, A. (2001). FDI and HumanCapital : A Research Agenda, Research
- FDI in multi-brand retail challenged in apex court: Available from: http://www.thehindu.com/business/Economy/fdi-in-multibrand-retail-challenged-in-apexcourt/article3927065.

eceAccessed on 02/10/ 2012

- Gupta, A. (2012). 'Foreign Direct Investment In Indian Retail Sector: Strategic issues and Implications', IJMMR, 1(1), 55-68.
- Henley, J.S.(2004). 'Chasing the dragon: accounting for the under-performance of India by comparison with China in attracting foreign direct investment', Journal of International Development, 16(7),1039-1052.
- Jain, M., Suklecha, M.L. (2012). "FDI in Multi-Brand Retail: Is it the need of the hour?', Zenith, International journal of Multi-disciplinary Research, 2(6), 108-131.
- Joseph, M., Soundararajan,N.,Gupta, M. and Sahu, S.(2008). Impact of Organized retailing in the paper-222. Asia Pacific Business Review, 18(3), 303-333.

Foreign Direct Investment and Indian Economy

Dr. Rajesh Dogra
Assoc. Prof. Govt. College Talwara, Punjab

Abstract

Foreign capital played an important role in the early stages of industrialization of most of the advanced countries of today, like the countries of Europe (including the Russia) and North America. Though the problems of development of developing countries of today are not very much similar to those faced by the advanced countries in the past, there is a general view that foreign capital, if properly directed and utilized, can assist the development of the developing countries. Economic growth is a function of, among other things, capital formation. In the developing countries, the per capita income and savings rate being very low, domestic capital formation is inadequate to give a 'big push' to the economy to take it to the 'take-off stage. Hence the domestic resources may be supplemented with foreign capital to achieve the critical minimum investment to break the vicious circle of "low-income-low savings-low investment-low income."Another way by which foreign capital helps accelerate the pace of economic growth is by facilitating essential imports required for carrying out development programmes, like capital goods, know-how, raw materials and other inputs and even consumer goods. The machinery, the know-how, and other inputs needed may not be indigenously available; further, the demand spurt created by large-scale investments may necessitate import of consumer goods. Capital is stated as the engine of economic growth. This statement has gained more importance in the recent times.

Conceptual Framework of FDI

Traditionally, the various sources of capital for developing countries were either the demand of their output (raw material) by industrial countries or foreign aid or loans from foreign banks. However, now-a-days, the official development assistance flows are steadily declining. Beside others, Foreign Direct Investment as a source of funds has gained very high importance, in recent years.

Foreign Direct Investment (FDI) is an investment involving a long-term relationship and reflecting a lasting interest and control of a resident entity in one economy in an enterprise resident in an economy other than that of the foreign direct investor. Individuals as well as business entities may undertake FDI. Such investments involve both the initial transaction between the two entities and all subsequent transactions between them and among foreign affiliates.

Foreign Direct Investment involves the ownership and control of a foreign company in a foreign country. In exchange for this ownership, the investing country usually transfers some of its financial, technical, managerial, trademark and other resources to the recipient country. The international transfer of funds need not be prerequisite for this exchange. The Government of India, in March 2008, revised the FDI definition in line with international practices.

The revised FDI data now includes 'equity capital' including that of unincorporated entities, non-cash acquisition against technology transfer, plant and machinery, goodwill, business development, control premium, and non-competition fees.

Considerable interest is now being shown in measures that might promote FDI and allow it to make a greater contribution to the development of the recipient countries. In determining the flow of foreign capital controls exercised by the host country over the conditions of entry of foreign capital, regulations of the operation of foreign capital and restrictions on the remittance of profits and the repatriation of capital are far more decisive.

Significance of Foreign Capital

Foreign capital played an important role in the early stages of industrialization of most of the advanced countries of today, like the countries of Europe (including the Russia) and North America. Though the problems of development of developing countries of today are not very much similar to those faced by the advanced countries in the past, there is a general view that foreign capital, if properly directed and utilized, can assist the development of the developing countries.

Economic growth is a function of, among other things, capital formation. In the developing countries, the per capita income and savings rate being very low, domestic capital formation is inadequate to give a 'big push' to the economy to take it to the 'take-off stage. Hence the domestic resources may be supplemented with foreign capital to achieve the critical minimum investment to break the vicious circle of "low-income-low savings-low investment-low income."

Another way by which foreign capital helps accelerate the pace of economic growth is by facilitating essential imports required for carrying out development programmes, like capital goods, know-how, raw materials and other inputs and even consumer goods. The machinery, the know-how, and other inputs needed may not be indigenously available; further, the demand spurt created by large-scale investments may necessitate import of consumer goods. Foreign investments may also help increase a country's export and reduce the import requirements if such investments take place in export-oriented and import competing industries. "Infrastructure provides a platform and creates the strategic context in which the firms can grow. The key characteristic is that it enables generating other investment opportunities.

In nutshell important advantages of FDI may include the following:

1. It helps increase the investment level and thereby the income and employment in the host country.
2. FDI facilitates transfer of technology to the recipient country.
3. It may kindle managerial revolution in the recipient country through professional management and the employment of highly sophisticated management techniques.
4. Foreign capital may enable the country to increase its exports and reduce import requirements.
5. Foreign investments may stimulate domestic enterprises because to support their own operations, the foreign investors may encourage and assist domestic suppliers and consume industries.
6. Foreign investment may also help increase competition and break domestic monopolies.

Dangers of FDI

It is not that FDI helps in the economic development; there is another side of this aspect. Since 1960, the discussion on the advantages and disadvantages of FDI has started and is still enduring. The capital flows to an industry in which an existing firm has monopoly power in the world market, an increase in output from the new competition lowers the price of the exportable, thus reducing the terms of trade and potentially lowering welfare in the host country. The components of Portfolio investment are equity and debt instruments. These flows include the investment activities of collective investment scheme and money market funds. Portfolio investment does not entitle an investor to legal control over a firm.

FDI Policies in India Since Independence

India has introduced many policy reforms to attract FDI. Restrictive investment regimes have been liberalized. In addition, various types of incentives are being offered to attract foreign direct investment. Changes in policy frameworks in India dealing with FDI inflows could be studied in four phases viz.

(i) "Cautious welcome policy" from independence to the emergence of crisis in the late sixties (1948-66);

(ii) "Selective and restrictive policy" from 1967 till the second oil crises in 1979.

(iii) "Partial liberalization policy" from 1980 to 1990 with progressive attenuation of regulations; and

(iv) "Liberalization and open door policy" since 1991-2013 & onwards, signifying liberal investment environment.

In nutshell, the continuing policy changes introduced since 1991 mark a radical departure from the past and reflect a positive approach towards foreign collaboration. The changes provide freedom to foreign investors to enter into Indian industry. In terms of openness, the prevailing Indian policy is not unfavorably placed in terms of competitiveness with other major FDI-receiving countries in Asia\World.

Now, it is established fact that capital and investment are the essential pillars of economic development of every country. Savings, capital and investment along with human resources are the essential hub of development.

Low GDP keeps the savings and investment rates low, which in turn, limit growth. Poor technological base of production is another factor impinging upon growth of the developing countries. FDI mitigates these constraints to growth of the developing and emerging countries.

FDI and foreign technology also brings with them the modem managerial practices. Market size, as manifested by population size and growth environment, including economic policy, specially the reform process, prevailing growth rates and future growth potential, beside others, may together affect the level and sectoral directions of inflows of FDI into the recipient countries.

Keeping in view the pivotal role played by FDI inflows, the government of India opened the Indian economy for foreign players in 1991 when the economic reforms process was initiated.

Emerging Trends In FDI: Indian Evidence

This paper aims at presenting trends and progress of FDI in India since 1991, an era of economic reforms and liberalization. The time series, secondary data is used for the purpose and the analysis is carried across state, sector and country. The analysis of phenomenon of FDI trends at the global level, in developing countries, China, India and SAARC countries have been made in next chapter.

India initiated economic policy reforms in 1991 and since then these reforms have played a critical role in the performance of the Indian economy. Among other things, the reforms have involved opening the economy, making it more competitive, getting the government out of the huge morass of regulation, empowering the states to take more responsibility for economic management and thereby creating a kind of competition between the states for foreign investors.

In the backdrop of the East Asian crisis, growth did slow down a little bit, but India has kept growing and has avoided the worst of the crisis.

From the narrow financial point of view two things that India did were quite helpful. One, it did keep some limit on the short-term capital inflows and did not go overboard in borrowing short-term from abroad. This helped India to avoid the financial reversals of some of its neighbours. Second, it kept the rupee flexible and the depreciation of the rupee definitely helped keep the Indian economy more competitive and kept economic growth going during this period

A comprehensive study of Bosworth and Collins (2008) provides evidence on the effect of capital inflows on domestic investment for 58 developing countries. The sample covers nearly all of Latin America and Asia, as well as many countries in Africa. The authors distinguish among three types of inflows; FDI, portfolio investment, and other financial flows (primarily bank loans).

When competing for FDI, policy makers have to be aware that various measures intended to induce FDI are necessary. These include liberalization of FDI regulations and various business facilitation measures. Other reforms, such as privation, tend to be more effective in stimulating FDI inflows, but need to ensure that FDI inflows are beneficial. Other determinants of FDI, which were sufficient in the past, may prove to be less relevant in the future.

FDI is a zero-sun game in which a country can attract FDI only at the expanse of another country. Additional FDI is likely to take place when new investment opportunities emerge in country opening up to the world.

Sector-Wise Trends of FDI

Since the mid-1990s, India has allowed "automatic" FDI approval in many sectors, gradually expanding the list over time. Where applicable, foreign investors do not need government licenses or approvals and simply notify the Reserve Bank of India (RB[) of their investments.

Other sectors require approval by either the Foreign Investment Promotion Board (FIPB) or the Cabinet Committee on Foreign Investments. Presently, foreign direct investment is freely allowed in all sectors including the services sector, except a few sectors where the existing and notified sectoral policy does not permit FDI beyond a ceiling.

The govt. of India has set for itself an ambitious target of achieving $10 bn, of actual FDI Inflows per year. In order to achieve the above target, it is crucial to raise FDI Inflows. FDI is stated as the engine of economic growth. FDI as a source of funds has gained very high importance.

FDI has evolved as a vital resource for the economic development of developing and under-developed countries. FDI flows to a country when business investors are attracted to make investments in it. India is not an exception to this. The understanding of the mindset of foreign business investors is very important for attracting more FDI Inflows in India.

Statewise Trends in FDI Inflow

The main factors, which determine the attractiveness of a state as an important FDI destination, are the extant of state Level reforms, the overall investment climate and infrastructure facilities. An attempt has also been made to examine the disparity in FDI coming to various states of our country.

In fact various states of India now have been showing considerable interest in attracting foreign investments. In this context, while range of interstate disparities in industrialization, location of projects has assumed a lot of significance.

Currently, a significant difference is noticed in economic performance between Northern and Southern Indian states. The Karnataka, Tamil Nadu and Andhra Pradesh are quite dynamic and are trying to get the infrastructure, and the policy regime right to attract large-scale investment.

In the north, in Bihar, Uttar Pradesh, we don't find the same kind of reform dynamism and the results are therefore poor in terms of economic growth. The states that are behind will find that there is the demand to catch-up with the states that are growing. This will spur a kind of competition among the Indian States and make the reform process go much faster.

"The progress of policy reforms and variations in reforms at the sub-national level in India" divided states into three categories as follows:

(i) Reform-oriented States: Andhra Pradesh, Gujarat Karnataka, Maharastra and Tamil Nadu.

(ii) Intermediate States: Haryana, Orissa and West Bengal.

(iii) Lagging Reformers: Assam, Bihar, Kerala, Madhya Pradesh, Punjab, Rajasthan and Uttar Pradesh.

It should be noted that provision of, better infrastructure and financial incentives to attract private investment flows at the state level were also emphasized in the perform era in India. However, these policy packages, meant for development of backward regions, became part and parcel of regional policies in the Plan documents with respect to achieve in balanced regional development of industries.

Higher intensity of competition amongst states to attract FDI entails an increased competition amongst states for "total fiscal resources" in an economy. Each state would try to utilize its own resources, supplementing it by trying to divert outside resources via the Central Government towards the region.

Conclusion

In order to achieve the objectives of the paper both secondary and primary data can be used. The prime sources of secondary data include SIA Newsletter, DIPP, GOI, UNCTAD-World Investment Reports, World Development Reports, Human Developments Reports, Reserve Bank of India Bulletins, FICCI Survey Reports, CII Survey Reports, etc. Internet has also remained as an important source of secondary data.

In the earlier policy phases in India, the attitude was quite rigid with respect to foreign equity ownership and control. It was insisted that FDI should be accompanied by technology transfer agreements. And, foreign ownership exceeding 40 percent of equity was granted only in exceptional cases.

The central question of this study is why foreign investments are coming into India. Taking the case of German investments during the post-liberalization period, the report has found three main reasons of German investments into India- availability of cheap labour coupled with toothless labour legislation; huge domestic markets of goods and services; and India's lax environmental and public health regulations with ineffective implementation by the state machinery.

Any policy to attract foreign investments in India needs to be guided by the overall development agenda keeping the concerns of people, domestic economy and environment in mind. The recent restructuring of FIPB and setting up of the Foreign Investment Promotion Council has been done only to accelerate the inflows of FDI into India.

Bibliography

- Ahmad arif almazari (2009), "The impact of FDI on developing countries", the journal of accounting and finance, vol.21 No.2 April – Sept. 2007, Page. 3-15.
- Aykut.D, Goldstein. A, (2013) "Developing country multinationals: South-South investment comes of age." United Nations (Edition) Industrial development for the 21st century: Sustainable development perspective, New York, United nations, pp.85-116
- Akkio Hagiwara (2012), "Recent FDI Trends and Policies in Developing Asia", Economic and Research Department, Asian Development Bank.
- Anwar, Syed Aziz (2009), "Reassessing Determinants of FDI in Some Emerging Economies", Foreign Trade Review.
- Agrawal pradeep (2010); "Economic impact: of FDI in South Asia", Indira Gandhi institute of Development Research, Mumbai.
- Bhatt, P.R (2008),Foreign Trade Review,VOL.XLIII.NO. 3,Quarterly Journal of Indian Institute Foreign Trade, OCT.-DEC. 2008,P.21-40.
- Bajpai, Nirupam and Jeffrey D, Sachs (2009), "The Progress of Policy Reform and Variations in Performance at the Sub-National Level in India", Development Discussion Paper No. 730, (November), Harvard Institute for international Development, Harvard University.
- Barry P. Bosworth and Susan M. Collins (2008), "Capital Flows to Developing Economics: Implications for Saving and Investment", Breakings Papers on Economic Activity: 1, Brookings Institution, pp. 143-69.

Real Estate and Foreign Direct Investment Its Impact on Indian Economy

Dr. Ashok Kumar Chaudhary
Associate Professor in Commerce
Govt. P. G. College Dharamshala Distt. Kangra (H.P.)
Prof. Raman Kumar
Assistant Professor in Commerce
Govt. College Shahpur Distt. Kangra (H. P.)

FDI in Housing Sector

India of today as acknowledge as one of the fastest growing economy in the world and in this current economic status, housing sector has emerged as one of the most appealing investment area for domestic as well as foreign investor. And this high growth curve in housing sector owes some credit to a booming economy and liberalized foreign direct investment regime in the housing sector.

The Govt. of India in the March 2005 amended existing norms to allow 100 percent FDI in construction business. This liberalized act cleared the path of foreign investment to meet the demand into development of the commercial and residential housing sector. It has also encouraged several large financial firms and private equity funds to launch exclusive funds targeting the Indian housing sector. Foreign Direct Investment (FDIs) in

India's booming real estate and housing market jumped 80 times between 2005 and 2010 figures show that in 2005, FDIs in housing sector was mere Rs. 171crores, that soared to Rs. 13,586 crores in 2009 -10 in April and May 2010, Rs. 2957crores in FDIs were pumped in to housing sector.

India has been witnessing more money being pumped in housing sector from abroad despite the recent downturn. Since 2005, Foreign Direct Investment worth Rs. 37248 crores has come into the housing sector in India, including Rs. 856 cores in 2009-10. It is no surprise that the largest number of building projects where FDIs is in play is in the country's commercial capital, Mumbai. Of the total, 1614 projects in which foreign investor have put in money since 2005, 422 were cleared by the Reserve Bank of India's Mumbai office, followed closely by 316 in Delhi. Other big cities like Bangalore (225 projects), Hyderabad (105 project), and Chennai (68 projects) also enjoy considerable attention of foreign real estate developers.

At present, the government allows FDIs in real estate, but does not permit foreign institutional investment. It is, however, considering a proposal not to view FDIs and FII and Distinct investment flows while specifying an overall limit. It is yet to be permit foreign venture capital investor in the reality sector. To ensure that the concept of special economic zone did not distort the reality market, the RBI has classified lending SEZs on par with commercial real estate, according to higher risk weight and provisioning. India in the next five years period is estimated to require investment worth US$25 billion with urban housing sector. This again opens up the opportunities for the foreign investment in the reality sector. The central government allows up to 100 FDIs for setting up of townships in 2002. However, the flows of FDIs investment has been slowed by the 100 acres criterion, since acquiring such a large chunk of land was impossible in metropolitan cities and even satellite cities and state capital.

Advantages of FDIs in Housing Sector

- FDIs flows in India can encourage the reality sector and thereby also create better employment opportunities in this sector.
- Technology advantages is possible in construction activity in India whether commercial or residential housing.
- To create healthy competitive market environment for both Indian and foreign investors.
- Better infrastructure facilities are possible with investment from foreign investor.
- Efficiency in funds management in India and enrich the quality standards for housing sector in India.

Disadvantages of FDIs

- There is a necessity to frame strategic for better utilization of FDIs inflow as is pressurizes in Indian economy.
- There is also a scope of losing the ownership and entity with the foreign investors in the business.
- The increased liquidity and consequent inflation due to excessive FDIs flow in India.

FDI Rules in Housing Sector

The government of India has setup certain guidelines for investors willing to apply in FDIs in real estate, which has the condition like area, investment options and target for completion of a project.

1. Minimum Area

In case of development of serviced in housing plots, 10 hectors (25 acres). In case of construction – development projects, buildup area of 50000 sq. m. in case of combination projects any of above conditions.

2. Investment

Minimum capitalization for wholly owned subsidies US$10 million. For JV with Indian partners- US$ 5 million to be brought in within 6 month of commencement of the business. Original investment cannot be repatriated before a period of three years from completion of capitalization. The investor may exist earlier with prior approval from Foreign Investment Promotion Board.

3. Time Frame & Rules

At least 50 percent of the projects are developed within 5 years from the date of obtaining all statutory clearness. Investor cannot sell underdeveloped plots- where roads, water supply, street lighting, drainage, sewerage and other conveniences are not available.

Guidelines for Foreign Direct Investment

No foreign investment is permitted in this sector except for development of integrated township and settlement where FDIs up to 100 percent is permitted with prior government approval. NRIs/OCBs are allowed to invest in the following activities.

1. Development of serviced plots and construction of buildup residential premises.
2. Invest in real estate covering construction of residential and commercial premises including business centers and offices.
3. Development of township.
4. City and regional level urban infrastructure facilities, including both roads and bridges.
5. Investment in manufacture of building material, which is also opened to FDIs.
6. Investment in housing financial institutions, which is also opened to FDIs as an NBFC.

The government has also imposed a lock in period of three years for repatriation of investment made in this sector after the minimum capitalization equipments are complete. Also, 50 percent of the projects must be complete in 5 years from the date of statutory clearance and investor is not permitted to sell underdeveloped plots.

Some of the foreign players who have already tied up with the Indian real estate developers are Lee Kim the Holding, CESMA International Pvt. Ltd., Even Lim, and Keppel land from Singapore, Salim group from Indonasia, Edaw Ltd from USA, Emaar group from Dubai, IJM Ho Hup construction company from Malaysia etc.

Methodology

The study is constructed with the following objectives.

1. To analyze the follows of FDIs in housing sector before global financial crises and till date.
2. To study the sources of FDIs in India.
3. To study the impact of FDIs on economic growth in India.

For the study only secondary data has been used. The trends of the FDIs in real estate sector are compared with the other sectors in India. The data from 2002 to 2013 has been considered. This data is used to assess the impact of FDIs in India and economic growth achieved through FDIs follows. This sector has attracted a cumulative foreign direct investment worth US $22007.67 million from April 2000 to Feb. 2013.

Analysis and Finding

Table 1 Housing and Real Estate in India (2005- 2010)

Years	Rs. In Crore	% of FDIs
2005-06	171	0.42
2006-07	2121	5.27
2007-08	8749	21.77
2008-09	12621	31.40
2009-10	13586	33.49

Years	Rs. In Crore	% of FDIs
2010-11	2957	7.35
2012-13	US$ 1260 Million	

Source: CIA World Fact Book

The above figures show that FDI's inflows in the housing sector have increased from Rs. 171 crores in 2005-06 to Rs. 13586 crores in 2009-10. It indicates that FDIs inflow has jumped 80 times between 2005 to2010. Even during the global recession period of housing sector in India has received a considerable amount of FDIs. But in 2010-11, FDIs to realty Sector has down to 7.35% and in 2011-12 it is going to increase up to 46.6 billion.

Table 2: Financial Year wise FDI Inflow Data

Sr. No.	Years	Total FDI Inflow (US $)	% Growth (US $)
1	2000-01	4029	—
2	2001-02	6130	(+) 52%
3	2002-03	5035	(-) 18%
4	2003-04	4322	(-) 14%
5	2004-05	6051	(+) 40%
6	2005-06	8961	(+) 48%
7	2006-07	22826	(+) 146%
8	2007-08	34835	(+) 53%
9	2008-09	35180	(+) 01%
10	2009-10	37182	(+) 06%
11	2010-11	37763	(+) 02%
Total	2011-12	46.6 billion	(+) 23.6%

Source: RBIs Bulletin Jan. 2011

In the year 2005-06 the total inflow were 48% but during 2006-07 it has tremendously increased by 146%, it was due to the implementation of 100% inflows policy which later in 2007-08 has increased by 53%, in 2010-11 by 2% and in 2011-12 increased by 23.6%.

Economic Growth with FDI in Housing in India

India has been experiencing the impact of FDI's form a very recent period. Due to the government policy on FDI's all real estate sectors; residential, commercial and retail are currently witnessing huge growth in demand. India, during the first half of 2005-06 fiscal has attracted more than three times foreign investment at US $7.96 billion during making it amongst the " dominate the host countries" for FDIs in Asia and the pacific (APAC). After the initiatives of the government, the foreign investors have been more attracted in investing in India and so the construction activities have been enhanced. The real estate sector has been more organized in India since then so improving competitive condition for both the domestic and foreign investors. FDI has helped the Indian economy grow, and the government continues to encourage more investment of this short.

Foreign Direct Investment (FDI) in India has played an important role in the development of the Indian economy. FDI in India has-in a lot of ways-enabled India to achieve a certain degree of financial stability, growth and development. This money has allowed India to focus on the areas that may have needed economic attention, and addressed the various problems that continue to challenge the country. India has continually sought to attract the FDIs from the world major investor. FDI is permitted through financial collaborations, through private equity or preferential allotments, by way of capital markets through euro issues, and in joint ventures. FDI is not permitted in the arms, nuclear, railway, coal and lignite or mining industries.

Table 3: Economic Growth Rate in India

Year	DGP- Real Growth Rate
2003	4.30
2004	8.30
2005	6.20
2006	8.40

Year	DGP- Real Growth Rate
2007	9.20
2008	9.00
2009	7.40
2010	7.40
2011	7.70
2012	7.90

Source: CIA World Fact Book

The above studies highlights on the fact that the housing sector has received 21.77% in 2007-08 which was just 5.27% in 2006. With the effect of permitting 100% FDIs, the inflows have increased to 31.90% in 2008-09 and 33.49% in 2009-10 and so the GDP has also increased from 6.20% in 2005 to 8.40% in 2006 and 9.20% in 2007. This indicates that FDIs has positively contributed to the economic growth.

Impact of Recession on FDI Inflows in India

The global recession has changed the patterns of FDI flows with three major developing economies- Russia, Saudi Arab and India- becoming the top 10 largest recipients, creating history of sorts. The study reveals that China is leading as the priority host economy for FDIs among the developing economies and also second largest FDI recipient in the world, followed by Hong Kong (4th), Russia (6th), Saudi Arabia (8th) and India (9th). In 2007, total FDI inflow in the world soared to a record high of almost 2,100 billion $, of which developed countries received 1444 billion $ which is 68.8% of total FDI inflow in the world, while in the same year, developing and transition economies received only 31.2% of the total inflow in the world. In addition to other factor, implies screening requirements and new limitations of foreign equity policies of government during crises is also impairing with the inflows. Even with the gradual the recovery of FDIs in short term, developed nations chances of attracting more FDIs are fraught with mounting fiscal deficits and debt levels. Moreover, the global trends of economic growth are pointing to a stable and more rapid recovery for the developing and transition economies the results of several business surveys also highlight an encouraging short- term review of FDI prospects in these economies.

Region- wise FDIs Inflow in India

FDI inflows in India are heavily concentrated around two cities, Mumbai (US $ 45,592 million) and Delhi (US $ 24,700 million). Banglore, Ahmedabad and Chennai are also receiving significant amount of FDI inflows. These five cities together account for 69% of total FDI inflows to India. Mumbai and Delhi together received 55%of the total FDI inflow to India during 2000 to 2011. (table. 4)

Table 4: Statement on RBI's Regional Office (with state covered)

Received FDI Inflow (from April 2000 to)

Rank	RBI Regional Office	State (s) Covered	FDI inflow	Share of Total.
1.	Mumbai	Maharashtra, Dadra & Nagar Haveli	45,592	35
2.	Delhi	Delhi part of U.P. & Haryana	24,700	19
3.	Bangalore	Karnataka	8,114	6
4.	Ahmadabad	Gujarat	996	5
5.	Chennai	Tamil Nadu, Pondicherry	6,645	5
6.	Hyderabad	Andhra Pradesh	5,749	1
7.	Kolkata	West Bengal, Sikkim, Andaman Nicobar	1,481	1
8.	Chandigarh	Chandigarh, Punjab, Haryana, Himachal	922	1
9.	Other		28,170	23
Grand Total		121369	100	

Source of FDI in India

The analysis of (table: 5) present the major investing countries in India during 2000 to 2013. Mauritius is largest investor in during this period. FDI inflows from Mauritius constitute about 42% of the total FDI in India and enjoying the top position on India's FDI map from 2000. This dominance of Mauritius is because of the Double Taxation Treaty i.e. DTAA. Double Taxation avoidance Agreement between the two countries, which favor routing of investment through this country. This (DTAA) type of Taxation Treaty has been made out with Singapore also. The US is the second largest investing country in India. While comparing the investment made by both (Mauritius and US) countries one interesting fact comes up which shows that there is a huge difference (between FDI inflows to India from Mauritius and US) in the volume of FDI received from Mauritius and US. FDI inflow from Mauritius is more than US. The other major countries are Singapore with a relative share of 9% followed by UK, Netherlands, Japan, Germany, Cyprus, France and U.A.E.

Table 5: Share of top Investing Countries, FDI Equity

Sr. No.	Country	Cumulative Inflow	%age of total FDI
1	Mauritius	238,876	42%
2	Singapore	51,984	9%
3	U.S.A.	42,190	7%
4	U.K.	28,298	5%
5	Netherlands	24,877	4%
6	Japan	23,075	4%
7	Cyprus	21,235	4%
8	Germany	13,013	2%
9	France	10,088	2%
10	U.A.E.	8,526	1%
Total		570,105	

Source: Fact Sheet on Foreign Direct Investment.

Conclusion

India has witnessed a steady growth in the economy with the FDIs inflows. Interestingly, given the booming property market across the country FDIs are not confined to metros and big cities alone. Thus since 2005, various real estate projects have been given a green signal by RBIs. But certain factors such as the economic conditions of the developing economies in the world are putting pressures on the recovery of FDIs flows. The policies for FDIs have changed overtime with the changing requirements. India's share in the global FDIs regime is still minuscule which need further liberalization in the policies.

Refrences

1. Lata M. Chakaravsrtthy (2005) "Foreign Direct Investment in India", ICFAI University presses.
2. Dr. Arabi. U, "Foreign Direct Investment (FDIs) flows and sustained growth: a case study of India and China."
3. Laura Alfaro, "Foreign Direct Investment and Growth: Does the sector matter." HARVARD Business School.
4. Singh, Lakhwinder (2007), "India's economic growth and role of Foreign Direct Investment."
5. TK Shandiliya Anil Kumar Thakur (2008), "Foreign Direct Investment in India: problem and prospectus." Deep and deep publication Pvt. 1st edition.
6. Suman Chatterjee (2009) "An economic analysis of Foreign Direct Investment in India."
7. Nirupa Bajpai and Nandita Das Gupta CGSD (2004), "what constitutes Foreign Direct Investment? Comparison of India and China." www.earth.columbia.edu.
8. Global Recession has changed FDIs patterns, India high on priority, HTTP://www.indiangroung.com/real_estate_fdis.aspx.
9. RBIs bulletin Jan 31.1.2011. (Table no 77): Foreign Direct Investment Inflows.
10. Sapna Hooda, "A study of FDI and Indian economy, Ph.D. this submitted to National Institute of technology, Haryana, Jain 2011.
11. www.indiahousing.com.

NPAs and Indian Banking Sector

Dr N N Sharma
Associate Professor
Govt. PG College Dharmsala (HP)
Email-nnsharma585@gmail.com

Abstract

The issue of non-performing assets (NPA), the root cause of the recent global financial crisis, hasbeen drawing the attention of the policy makers and academicians alike. The problem of NPAs,which was ignored till recently, has been given considerable attention after liberalization of the financial sector in India. This exploratory paper examines the trends of NPAs in India fromvarious dimensions and explains how mere recognition of the problem and self-monitoring hasbeen able to reduce it to a great extent. The best indicator for the health of the banking industry in a country is its level of Non-performing assets (NPAs). NPAs are one of the major concerns for banks in India. It reflects the performance of banks. Reduced NPAs generally gives the impression that banks have strengthened their credit appraisal processes over the years and growth in NPAs involves the necessity of provisions, which bring down the overall profitability of banks. The Indian banking sector is facing a serious problem of NPA.The magnitude of NPA is comparatively higher in public sectors banks. To improve the efficiency and profitability of banks the NPA need to be reduced and controlled. This paper deals with understanding the concept of NPAs,India ranks of NPA in BRICS , its magnitude and major causes for an account becoming non-performing and strategies for managing NPA in Indian banks.

Keywords: Commercial Banks, NPA (Non performing asset), BRICS (Brazil, Russia, India, China and South Africa)

Introduction

The Indian Banking industry, which is governed by the Banking Regulation Act of India, 1949 can be broadly classified into two major categories, scheduled banks and non-scheduled banks. Scheduled banks comprise commercial banks and the co-operative banks. In terms of ownership, commercial banks can be further grouped into nationalized banks, the State Bank of India and its associate banks, regional rural banks and private sector banks (the old/ new domestic and foreign).Amongst the various desirable characteristics of a well-functioning financial system, the maintenance of a few non-performing assets (NPA) is an important one. NPAs beyond a certain level are indeed cause for concern for everyone involved because credit is essential for economic growth and NPAs affect the smooth flow of credit. Banks raise resources not just on fresh deposits, but also by recycling the funds received from the borrowers. Thus, when a loan becomes non-performing, it affects recycling of credit and credit creation. Apart from this, NPAs affect profitability as well, since higher NPAs require higher provisioning, which means a large part of the profits needs to be kept aside as provision against bad loans. Therefore, the problem of NPAs is not the concern of the lenders alone but is, indeed, a concern for policy makers as well who are involved in putting economic growth on the fast track.

In India due to the social banking motto, the problem of bad loans did not receive priority from policy makers initially. However, with the reform of the financial sector and the adoption of international banking practices the issue of NPAs received due focus. Thus, in India, the concept of NPA came into the reckoning after reforms in the financial sector were introduced on the recommendations of the Report of the Committee on the Financial System (Narasimham, 1991) and an appropriate accounting system was put in place.

Broadly speaking, NPA is defined as an advance where payment of interest or repayment of Installment of principal (in case of term loans) or both remains unpaid for a certain period2. In India, the definition of NPAs has changed over time. According to the Narasimham Committee Report (1991), those assets (advances, bills discounted, overdrafts, cash credit etc.) for which the interest remains due for a period of four quarters (180 days) should be considered as NPAs. Subsequently, this period was reduced, and from March 1995 onwards the assets for which the interest has remained unpaid for 90days were considered as NPAs.

This paper attempts to provide an overview of the NPA problem in India concentrating on the various dimensions involved.

Objectives of Study

1) To study the role and concept of Non Performing Assets in Banking Sector.
2) To study the trends of Non Performing asset classification in Indian Banking Sector.
3) To study the Indian Banking Sector NPAs in comparison with global countries (BRICS).
4) To study the Gross and Net NPAs of PSU with Pvt. Banks in India.

Sources of Data

The study is based on published data available in respect of Indian Capital Market. The sources of data include the annual data of Annual reports of banks, RBI, ICRA Research, report of

RBI, CSO, World Bank and World Development Indicators etc. The collected data has been examined with the help of statistical tools and techniques such as average, time series and percentage.

NPAs at the Global Level

In order to get a global picture it is essential to look at the NPAs in the different countries of the world. Since the concept of NPA developed in India only in the post -reform era, it would be useful to look at recent figures rather than adhere to a historical account. A closer look at the Non-performing Loans (NPL), as they are called in many nations, reveals that in 2003 the NPL at the global level was US$1,300 billion. India ranks fourth with NPL of around US$ 30 billion (2.3 per cent of the global NPL), while Japan has the highest NPL of US$ 330 billion (25.4 per cent of the global NPL) and Turkey has the lowest NPL of US$ 8 billion (0.6 percent of global NPL, Table 1).

Table 1

Country Name	2005	2006	2007	2008	2009	2010	2011	2012
BRICS								
Brazil	3.5	3.5	3	3.1	4.2	3.1	3.5	3.6
Russian Federation	2.6	2.4	2.5	3.8	9.5	8.2	6.6	6.7
India	5.2	3.3	2.7	2.4	2.4	2.5	2.3	3
Hong Kong SAR, China	1.4	1.1	0.8	1.2	1.6	0.8	0.7	0.6
South Africa	1.5	1.1	1.4	3.9	5.9	5.8	4.7	4.6

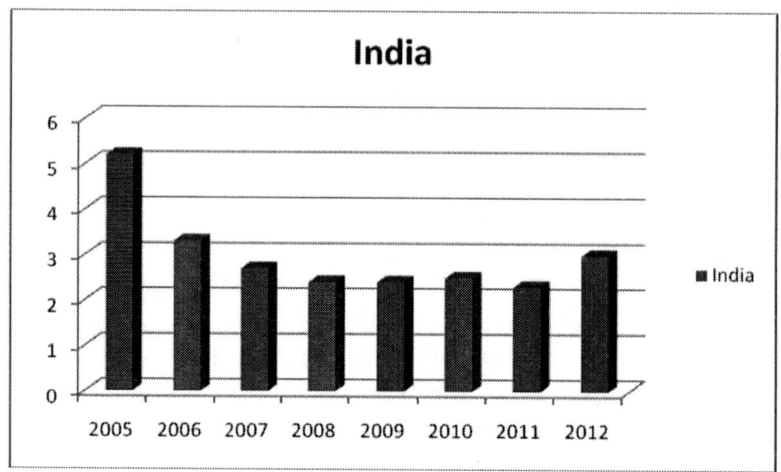

Fig-1

25
20
15
10
5
0
2005 2006 2007 2008 2009 2010 2011 2012
South Africa
Hong Kong SAR, China
India
Russian Federation
Brazil
BRICS

Fig-2

Bank nonperforming loans to total gross loans (%) (other than BRICS)

Table-2

Country Name	2005	2006	2007	2008	2009	2010	2011	2012
Canada	0.5	0.4	0.4	0.8	1.3	1.2	0.8	0.6
Switzerland	0.5	0.3	0.3	0.9	1	0.9	0.8	

Country Name	2005	2006	2007	2008	2009	2010	2011	2012
Germany	4	3.4	2.7	2.9	3.3	3.2	3	
Spain	0.8	0.7	0.9	2.8	4.1	4.7	6	
France	3.5	3	2.7	2.9	4.2	4.3	4.3	
United Kingdom	1	0.9	0.9	1.6	3.5	4	4	
Singapore	3.8	2.8	1.5	1.4	2	1.4	1.1	1
Chile	0.9	0.8	0.8	1	2.9	2.7	2.4	2.4
Denmark	0.4		0.6	1.2	3.3	4.1	3.7	4
Indonesia	7.4	6.1	4	3.2	3.3	2.5	2.1	2.1
Italy	5.3	4.9	5.8	6.3	9.5	10	11.7	
Jordan	6.6	4.3	4.1	4.2	6.7	8.2	8.5	
Colombia	2.7	2.7	3.2	3.9	4	2.9	2.5	3
Belgium	2	1.3	1.4	1.7	2.7	2.8	2.8	
Australia	0.2	0.6	0.6	1.3	2	2.2	2	1.9
Austria	2.6	2.7	2.2	1.9	2.3	2.8	2.7	2:7
Japan	1.8	1.5	1.5	1.4	1.6	2.5	2.4	
Uruguay	3.6	3.7	1.1	1	1.2	1	1.3	1.5

Source:data.worldbank.org

This time duration given for an asset to consider it as a NPA varies from country to country and can change over time within a particular country.

While comparing the NPA levels of different countries, it should be remembered that the Features relating to NPA reporting/ evaluation practices are not uniform across the globe. In some Countries, the NPA level may be low because losses are written off at an early stage. In some of the developing countries belonging to the Asia-Pacific Economic Co-operation (APEC), a loan is classified as non-performing only after it has been in arrears for at least six months. In India, currently, an asset is considered NPA if it is due for 90 days. Besides, in India due to the lengthy legal process, a considerably longer time is taken to recover the loan and due to many safeguards/procedures even after a NPA is written off, banks continue to hold them in their books often with the provisions made for those loans.

Even the classification of NPA into Gross NPA and Net NPA is not uniform because in some countries general provisions are made, whereas in India, NPAs are considered GNPA for some time even after making provisions. Thus, while comparing the NPA of India with other countries one should keep in mind that in many respect s asset classification norms in India are considerably more stringent than the best of international practices.

In addition, countries also do differ in various other respects, so a strict comparison across countries cannot be made. Nonetheless, the global picture reflect s a comprehensive view of NPAs across the world.

NPA Norms

Though the issue of NPA was given more importance after the Narasimham Committee Report (19 highlighted its impact on the financial health of the commercial banks and, subsequently, various asset classification norms were introduced, the concept of classifying bank assets based on its quality began during 1985-86. A critical analysis to monitor credit comprehensively and uniformly was introduced in 1985-86 by the RBI by way of the Health Code System in banks. This system, inter alia, provided information regarding the health of individual advances, the quality of the credit portfolio and the extent of advances causing concern in relation to total advances. It was considered that such information would be of immense use to banks for control purposes. The RBI advised all commercial banks (excluding foreign banks, most of which had similar coding system) on November 7, 1985, to introduce the Health Code System indicating the quality (or health) of individual advances under the following eight categories, with a health code assigned to each borrowal account (source: RBI):

1. Satisfactory - conduct is satisfactory; all terms and conditions are complied with; all accounts are in order and safety of the advance is not in doubt.
2. Irregular- the safety of the advance is not suspected, though there may be occasional Irregularities, which may be considered as a short term phenomenon.
3. Sick, viable - advances to units that are sick but viable - under nursing and units for which nursing/revival programmers' are taken up.
4. Sick: nonviable/sticky - the irregularities continue to persist and there are no immediate prospects of regularization and the accounts could throw up some of the usual signs of incipient sickness
5. Advances recalled - accounts where the repayment is highly doubtful and nursing is not considered worthwhile and where decision has been taken to recall the advance.
6. Suit filed accounts - accounts where legal action or recovery proceedings have been initiated
7. Decreed debts - where decrees (verdict) have been obtained.
8. Bad and Doubtful debts - where the recoverability of the bank's dues has become doubtful on account of short-fall in value of security, difficulty in enforcing and realizing the securities or Inability/unwillingness of the borrowers to repay the bank's dues partly or wholly. The NPA would be defined as advance, as on the balance sheet date in the following circumstances:
    1. In respect of overdraft and cash credits, accounts remain out of order for a period of more than 180 days,
    2. In respect of bills purchased and discounted, the bill remains overdue4 and unpaid for a period of more than 180 days,
    3. In respect of other accounts, any account to be received remains past due for a period of more than 180 days.; (i) Standard, (ii) Sub-standard, (iii)Doubtful and (iv) Loss.

Broadly, sub-standard assets would exhibit problems and include assets classified as non-performing for a period not exceeding two years. Doubtful assets are those that remain as such for more than two years and include loans that are overdue for more than two years.

An amount is considered overdue when it remains outstanding 30 days beyond the due date.

Loss assets are accounts where loss has been identified but amounts have not been written off.

According to international norms, commercial banks need to keep aside a portion of their income as a provision against bad loans. The amount of the provision depends on the type of NPAs and the time duration. Now Indian banks need to make provisions for all bad loans.

Table- 3

Bank Group Wise Classification of Loan Assets (2007 to 2012)

Bank	Standard		Sub Standard		Doubtful		Loss	
	Asset %		Asset %		Asset %		Asset %	
	Amt.	share	Amt.	share	Amt.	share	Amt.	share
Public Sector								
2007	13353	97.2	139.45	1	199	1.5	45.1	0.3
2008	16568	97.7	168	1	190	1.1	36.6	0.2
2009	20560	97.7	195	0.9	207	1	38	0.2
2010	24550	97.7	276	1.1	246	1	49	0.2
2011	29888	97.7	336	1.1	319	1	55	0.2
2012	34379	96.6	603	1.7	470	1.3	50	0.1
Pvt. Sector								
2007	3826	97.6	43.6	1.1	39	1	9.41	0.2
2008	4593	97.3	72	1.5	44	0.9	12.4	0.3
2009	5028	96.8	105	2	50	1	13.45	0.3
2010	5671	97	87	1.5	65	1.1	21.6	0.4
2011	7143	97.5	43	0.6	107	1.5	28	0.4
2012	8621	97.9	51	0.6	103	1.2	28.72	0.3

Source: Banking of supervision RBI

Table-4

	Gross		Total Advances
	NPA	% Share	
Public Sector			
2007	384	2.8	13738
2008	396	2.3	16964
2009	440	2.1	20999
2010	573	2.3	25124
2011	710	2.3	30599
2012	1125	3.2	35504
Pvt. Sector			
2007	92.39	2.4	3919
2008	130	2.7	4723
2009	169	3.2	5196
2010	174	3	5845
2011	179	2.5	7323
2012	183	2.1	8805

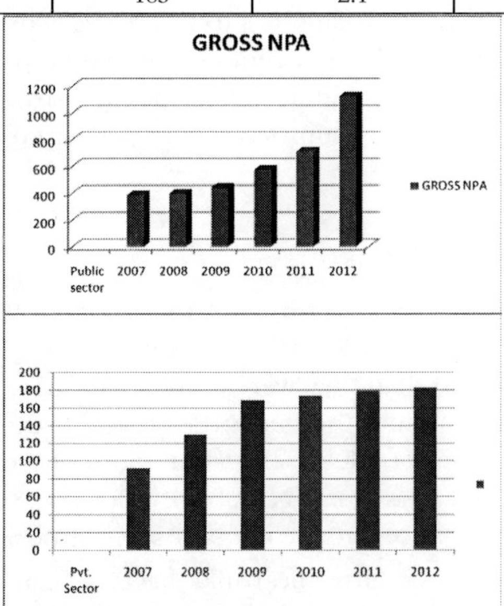

Fig-5

Gross NPA and Net NPA

Gross NPA is a advance which is considered irrecoverable, for bank has made provisions, and which is still held in banks' books of account. Net NPA is obtained by deducting items like interest due but not recovered, part payment received and kept in suspense account from Gross NPA.

The Reserve Bank of India states that, compared to other Asian countries and the US, the gross non-performing asset figures in India seem more alarming than the net NPA figure.

The problem of high gross NPAs is simply one of inheritance. Historically, Indian public sector banks have been poor on credit recovery, mainly because of very little legal provision governing foreclosure and bankruptcy, lengthy legal battles, sticky loans made to government public sector undertakings, loan waivers and priority sector lending.

Net NPAs are comparatively better on a global basis because of the stringent provisioning norms prescribed for banks in 1991 by Narasimham Committee. In India, even on security taken against loans, provision has to be created. Further, Indian banks have to make a 100 per cent provision on the amount not covered by the realizable value of securities in case of "doubtful" advance, while in some countries, it is 75 per cent or just 50 per cent.

Non-performing assets

The best indicator of the health of the banking industry in a country is its level of NPAs. Given this fact, Indian banks seem to be better placed than they were in the past. A few banks have even managed to reduce their net NPAs to less than one percent (before the merger of Global Trust Bank into Oriental Bank of Commerce, OBC was a zero NPA bank). But as the bond yields start to rise the chances are the net NPAs will also start to go up.

This will happen because the banks have been making huge provisions against the money they made on their bond portfolios in a scenario where bond yields were falling. The Indian banking sector features a large number of players competing against each other, the top 10 banks accounted for a significant 57% share of the total credit as on March 31, 2011.

Key Players In Indian Banking Sector

NAME OF BANK	MARKET SHARE (2011)	NIM	GROSS NPA (March 31, 2011)
STATE BANK OF INDIA	18%	2.90%	3.70%
PUNJABNATIONALBANK	6%	3.50%	1.80%
BANK OF BARODA	5%	2.80%	1.40%
ICICI BANK	5%	2.30%	4.20%
BANK OF INDIA	5%	2.50%	2.20%
CANARA BANK	5%	2.60%	1.50%
HDFC BANK	4%	4.20%	1.10%
IDBI BANK	4%	1.80%	1.80%
AXIS BANK	3%	3.25%	1.10%
CENTRAL BANK OF INDIA	3%	2.70%	2.20%

Table-6

NIM: net interest margin

Source: Annual Reports, Results of banks, ICRA Research

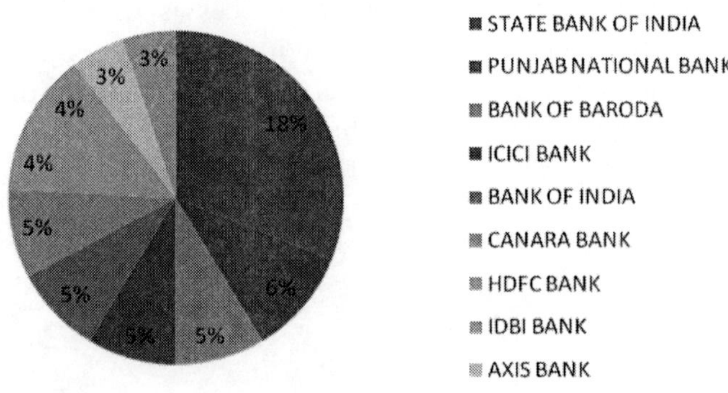

Fig-7

The non-performing assets of the banking sector rose sharply to 1.28 per cent in 2011-12 from 0.97 per cent a year ago due to high interest rate and slowdown in the economy. The NPAs (non-perfomring assets) or bad loans of the public sector banks rose to 1.53 per cent in 2011-12, up from 1.09 per cent in the previous year, said the latest RBI report.

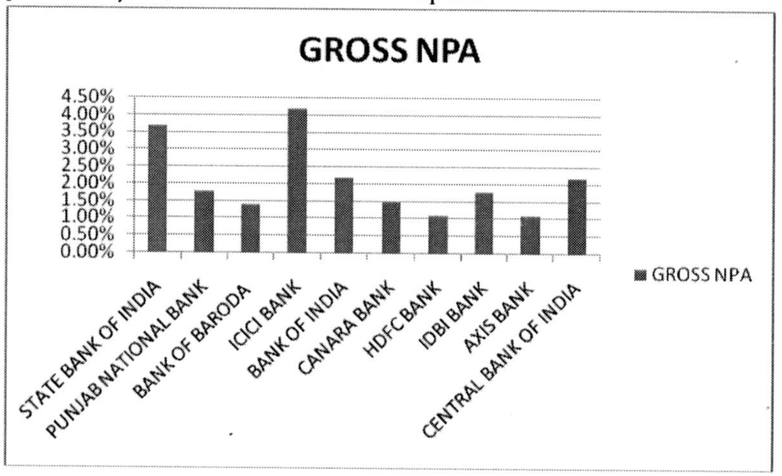

Fig-8

As per the Profile of Banks: 2011-12 released by the RBI, the NPA for India's largest public sector lender SBI along with its associates rose to 1.76 per cent from 1.49 per cent in 2010-11. Reduced NPAs generally gives the impression that banks have strengthened their credit appraisal processes over the years. This does not seem to be the case. With increasing bond yields, treasury income will come down and if the banks wish to make large provisions, the money will have to come from their interest income, and this in turn, shall bring down the profitability of bank

Table :7 Trend in Asset Quality Indicators

PSBs	FY06	FY07	FY08	FY09	FY10	FY11
Gross NPA (%)	3.6	2.7	2.2	2	2.2	2.3
Net NPA (%)	1.3	1.1	1	0.9	1.1	1.1
Net NPAs/Net Worth (%)	13.1	12.1	11.2	11.4	13.5	13.4
Private banks	FY06	FY07	FY08	FY09	FY10	FY11
Gross NPA (%)	2.1	2.1	2.4	2.9	2.7	2.3
Net NPA (%)	0.9	0.9	1.1	1.3	1	0.6
Net NPAs/Net Worth (%)	6.3	7.8	6.1	7.5	5.3	3.2

Source: Annual reports of banks, RBI, ICRA Research

Over the last two years, PSBs Gross NPAs rose from 2% to 2.3%, while private banks NPAs declined from 2.9% to 2.3%. The Gross NPA percentage of the PSBs got impacted by slippages from restructured accounts, "agri debt relief", and slippages because of automation of asset classification. Better provisioning coverage and a stronger capitalisation profile allowed private banks report better solvency (Net NPA/Net Worth) than PSBs during last few years.

Impact of NPAs on Banking Operations

The efficiency of a bank is not always reflected only by the size of its balance sheet but also the level of return on its assets.

The NPAs do not generate interest income for banks but at the same time banks are required to provide provisions for NPAs from their current profits.

1. The NPAs have destructive impact on the return on assets in the following ways.
2. The interest income of banks reduced it is to be accounted only on receipt basis.
3. The current profits of the banks are eroded because the providing of doubtful debts and writing it off as bad debts and it limits the recycling funds.

4. The capital adequacy ratio is disturbed and cost of capital will go up.
5. The economic value addition (EVA) by banks gets upset because EVA is equal to the net operating profit minus cost of capital

Conclusion

The problem of NPAs can be achieved only with proper credit assessment and risk management mechanism. In a situation of liquidity overhang, the enthusiasm of the banking system to increase lending may compromise on asset quality, raising concern about their adverse selection and potential danger of addition to the stock of NPAs. It is necessary that the banking system is to be equipped with prudential norms to minimize if not completely to avoid the problem of NPAs. The NPA is the root cause of the global financial crisis that we observed recently. The world is still trying to recover from the after-effects of the crisis. The problem of NPA has received considerable attention after the liberalization of the financial sector in India. Accounting norms have been modified substantially and mechanisms are in place for reduction of bad loans. NPAs affect profitability as well, since higher NPAs require higher provisioning, which means a large part of the profits needs to be kept aside as provision against bad loans. Our discussions with banks, however, show that such decline is mainly due to the awareness of the problem of bad loans at the bank level. It remains true that NPA in the priority sector is still higher than that of the non-priority sector. Within the priority sector, the SSI's performance is the worst. However, even this sector has shown reduction in bad loans over time. In the process of reducing NPAs, will banks shun the poor borrowers? In this context, the self-help group model can be applied to some of the sectors to help the poor access loans and ensure repayment for the banks. So this paper concludes that the Indian being part of emerging economy (BRICS) Indian banking sector is facing a serious problem of NPA.The magnitude of NPA is comparatively higher in public sectors banks. To improve the efficiency and profitability of banks the NPA need to be reduced and controlled.

References

Bardhan, P (1989). The Economic Theory of Agrarian Institutions. Oxford, NY: Claredon Press.

Bell, C and T N Srinivasan (1989). Some Aspects of Linked Products and Credit Market

Risk Neutral Agents. In Pranab K Bardhan (ed), The Economic Theory of Agrarian Institutions.

Oxford: Oxford University Press.

Battese, GE and T J Coelli (1995). A Model for Technical Inefficiency Effects in a Stochastic Frontier

Production Function for Panel Data. Empirical Economics, 20 (2): 325-32.

http://www.wdi.umich.edu/files/Publications/WorkingPapers/wp357.pdf

Chaitanya V Krishna (2004). Causes of Non-performing Assets in Public Sector Banks. Economic Research, 17 (1): 16-30.

Chakravarty, S (1985). Report of the Committee to Review the Working of the Monetary System.Mumbai: Reserve Bank of India.

Das Abhiman (2002). Risk and Productivity Change of Public Sector Banks. Economic and PoliticalWeekly, 37 (5): 437-48.

Gang, I N (1995). Small Firms in India: A Discussion of Some Issues. In Mookherjee, D (eds),Indian

Industry: Policies and Performance. New Delhi: Oxford University Press.Ghosh, S (2005). Does Leverage Influence Bank's Non-Performing Loan?: Evidences from India.

[Online] Available : http://203.115.117.202/Arcil1/ knowledge_centre/publications/papers/NPA_S1_Arcil-Positioning.pdf

[Online] Available : http://www.cdrindia.org/

[Online] Available : www.rbi.com

Report on trend and progress of banking in India 2004- 05,2006-07, 2009-10. pdf

[Online] Available : www.cibil.com

Trends of Primary Market in India: An Overview

Sahil Mahajan
Asstistant Professor, Govt. P. G. College, Dharamshala
Dept. of MBA
Email: sahil7.overseas@gmail.com

Abstract

The primary market enables the government as well corporate in raising the capital that is required to meet their requirements of capital expenditure. Primary Market helps to translate savings of different sectors into economy and helps in capital formation of the country. The most common primary mechanism for raising capital is an Initial Public Offer (IPO), under which shares are offered to the public as a precursor to trading in the secondary market of an exchange. The new issue market deals with the new securities which were not previously available to the investing public, i.e., the securities that are offered to the investing public for the first time. Primary market helps in capital formation as it provides attractive issue to the potential investors and with this company can raise capital at lower costs. There is a flourishing market for public issues in India after opening up of Indian Economy. The instruments commonly offered are equity, debentures, and a variety of convertibles including debentures bundled with warrants. Both private and public sector companies make public issues. An initial public offer (IPO) is the selling of securities to the public in the primary market by the unlisted companies either a fresh issue of securities or an offer for sale of existing securities are both for the first time to the public. This paper analyses the recent trends in New Issue Market and Industry/Sector wise break up of capital raised from Primary Market in term of number of issues and amount of capital raised. The performance of capital raised from Primary Market in India during the last twelve years has been studied with the help of secondary data collected from NSE, BSE, SEBI and other relevant data sources. This paper also studies to attempt the Industry-wise as well as Size of Classification of Capital Raised through Primary Market in India. This paper aims to analyses the recent trends of Resources Mobilized from the Indian Primary Market and growth pattern of F.I.Is in Indian Primary Market

Keywords: Initial Public Offer (IPO), Short-term returns, F.I.Is (Foreign Institutional Investors), Performance Review

Introduction

Primary market is the part of capital market where issue of new securities takes place. Public sector institutions, companies and governments obtain funds for further growth of the company after the sale of their securities or bonds in primary market. The selling process of new issues in primary market is called as Underwriting and this process is done by a group of people called underwriters or security dealers. From a retail investor's point of view, investing in the primary market is the first step towards trading in stocks and shares.

The industrial securities market in India consists of New Issue Market and Stock Exchange. The new issue market deals with the new securities which were not previously available to the investing public, i.e., the securities that are offered to the investing public for the first time. It is also known as Primary Market. There is a flourishing market for public issues in India. The instruments commonly offered in the primary market are equity, debentures, and a variety of convertibles including debentures bundled with warrants. Public issues are made by both private and public sector companies. Unlike many other countries, where issues are privately placed, public issues in India are directly marketed to retail investors all over the country. Investment returns of the Indian primary market have been condensed largely during 2007-08 and 2008-09. Associated Chambers of Commerce and Industry of India (ASSOCHAM) found that retail investors and financial institutions including foreign institutions (FIIs), are gradually withdrawing from the capital market particularly from initial public offerings (IPOs).

Indian Financial Market

Development of an economy is based on sound financial system. It's a well-known fact that finance is the lifeline for any business enterprise. The efficient functioning and success of business operations depend upon the availability of adequate fund at the right time and required amount of funds as and when required. Financial Market is the place where the investors and fund seekers meet for mutual benefits. Indian stock market has about 7,000 listed companies in 19 stock exchanges. The number of listed companies in India is similar to that of United States. .Financial Market is divided into Money market and Capital market. Money market refers to open market operations in highly marketable short-term debt instruments and the capital market deals in long-term debt issues and stocks. Capital market deals in financial assets excluding coin and currency - is essentially a market for securities, which have either long-term or infinite maturities consists of two segments:

Primary market

Secondary market

Role of Primary Market

Capital formation - It provides attractive issue to the potential investors and with this company can raise capital at lower costs.

- Liquidity - As the securities issued in primary market can be immediately sold in secondary market the rate of liquidity is higher.
- Diversification - Many financial intermediaries invest in primary market; therefore there is less risk if there is failure in investment as the company does not depend on a single investor. The diversification of investment reduces the overall risk.
- Reduction in cost - Prospectus containing all details about the securities are given to the investors hence reducing the cost is searching and assessing the individual securities.

Features of Primary Market

- It is the new issue market for the new long term capital.
- Here the securities are issued by company directly to the investors and not through any intermediaries.
- On receiving the money from the new issues, the company will issue the security certificates to the investors.
- The amount obtained by the company after the new issues are utilized for expansion of the present business or for setting up new ventures.
- External finance for longer term such as loans from financial institutions is not included in primary market. There is an option called 'going public' in which the borrowers in new issue market raise capital for converting private capital into public capital.

Review of Literature

Chakrabarti (2001) has observed that foreign institutional investors do not appear to be at an informational disadvantage compared to domestic investors in the Indian markets. Using a monthly data-set for the period May 1993 to December 1999, he has found that FII net inflows are not only correlated with the returns in Indian equity market but are more likely the effect than the cause of the Indian equity market returns. Contrary to the general perception of foreign investors' activities having a strong demonstration effect and driving the domestic stock market in India, evidence from causality tests conducted by Mukherjee, Bose and Coondoo (2002) suggests that FII flows to and from the Indian market tend to be caused by returns in the domestic equity market and not the other way round. In a subsequent study, Bose and Coondoo (2004) have found mild evidence of bi-directional causality between returns on the BSE stock index and FII net inflows and reasoned that it may have been due to heightened FII inflows caused by an upsurge in global equity markets.

In the Indian context Shah (1995) study provides evidence on the short run performance only while Madhusoodanan and Thiripalraju (1997) from a study on IPOs offered on BSE during the period 1992 to 1995shows that under pricing was higher than the international experiences in the short run and in the long run too they yield higher returns compared to the negative returns recorded from the international markets. Krishnamurti and Kumar (2002) working on a sample of IPOs that hit the market between 1992 and1994 demonstrate that the under pricing is to the extent of 72.34% (market adjusted returns). Kakati (1999) analyzed the performance of a sample of 500 IPOs that came to the market during January 1993 to March 1996and documents that the short run under pricing is to the tune of 36.6% and in the long-run the overpricing is40.8%.

Research Methodology

The research Indian Primary Market, a review has been carried out to find the performance of Primary Market/ IPO in India between 2001-2012.Primary Market/New Issue Market provides capital for meeting the growing capital requirements in different industries. The present study is of analytical nature and makes use of secondary data. The relevant secondary data are collected from various publications of Government of India; Hand Book of Statistics of Security Market, SEBI, BSE, NSE, Reserve Bank of India, websites, annual reports, World Bank reports, DIPP, research reports etc The present paper is attempt is to identify some of the important changes that have taken place in the recent past particularly after opening up of Indian economy.

Objectives of Study

1) To study the recent trends and pattern of growth of Indian Primary Market
2) To study and analyses the Industry and Size Wise Resources Mobilized from the New Issue Market / Primary Market.
3) To study the role and growth pattern of F.I.Is in Indian Primary Market.

Indian Primary Market and its Framework:

The new issue market deals with the new securities which were not previously available to the investing public, i.e., the securities that are offered to the investing public for the first time. The market, therefore, makes available a new block of securities for public subscription. All financial institutions which contribute, underwrite and directly subscribe to the securities are part of new issue market. There are various intermediaries like registrars, custodians and merchant bankers that are involved in this activity of issuing new securities. The functions of New issue market and methods of floating these new issues are following.

Methods of Floating New Issue

The various methods which are used in the flotation of securities in the new issue market are :

1. Public issues
2. Offer for sale
3. Placement
4. Rights issues

Fig no-1 Kinds of Issues in Indian Primary Market

1. Public Issues

Under this method, this issuing company directly offers to the general public/ institutions a fixed number of shares at a stated price through a document called prospectus. This is the most common method followed by joint stock companies to raise capital through the issue of securities. The prospectus must state the following:

- Name of the company
- Address of the registered office
- Existing and proposed activities
- Location of the industry
- Names of Directors
- Minimum subscription
- Names of brokers/ underwriters/ bankers/ managers and registrars to the issue.

2. Offer For Sale

This method of offer of sale consists in outright sale of securities through the intermediary of Issue Houses or share-brokers. In other words, the shares are not offered to the public directly. This method consists of two stages: The first stage is a direct sale by the issuing company to the issue house and brokers at an agreed price. In the second stage, the intermediaries resell the above securities to the ultimate investors. The issue houses or stock brokers purchase the securities at a negotiated price and resell at a higher price. The difference in the purchase and sale price is called spread. It is otherwise called Bought out deals (BOD).

This method is used generally in two instances:

1. Offer by a foreign company of a part of it to Indian investors.
2. Promoters diluting their stake to comply with requirements of Stock exchange at the time of listing of shares.

3. Placement

Under this method, the issue houses or brokers buy the securities outright with the intention of placing them with their clients afterwards. Here the brokers act as almost wholesalers selling them in retail to the public. The brokers would make profit in the process of reselling to the public. The issue houses or brokers maintain their own list of clients and through customer contact sell the securities. There is no need for a formal prospectus as well as underwriting agreement.

4. Rights Issue

It is a method of raising funds in the market by an existing company. A right means an option to buy certain securities at a certain privileged price within a certain specified period. Shares, so offered to the existing shareholders are called rights shares. The ratio in which the new shares or debentures are offered to the existing share capital would depend upon the requirement of capital. The rights themselves are transferable and sale-able in the market. Section 81 of the Companies Act deals with rights issue. The cost of issue is minimum. There is no underwriting, brokerage, advertising and printing of prospectus expenses. It prevents the directors from issuing new shares in their own name or to their relatives at a lower price and get controlling right.

Players In The Primary Market

There are many players in the new issue or primary market. The important of them are:

1. Merchant Bankers - They are the issue managers, co-managers, and are responsible to the company and SEBI. They are registered by SEBI under category I, II, III and IV based on the capital adequacy and track record.
2. Registrars to the issue - They are an important category of intermediaries who undertake all activities connected with new issue management. They are appointed in consultation with the merchant bankers. A net worth of Rs. 6 Lakhs is essential for Registrars.
3. Collecting and coordinating Bankers - They collect information on subscriptions and co-ordinate the collection work.
4. Underwriters and Brokers - Brokers along with the network of sub-brokers market the new issues. They send their own circulars and applications to the clients and do follow up work to market securities.

Trends of Primary Market in India:

Indian Capital Market clearly on upswing trends particularly after opening up of economy i.e LPG in year 1991.Above data clearly indicates that with increase of market capitalization in both BSE and NSE proved the level of investors' confidence in growth story of India. There has been increasing trend both in primary as well in secondary market. A steady growth rate of GDP coupled with a high savings and investment rate, coupled with improved governance and favorablé regulatory environment has built the momentum and kept the financial markets afloat The level of investment by F.I.Is in Indian Capital Market also act as clear indicator of growth story of Indian Capital Market. The recent trends also analyses the Industry-wise & Size wise Classification of Capital Raised through Primary Market in India Growth Story of Indian Stock Market:

Table no.1

	1994	Apr11-Dec 12
Cash market segment		
Stock Exchanges	21	19
Brokers	6413	8922
Corporate brokers	143	4478
Sub Brokers	202	77163
Listed co . In BSE	3585	16961
Market capitalization in BSE(cr.)	368071	5348645
Avg Daily Turnover in BSE(cr.)	388	7928
Listed co . In NSE	135	1640
Market capitalization in NSE	363650	5232273
Daily Turnover in NSE	17	10669

Source:SEBI, Hand Book of Statistics of Security Market

Above table clearly represents that Indian Capital Market is on growing trend, as the brokers, sub brokers and corporate brokers are on increasing trend as compare from 1994 to 2012.On other hand listed companies in BSE/NSE have also shown tremendous growth as compare from 1994 to 2012.

The market capitalization of both BSE/NSE has also on increasing trend. This clearly shows the Growth story of Indian Stock Market.

Table no.-2

Annual Averages of Share Price Indices and Market Capitalization

Mkt. Capitalization (In Crs.)

Year	Sensex	Nifty	BSE	NSE
2004-05	5741	1805	1698428	1585585
2005-06	8280	2513	3022191	2813201

Year	Sensex	Nifty	BSE	NSE
2006-07	12277	3572	3545041	3367350
2007-08	16569	4897	5138014	4858122
2008-09	12366	3731	3086075	2896194
2009-10	15585	4658	6165619	6009173
2010-11	18605	5584	6839084	6702616
April11-12(dec)	17506	5257	5348645	5232273

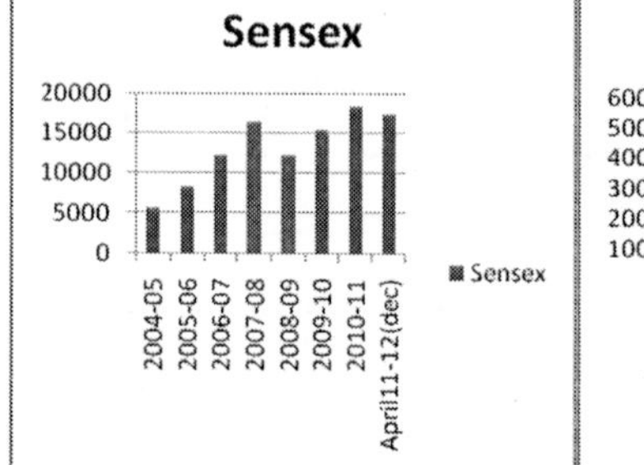

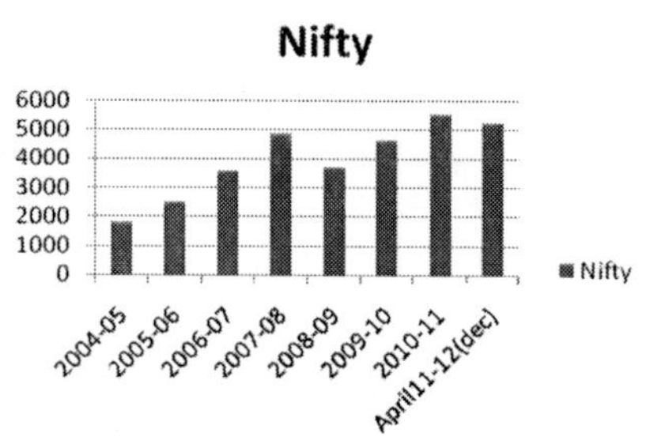

Figure no. 2&3: Annual Averages of Share Price Indices of Sensex & Nifty

Above table clearly interprets that increasing trend of market capitaliastion of both BSE/NSE as well as the volatility of market indicies of both BSE/NSE.The volatility may be of internal as well as external factors affecting the Stock market.

Size Wise Classification of Capital Raised From Primary Market (In Crores)

Table no. 3

Year	No.	Amount
2002-03	26	4070
2003-04	57	23272
2004-05	60	28256
2005-06	139	27382
2006-07	124	33508
2007-08	124	87029
2008-09	47	16220

Year	No.	Amount
2009-10	76	57555
2010-11	91	67609
2011-12(dec)	52	31685

Source: SEBI

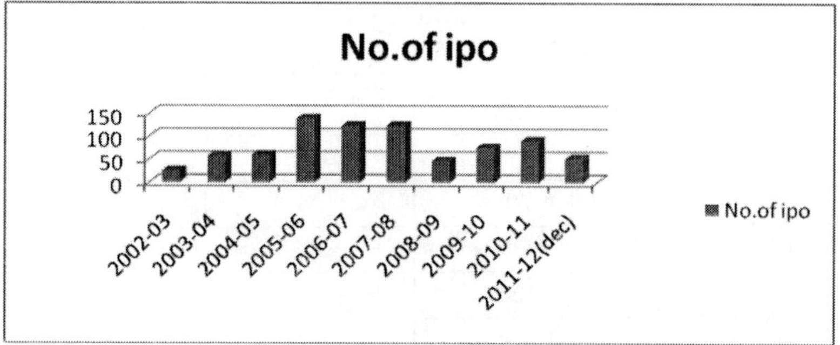

Fig no.-4 Number of IPOs

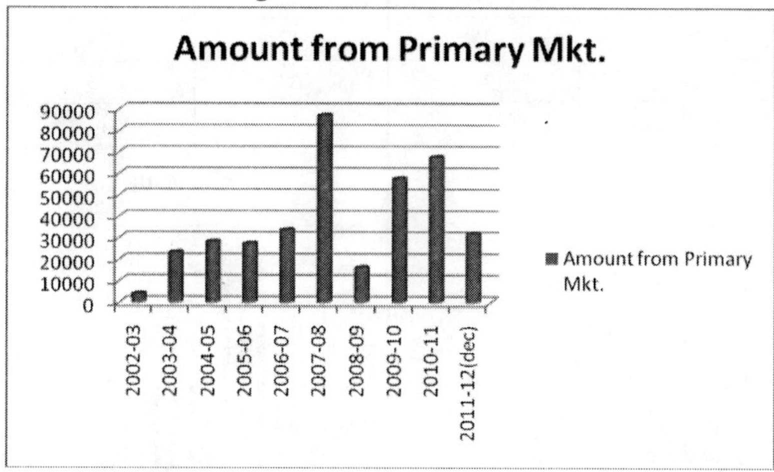

Fig no-5 Amount of capital raised from Primary Market

Investment decision in IPOs is appeared to be very attractive and encouraging to many of the retail investors. Before investing in an IPO, investors need to have an understanding of company, including various aspects of its business, its track record in executing projects, future earning potential, future orders, adaptability with the changing micro and macro economic and political environment, credentials of promoters and the valuation compared with its peers.

Resource Mobilized from Primary Market (Including Public Issue & Right Issue)

Table no-4

Year	Number	Public Issue	Right Issue
2002-03	26	14	12
2003-04	57	35	22
2004-05	60	34	26
2005-06	139	103	36
2006-07	124	85	39
2007-08	124	92	39
2008-09	47	22	25
2009-10	76	47	29
2010-11	91	68	23
2011-12(dec)	52	42	10

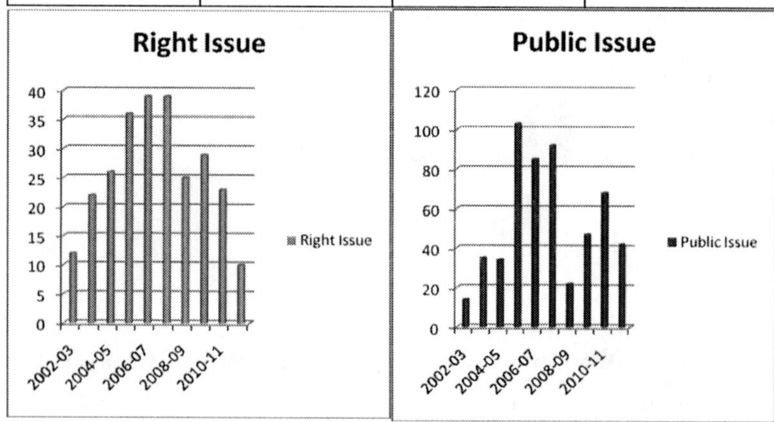

Source: SEBI, Hand Book of Statistics of Security Market

Fig no.6 & 7 Resource mobilized through Right Issue & IPO market

Above graphs clearly analyses that both public issue and right issues are plays an important role in resource moblisation. It also interprets that percentage of public issue is much more as compared with Right issues from 2001 to 2012.But there is sudden fall in numbers in 2008-09 & 2011-12 due to global cues and slow down in the Market.

Industry-wise distribution, Size-wise distribution (Table no-5)

Above table interprets that the industry wise distribution and size wise distribution of amount generated from Primary market. It analyses that sectors from which amount to be collected comprises with Finance ,Cement ,Chemical ,Electronic ,Engineering ,Food Processing,Healthcare,Information Technology, Paper & Pulp, Plastic,Power,Printing, Telecommunication , Textile sectors. Among above sectors Banking/FI holds the major stake but it also reveals that IPO collection in different sectors have been on decreasing trend as compare to previous year.

The banking sector contributed the maximum share (25.5 percent) of the total resources mobilized during 2010–2011, with 18 issues mobilizing ` 172,480 million but in year 2011-12 it has been decreased to 20039 and number of IPOs have been decreased to 12. The finance sector was at the leading position in the league with ` 76,990 million, accounting for 47.11 percent of the total resources mobilized in the first six months of FY 2012. In 2010–2011, the finance sector contributed only 3.30 percent to the total resources. Over the years, several industries have emerged as the major contributors of the resources mobilized

Size Wise Classification of Capital Raised from Primary Market (in Crore)

	2008-09		2009-10		2010-11		April2011-12dec	
Sector	No.	Amount	No.	Amount	No.	Amount	No.	Amount
Banking/FIs -	0	0	6	3138	18	17248	12	20039

	2008-09		2009-10		2010-11		April2011-12dec	
Sector	No.	Amount	No.	Amount	No.	Amount	No.	Amount
Cement & Construction	3	80	8	2780	3	2841	1	60
Chemical	4	218	1	36	5	247	0	0
Electronics	0	0	1	1156	0	0	1	121
Engineering	0	0	1	50	5	1394	1	217
Entertainment	2	1156	9	2461	4	715	0	0
Finance	3	1966	2	1826	3	2210	9	7699
Food Processing	0	0	2	443	1	1245	0	0
Healthcare	3	144	3	1059	3	292	1	65
Information Technology	1	42	6	540	1	170	2	138
Paper & Pulp	0	0	1	35	0	0	2	727
Plastic	0	0	1	39	0	0	1	246
Power	2	958	6	25293	4	9469	0	11
Printing	0	0	0	0	1	52	1	46
Telecommunication	2	100	0	0	0	0	0	
Textile	5	710	3	237	3	207	0	0
Others	22	10845	26	18461	40	31519	21	2316
Total	47	16220	76	57555	91	67609	52	31685

Year	Total		< 5Crore		> 5Cr. to<10 Crore		> 10 Cr. to < 50 Cr.		> 50 Cr. to < 100 Cr.		> 100 Crore	
	No.	Amt.	No.	Amt.	No.	Amt.	No.	Amt.	No.	Amt.	No.	Amt.
2000-01	151	6108	66	186	25	165	34	764	8	507	18	4486
2001-02	35	7543	3	8	3	20	8	199	3	177	18	7140
2002-03	26	4070	2	7	1	8	10	255	0	0	13	3801
2003-04	57	23272	6	16	5	36	16	330	5	351	25	22539
2004-05	60	28256	2	3	5	44	17	461	11	723	25	27025
2005-06	139	27382	6	20	4	32	47	1325	33	2189	49	23815
2006-07	124	33508	3	10	6	45	40	1129	31	2386	44	29938
2007-08	124	87029	4	16	1	6	33	920	25	1669	61	84418

Year	Total		< 5Crore		> 5Cr. to< 10 Crore		> 10 Cr. to < 50 Cr.		> 50 Cr. to < 100 Cr.		> 100 Crore	
	No.	Amt.	No.	Amt.	No.	Amt.	No.	Amt.	No.	Amt.	No.	Amt.
2008-09	47	16220	1	3	7	21	21	509	6	445	18	15255
2009-10	96	57555	1	2	24	18	18	596	9	636	45	56298
2010-11	91	67609	1	2	11	13	13	455	20	1406	55	65735
2011-12	71	48468	2	9	14	18	18	510	14	1018	35	46916

Table no-6 Size Wise Classification of Capital raised

Above table clearly interprets that the Size wise capital mobilized from New issue Market /Indian Primary Market has shown the tremendous growth .As the IPOs size of the more than 100 crore has shown the increasing trend, it analyses that Indian Primary Market capital mobilized is touching new heights as compared to previous years collection. This also analyses that the confidence of investors as well as flow of FIIs in Indian Primary Market is on great heights. As compare to previous year's capital mobilizations there is growth in the Size wise capital mobilized from New issue Market /Indian Primary Market.

Growth of FIIs in Indian Primary Market:

The growth of institutional investors in the market is having its own advantages as well as its own share of problems on the brighter side almost always purchase stocks on the basis of fundamentals. FIIs have been investing on financial instruments in India and providing incentives for financial innovations in the country. Recently, they have become the movers and shakers of the market. Given this growing importance of FIIs for the Indian economy, it is essential that the dynamics of such cross-border portfolio investment in the context of economic growth of the country. Also, the increasing presence of this class of investors leads to reform of securities trading and transaction systems, nurturing of securities brokers, and liquid markets. If we see the numbers of FII flows, It is increasing every year expect some of rare years where global factors like slowdown have effected Indian Primary market too.

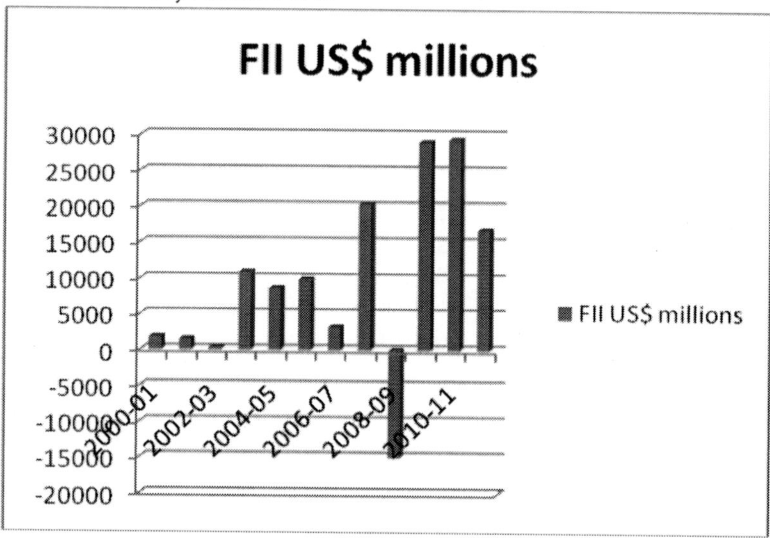

Fig no.-8 Inflow of FIIs in Indian Primary Market

Table no-7

Year	FII U.S. $ millions
2000-01	1847
2001-02	1505
2002-03	377
2003-04	10918
2004-05	8686
2005-06	9929
2006-07	3225
2007-08	20328
2008-09	-15017
2009-10	29048
2010-11	29422
2011-12	16813

Source:SEBI

Regulatory Framework for the Primary Market

The regulatory framework for primary markets in Indian comprises of the SEBI Act, 1992. SEBI regulations and rules for various intermediaries, for the issue of capital by management tie up with certain provisions of the companies Act, 1956. The following are the important enactments relating to the primary market in India (Table :9)

Enactments Relating to the Indian Primary Market Serial

a	SEBI (Disclosure and Investor Protection) Guidelines, 2000
b	SEBI (Merchant Bankers) Rules and Regulations, 1992
c	SEBI (Banker to the Issue) Rules and Regulations, 1994
d	SEBI (Registrar to an Issue) Rules and Regulations, 1993
e	SEBI (Underwriters) Rules and Regulations, 1993
Table no. 9	
Major Reforms in the Primary Market	Type of Reform
1	Merit-based regime to disclosure-based regime. Investor Protection. Guidelines issued.
2	Pricing of public issues determined by the market.
3	System of proportional allotment of shares introduced.
4	Banks and public sector undertakings allowed to raise funds.
5	Accounting standards close to international standards
6	Corporate Governance Guidelines issued.
7	Discretionary allotment system to QIBs has been withdrawn
8	Mutual funds are encouraged in both the public and private sectors have been given permission to invest overseas and Guidelines were issued forivate placement of debt.
9	SEBI to promote Self-Regulatory Organizations.
10	Allocation to retail investors increased from 25 percent to 35 percent.
11	Separate allocation of 5 percent to domestic mutual funds within the QIB category.

12	Freedom to fix face value of shares below Rs. 10 per share only in cases here with the issue price is Rs. 50 or more.
13	Shares allotted on preferential basis are subjected to lock-in period of six months to prevent sale of shares.

Source: Securities and Exchange Board of India (SEBI).

Further Primary Market Reforms:

(i) The improved disclosure standards, introduction of prudential norms, and simplification of issue procedures.

(ii) Companies required disclosing all material facts and specific risk factors associated with their projects while making public issues.

(iii) Listing agreements of stock exchanges amended to require listed companies to furnish annual statement to the exchanges showing variations between financial projections and projected utilization of funds in the offer document and actual figures. This is to enable shareholders to make comparisons between performance and promises.

(iv) SEBI introduces a code of advertisement for public issues to ensure fair and truthful disclosures.

(v) Disclosure norms further strengthened by introducing cash flow statements.

(vi) New issue procedures introduced—book building for institutional investors—aimed at reducing costs of issuing shares.

(vii) SEBI introduces regulations governing substantial acquisition of shares and takeovers and lays down conditions under which disclosures and mandatory public offers are to be made to the shareholders.

Conclusion:

The new issue market deals with the new securities which were not previously available to the investing public, i.e., the securities that are offered to the investing public for the first time. The market, therefore, makes available a new block of securities for public subscription. All financial institutions which contribute, underwrite and directly subscribe to the securities are part of new issue market. There are various intermediaries like registrars, custodians and merchant bankers that are involved in this activity of issuing new securities.Over the years, SEBI and government have come up with a series of regulatory measures to give boost to new issue market. A lot of merchant bankers don't follow the code of conduct and as a result are debarred, however these cases have reduced. As per the 1997 amendment to the SEBI Rules and Regulations, 1992 only corporate bodies will be allowed to function as merchant bankers. Primary market is the part of capital market where issue of new securities takes place. The selling process of new issues in primary market is called as Underwriting and this process is done by a group of people called underwriters or security dealers. From a retail investor's point of view, investing in the primary market is the first step towards trading in stocks and shares. Its functioning affects the level of investor confidence among investors. Moreover the global developments are affecting the growth and development of economy including the regulations and working of capital markets.

Sebi has taken several initiatives to improve operational efficiency and transparency in Indian Primary Market. It attempts to bring confidence among not only Indian investors but also FIIs (Foreign Institutional Investors) where cooperates can raise capital in cost effective manner. It also analyses that FIIs plays an important role in Indian Capital Market and they are the strong pillar in inflow of funds in Indian Primary Market. As both FIIs and Indian Primary Market are correlated with each other.

This paper attempts to analyze from different publish data relating to number of issues raised from the time period 2001 to 2012.Industry wise break up of capital raised from Primary Market indicates that Banking/Financial Institution Sector continued to dominate the Primary Market in term of number of issues and amount of capital raised. On the other hand Size wise distribution of capital raised from Primary Market analyses that from time period of 2001 to 2012 there has been tremendous growth even though it has touched the more than 100 crore amount too. Being India part of emerging economy and part of BRICS, Indian Primary Market plays an important role in capital mobilization and growth of Indian Economy.

References

- Aggrawal, R and P. Rivoli,(1989), 'Fads, in the Initial Public Offering Market', Financial Management Vol.19, 45-57
- AGGARWAL, Reena. Stabilization Activities by Underwriters after Initial Public Offerings.The Journal of Finance, 40, 1075-1099, 2000.
- Barry, C B and Jennings. R.H (1993), 'The Opening Price Performance of Initial Public Offerings Of Common Stock', Financial Management, Vol. 22, 54-63.
- Jaitly, Shailesh and SHARMA, Ruchira (2004), Pricing of IPOs and their after issue performance in the Indian equity market. Managerial Finance, 30, 29-45,.
- Krishnamurti Chandrasekhar and Pradeep Kumar (2002), 'The Performance of Indian IPOs',Managerial Finance; Vol. 28, 39-51
- Raj Chaitanya (2003). "Foreign Institutional Investments", Money and Finance" Vol. 2, No. 7, October-December, pages 61-81.
- Hand Book of Statistics in Indian Security Market 2011
- Hand Book of Statistics in Indian Security Market 2012
- Stock Exchange Official Directory, Vol.2 (9) (iii), Bombay Stock Exchange, Bombay
- http://business.mapsofindia.com/india-market/debt.html
- http://www.dbie.rbi.org.in
- http://www.sebi.gov.in/
- http://www.tradingeconomics.com
- Bank for International Settlements, 2006
- RBI; National Stock Exchange of India Limited
- http://www.equitymaster.com
- http://www.businessdictionary.com/definition/stock-exchange.html

- http://www.yeahindia.com/c-india1.htm
- http://en.wikipedia.org/wiki/Capital_market
- http://kalyan-city.blogspot.com/2010/09/reforms-developments-in-indian-capital.html
- http://www.pwc.com/in/en/publications/india-captial-market-11-feb.jhtml
- http://business.gov.in/business_financing/capital_market.php
- http://www.economywatch.com/market/capital-market/indian.html

Econometric Investigation of Volatility in Indian Currency Market

Dr. Sanjeev Gupta

Associate Professor & HOD, Department of Accounting and Finance (A&F), School of Business & Management Studies, Central University of Himachal Pradesh

Email Id:sanjeeveco@hotmail.com

Ph.No-09418048812

Sachin Kashyap

Research Scholar, School of Business & Management Studies, Central University of Himachal Pradesh

Email Id: sachinkashyap1981@gmail.com

Ph.No- 08628808815, 09915800815

Abstract

Volatility in the exchange rate is an important contributor to risks. It affects the export & import fluctuations, balance of payment, profits of the multinational corporations etc. Excessive fluctuation in the exchange rate affects the foreign exchange policy, currency value and fiscal instability of the country. Present paper is an endeavour to measure volatility in the foreign exchange market in India. GARCH family of models have been used to measure volatility clustering on time series data of US dollar and Euro on daily basis in terms of Indian rupees. The results of the study show that volatility is highly persistent in the Indian foreign exchange market.

Keywords-Exchange rate, Heteroscedasticity, Volatility, ARCH-LM Test, Forecasting

Introduction

Foreign exchange rate fluctuations is a critical factor which impacted all the player of foreign exchange market such as investors, bankers, financial institutions, exporters, importers, business concerns, foreign employees, NRIs, tourists and policy makers and other service providers etc., who deal with multiple currencies of all over the world. The accurate forecasting and trends of foreign exchange rate movements will give valuable information to various players of foreign exchange rate market.

Due to the failure of Bretton Wood system of fixed exchange rates among currencies of major countries, last few decades witnessed a movement of many countries from fixed exchange rate regime to floating exchange rate system So this shifting to floating exchange rate from fixed exchange rate would open a platform for an extensive debate among different stake holders such as risk mangers of corporate firms, policy makers, academicians and financial economist etc., about volatility in the foreign exchange market and its characteristics which influence on economic affairs such as balance of payment and risk management policies, international trade, inflation etc.

Volatility refers to the amount uncertainty of changes and risk in the value of asset, security, investment. Foreign exchange rate volatility refers to the quantity of fluctuations or measure of risk due to variations in the foreign exchange rate. There are two types of measures of volatility, historical volatility and implied volatility. Historical volatility is the amount of deviations in the past market or asset price or exchange rate movements. On the other hand Implied volatility is forward looking and it projected through potential movement of a an asset or a market or exchange rate by estimating of what is going to be happen in the future. Volatility in the exchange rate market has gained significant scope in empirical finance research studies after the collapse of Bretton wood exchange rate system in 1973 and subsequent movement from fixed exchange rate system to floating exchange rate system.

Evolution of Indian Foreign Exchange Rate System

After successful independence India followed a exchange rate system linked to the British Pound Sterling. This system of exchange rate regime continues til1970's, this period represented by the breakdown of Bretton wood Exchange system around the world.

In 1975 the system of Indian Rupee linking with Pound sterling were broken and India managed a controlled floating exchange rate regime in which Indian Rupee linked to a number of currencies constituting the basket currencies of which India is major trading partners. During 1990-91 Indian economy experienced major macroeconomic problems like problems of balance of payment, trade deficit and foreign exchange rate reserve etc., which motivated the Government of India and Reserve Bank of India(RBI) to undertake on number of structural adjustments to correct the economic pressure.

In order to regulate the exchange rate system the Reserve Bank of India started a sequential process from downward adjustment in 1991 and followed by a dual (market determined and official) system of exchange rate called Liberalised Exchange Rate Management System (LERMS) in 1992. But this system faced inherent practical difficulty in implicit tax on exports proceedings. Hence in1993, the Government of India and RBI introduced a unified market driven foreign exchange rate system and now India followed this system of market determined foreign exchange rate.

Data and Methodology

A number of empirical studies have been undertaken to investigate or estimating the volatility across different countries. Engle (1982) developed an Auto Regressive Conditional Heteroscedastic (ARCH) model and his student Bollerslev (1986) and Taylor (1986) were contribute an advanced ARCH model of Genaralised Auto Regressive Conditional Heteroscedastic (GARCH) model. These models and its variant improved models of EGARCH, TGARCH etc., are frequently and popularly used to estimate volatility in financial and economic research.

To investigate foreign exchange rate volatility of Indian market, this study used time series data of daily Exchange Rate of Indian Rupee against US Dollar and Euro from January 1, 2002 to October 31,2013. Result in total observations of 2785. The daily exchange rate of Indian rupee against US Dollar was collected from Reserve bank website.

As in most of empirical foreign exchange rate volatility studies, the variable used to model foreign exchange rate volatility is percentage daily exchange rate return of Indian Rupee Versus US Dollar and Euro which is the first difference in natural logarithm of the exchange rate of successive days calculated by following equation:

Where Rt is the percentage of daily foreign exchange rate return of Indian Rupee versus US Dollar and Euro, Et is the current day foreign exchange rate of USD/INR and Euro/INR and Et-1 is the previous day foreign exchange rate of USD/INR and Euro/INR respectively. The descriptive statistics of daily foreign exchange rate (USD/INR and Euro/INR) series and daily return series of USD/INR and Euro/INR were shown in Table 1.

Table 1. Descriptive

Statistics	**USD**	**Euro**
Mean	47.07895819	60.1628
Standard Error	0.086203216	0.152721
Median	46.04	58.68
Mode	48.7	56.77

Statistics	**USD**	**Euro**
Standard Deviation	4.623739917	8.191615
Sample Variance	21.37897082	67.10255
Kurtosis	2.174371241	0.466459
Skewness	1.220230797	0.402116
Range	29.0911	49.8082
Minimum	39.27	41.66
Maximum	68.3611	91.4682

FDI in Retail Sector and Indian Economy-A Critical Appraisal

Madan Lal Guleria
Associate Professor, Department of Commerce
Govt. P G College Dharamshala

Abstract

The retail industry is definitely one of the pillars of the Indian economy. It contributes a lot to the national GDP. Retail sector in India is one of the major employment providers. The move for opening up the retail sector to FDI has become a hotly debated issue. Opening up of FDI in multi brand retail in India could possibly be a mixed blessing for domestic players. The proponents of allowing FDI in retail sector are of the view that it will increase transfer of technology, enhance supply chain efficiencies, increase employment opportunities and curtail inflation etc. Opponents feel that liberalization would jeopardize the unorganized retail sector and would adversely affect the small retails, farmers and consumers and give rise to monopolies of large corporate houses, which can adversely affect the pricing, and availability of goods Permitting FDI in retail sector can displace the unorganized retailers leading to loss of livelihood.

Keywords: FDI, Single-Brand, Multi-Brand, Liberalization, Privatization Globalization, Retail Sector

Introduction

Capital is the engine of economic development and this statement is gaining importance in the recent times. Traditionally the various sources of capital for developing countries were either the demand of their output by industrial countries, or foreign aid, or loans from foreign banks. In today's scenario where official development assistance flows are steadily declining, high interest rates and portfolio investment involve risks, foreign direct investment is considered to be the major source of funds which may contribute in increasing the economic growth rate of the developing countries. Recently the liberal and open Government policy reforms in FDI are to integrate the Indian Economy to the world economy.

FDI has been instrumental in the economic growth of the developed countries. This has inspired the developing countries to reform their economic policies to attract FDI. Since 1991 the Government of India has been laying down the road map for FDI reforms to encompass relaxation of procedural as well as investment norms. FDI provides financial resources for investment in the host country. Hence investment saving gap can be bridged by attracting FDI.

The Spurt in globalization is putting pressure on the existing infrastructure like telecom, roads, power and ports to serve business in a cost effective and efficient manner. Huge resources are required for fast development of infrastructure. This is only possible by attracting FDI in infrastructure sectors.

FDI facilitates technology upgradation and introduction of modern production and management practices. Thus it is anticipated that with the economic reforms and adequate supply of capital, India can come out the vicious circle of poverty and help creating more jobs.

Objectives of The Study

The objectives of the study are

1. To study the concept of FDI, Retailing, Brand , Single Brand and Multi Brand
2. To study the rationale behind allowing FDI in retail sector
3. To study the FDI policy towards FDI in Retail Sector (Single-Brand and Multi-Brand)
4. To make a critical appraisal of FDI in Retail and Indian Economy

Nature and Source of Data

The present study "FDI in Retail Sector and Indian Economy-Critical Appraisal" is based on secondary source of data. In order to enrich the study different books, various economic surveys of India, Ministry of Commerce and Industry data, RBI bulletins, Journals and newspapers have been consulted. The related websites have also been searched for information/data.

Concept of FDI, Retailing, Brand, Single Brand Retailing and Multi Brand Retailing

FDI is the outcome of the mutual interests of multinational firms and host countries. According to the international Monetary Fund (IMF), FDI is defined as "investment that is made to acquire a lasting interest in an enterprise operating in an economy other than that of the investor. The investor's purpose being to have an effective voice in the management of the enterprise. The essence of FDI is the transmission to the host country of a package of capital, managerial skill and technical knowledge. FDI is generally a form of long term international capital movement, made for the purpose of productive activity and accompanied by the intention of managerial control or participation in the management of a foreign firm.

Superiority of FDI over other forms of capital inflows

FDI is widely considered as essential element for achieving

sustainable development. Developing countries are strongly advised to rely primarily on FDI in order to supplement national savings by capital inflow and promote economic development.

FDI is perceived superior to other types of capital inflows for the following reasons:

1. FDI inflows are usually preferred over other forms of external finance because they are non-debt creating, non-volatile and their returns depend on the performance of the projects financed by the investors. FDI also facilitates international trade and transfers of knowledge, skills and technology.
2. In contrast to foreign lenders and portfolio investors, foreign direct investors typically have a long term perspective when engaging in a host country. Hence FDI inflows are less volatile and easier to sustain at times of crisis.
3. While debt inflows may finance consumption rather than investment in host countries, FDI is more likely to be used productively.
4. FDI is expected to have relatively strong effects on economic growth as FDI provides for more than just capital. FDI offers access to internationally available technologies and management know how and may render easier to penetrate world market.
5. The risk sharing properties of FDI are undisputed. This suggest that FDI is the appropriate form of external financing for developing countries, which have less capacity than highly developed economies to absorb external shocks. Likewise, the evidence supports the predominant view that FDI is more stable than other types of capital inflows.

However, positive growth effects of FDI cannot be taken for granted. In the ultimate analysis, it all depends on time-varying and location–specific factors whether FDI and growth are positively correlated or not.

Concept of Retailing

The word 'retail' has been derived from the French word retailer which mean 'to cut a piece off' or 'to break bulk'. In common words, it means relating to the sale of goods directly to consumers. It is the sale of goods to end users, not for resale, but for use and consumption by the purchasers. Retailing is the interface between the producer and the individual consumers buying for personal consumption. It is the last link that connect the individual consumer with the manufacturing and the distribution chain.

The retail sector in India can broadly classified into organized and unorganized retail sector. Organized retailing refers to trading activities undertaken by licensed retailers, i.e. those who are registered for sales tax, income tax etc. These include the corporate backed hypermarkets and retail chains and also the privately owned large retail businesses. It refer to businesses employing more than 10 persons. Unorganized retailing refer to the traditional formats of low-cost retailing such as the local kirana shops, paan/beedi shops, convenience stores.

Concept of Brand

It means, 'trade mark' design, distinctive name identifying a product or a manufacturer, an identifying symbol, words or mark that distinguishes a product or company from its competitors. Brands help the customers to identify specific products from among identical commodities. Brands have significant impact on developing customer perception and expectation.

Concept of Single Brand Retail

There is no clear-cut definition of the term 'Single Brand Retail' in any Indian government circular or notification. Single brand retail generally refer to the selling of goods under a single brand name. It involves selling products under one brand which are also sold internationally. FDI in 'Single brand' retail implies that a retail store with foreign investment can only sell one brand. Nike is one of the examples.

Multi Brand Retail

The Government of India has not clearly defined the term "multi-brand retail". FDI in multi-brand retail implies that a retail store with a foreign investment can sell multiple brands under one roof. Opening up FDI in multi brand retail will mean that global retailers including Wal-Mart, Carrefour, and Tesco can open stores offering a range of household items and /grocery directly to consumers. Multi brand retail comes in different formats like supermarket, hypermarket, and the ubiquitous shopping malls.

FDI in retail Sector in India: its rationale

1. FDI in Single and Multi brand retail will pave the way for improving supply chain infrastructure and logistics.
2. It will curb inflation.
3. It will result in reduced cost to the ultimate consumer and enable a fair return to the farmers.
4. Economy will get the benefit with capital inflows from global giants that will develop the front- end and back – end infrastructure in different segments.
5. It would act as an important employment absorber for the present social system.
6. The consumer will get access to some of the major global brands. Entry of foreign brands would also improve the quality and variety of products.

Retail business in India and global retailer

The retail sector has been at the helm of India's growth story. The Indian retail market has seen considerable growth in the organized segment. After the waves of liberalization, privatization and globalization (LPG) marketing scenario particularly retailing has changed radically. Around 40 million people are engaged in retail trade in India. Small and medium enterprises dominate the Indian retail scene. Combination of organized and unorganized sectors, this industry is one of the fastest growing industries in India, especially over the last few years. According to the 8th Annual Global Retail Development Index (GRDI) of A T Kearney, Indian retail industry is most promising emerging market for investment

Reasons

1. High consumer spending over the years by the young population
2. Rising disposable income.
3. Rise in the purchasing power of Indians.
4. Improvements in infrastructure.
5. Liberalization of Indian economy.
6. Increase in urbanization.
7. Rise of self-employed class.
8. Shift in consumer demand to foreign brands.
9. The internet revolution making the Indian consumer more accessible to the growing influence of domestic and foreign retail chains.
10. Strategic location and geography.
11. Vast growing economy.

The Current scenario of retailing in India

The importance of retail can be appreciated from the following scenario of retail business in India

- Retail sector in India is estimated to account for about 10 percent share in GDP, as compared to 8 percent in China, 6 percent in Brazil and 10 percent in USA.
- India may be called the nation of the shopkeepers because,

with 15 million outlets, it has the highest density of retail outlets in the world.

- Indian retail sector is highly fragmented in nature, only 4 percent of Indian retail outlets are larger than 500 Sq. feet.
- Organized retail is just the 5 percent of the total retail market where as 95 percent of the total retail trade in India is in the unorganized sector.
- Unorganized retail industry in India is second largest employer after agriculture, employing about 8 percent of total work force (around 40 million persons).

Investors' Outlook Towards Indian Retail Sector

The critics of the Indian economy say that India is passing through a gloomy period where there is a dip in many macroeconomic indicators- yet the issue sector's perspective about the country and more over the retail sector has been very positive. The 2012 A.T. Kearney FDI confidence index, which examines the country wise future prospects for FDI flows, ranks India as the second best country in its global ranking. India scored 1.73 on a scale of 3 and is behind only to China. It is evident that with the successful survival of global recession, India has earned the investors' confidence over the developed retailers

Table 1: Global Retail Development Index in 2011

2011 Rank	Country	Market Attrac-tiveness	Country Risk	Market Satura-tion	Time Pressure	GRDI Score
1	Brazil	100	79.4	42.9	63.9	71.5
2	Uruguay	85	73.8	63.6	39.6	65.5
3	Chile	84.3	100	30.3	44.3	64.7
4	India	28.9	59.9	63.1	100	63
5	Kuwait	80.4	80.6	57.3	27.1	61.3
6	China	49.5	76.5	31	87.7	61.2

7	Saudi Arabia	70.9	80.7	50.6	35.7	59.5
8	Peru	39.8	61.5	72	59.5	58.2
9	UAE	87.6	88.9	12.6	42.9	58
10	Turkey	83.8	65.5	45	37	57.8

Source:-Compiled from the data available in the 2011 A.T. Kearney GRDI

The 2011 A.T. Kearney Global Retail Development Index (GRDI) put India in the fourth position (vide table 1) among the 30 developing countries in terms of the retail sector's prospects in those nations. India is lagging behind Brazil. Uruguay and Chile with an overall GRDI score of 63.0 on a scale of 100.

The GRDI score has been calculated based on four variables:

i. Country and business risk,

ii. Market attractiveness

iii. Market saturation

iv. Time Pressure

The study showed that Indian retail sector is advancing very quickly and poses a short term opportunity for the investors. There exists a huge opportunity in the organized retailing in India in supermarket segment which will help the investors reap dividend in long term as well.

FDI Policy Towards FDI in Retail Sector (Single and Multi-Brand)

The recent clamor about opening up the retail sector to FDI becomes a very sensitive issue. The FDI policy with regard to allowance of FDI in retail sector taken by the government of India is

A. FDI policy toward single-brand retail

FDI in single-brand retail trading was allowed up to 100 percent under the Government route subject to the fulfillment of following conditions

- Products to be sold should be of 'Single-Brand' only

- Products should be sold under the same brand in one or more countries other than India
- Only products which are branded during manufacturing would be covered.
- The foreign investor should be the owner of the brand

B. FDI policy toward multi-brand retail

Previously, India did not allow any FDI in multi-brand retail operation in India. The changes in FDI policy prove that 51 percent FDI in multi-branding retail sector with the foreign investment permotion Board (FIPB) approval would be allowed, inter alia, subject fulfillment of the following conditions

- Minimum amount to be brought in, as FDI, by the foreign investors would be 100 million US $.
- At least 50 percent of the total FDI brought in shall be invested in back-end infrastructure.
- 30 percent of the procurements of manufacturing product should be from small industries.
- The retail stores will only be allowed in cities with a population of more than 10 lakhs people as per the 2011 Census. As of now, there are only 53 such cities in India.
- The Government reserves the first right to procure agricultures products.
- Fresh agricultural produce including fruits, vegetables, flowers, grains, pulses, fresh poultry. Fishery and meat products may be unbranded.

FDI in Retail Sector in Indian Economy- Critical Appraisal

Arguments in Favour:

- FDI in retail sector is a major step towards providing liberation to the farmers from middlemen and ensuring remunerative prices for their product.
- It will help in creating 10 million jobs and billions of dollars

in investments and will not affect smaller and domestic retailers.

- Minimum investment in multi-brand retail will be 100 million American dollars. This is minimum and not the maximum. 50% will be in developing rural infrastructure and 30% of sourcing will be from small and medium enterprises. This signals the development of infrastructure and the initiative to give fresh blood to SMEs.
- Retail trade in India is a capital starved sector. Provision of FDI provides an effective solution to the problem of capital deficiency.
- Foreign retail chains would bring the much needed investment in the back-end infrastructure, like cold storage, which the country currently lacks.FDI in multi-brand retail trade will help reduce wastages in the farm produce sector.
- This will bring modern technology to the country.
- The deep pocket and expertise of Wal-Mart's to establish supply chain will make rural areas and farmers prosperous.
- With entry of foreign retailers, consumers will experience more variety of products with improved quality.
- Expectations are that it would create jobs not only in the retail industry but also in related areas like real estate and construction.

Argument Against:

The entry of MNC like Wal-Mart, Tesco and Carrefour will throw hundreds of thousands of the neighborhood kirana storeowners out of business and that will result in millions of job losses. A total of 58.8 millions of small and marginal farming families that is over 32crore rural people live on farming in India. Their farm size is 5 acres or less. In contrast, some developed countries' farm size as compared to our country is notable:

Country's Name	Farm Size (acres)
Canada	1,798
USA	1,089

Country's Name	Farm Size (acres)
Australia	17,975
France	274
UK	432

So a country like ours should not allow FDI in retail sector.

In UK, it was reported that 3 retail chains controlled 65% of the entire retail market. Similarly, in Thailand, over 30% of the local shops were forced to shut within 10 years of the entry of foreign retailers. If this happens, FDI should not be allowed in the retail sector.

The foreign retail majors will hurt domestic players with the practice of predatory pricing and becomes monopolies.

The FDI in retail sector would make the country economically subservient to foreigners.

It will destroy food security in rural India.

It would destroy the livelihood of crores of small retailers. More than 5crore traders and 20 crore people are directly dependent on retail trade for their livelihood. There are 22 crore hawkers and street vendors in the country. The move will hit the domestic retail sector hard. This step will be disastrous.

Conclusion

The retail industry is definitely one of the pillars of the Indian economy. It contributes a lot to the national GDP. Retail sector in India is one of the major employment providers. The move for opening up the retail sector to FDI has become a hotly debated issue. Opening up of FDI in multi-brand retail in India could possibly be a mixed blessing in domestic players. The proponents of allowing FDI in retail sector are of the view that it will increase transfer of technology, enhance supply chain efficiencies, increase employment opportunities and curtail inflation etc.

Opponents feel that liberalization would jeopardize the unorganized retail sector and would adversely affect the small retailers, farmers and consumers and give rise to monopolies of large corporate houses, which can adversely affect the pricing, and availability of goods. Permitting FDI in retail sector can displace the unorganized retailers leading to loss of livelihood. So utmost care needs to be taken by the government so that the people engaged in retail sector are not affected. No denying the fact that India needs a widespread and efficient supply chain. It is highly improbable that a few retail giants can enable the desired outcome. If FDI in multi brand (51%) retail is allowed, it will pave the way for global groups such as Wal-Mart, Carrefour and Tesco to open super market in India. The entry of such top retailers may displace lakhs of people who are associated with this sector. The Indian economy needs reform but, most importantly there should be focus on the poor. FDI in multi-brand retailing must be dealt cautiously as it has direct impact on a large chunk of the population.

The proliferation of foreign capital into multi-brand retailing needs to be anchored in such a way that it results in a win-win situation for India. The move needs to be monitored in the wake of the current opposition by several political parties. All that is needed here is a strong political will and effective implementation of the policy.

References

1. Bhatia, S. C. Retail Management, Atlantic Publisher & Distribution, New Delhi, 2008.
2. Kumar D., FDI and Retail Sector in India, Dominant Publishers and Distributors, New Delhi 2009.
3. Economic Survey, 2009-10 & 2010-11, Ministry of Finance, GOI, New Delhi.
4. Verma, Manshu (2011). "FDI in multi-brand retail is great", The Economy Nov, 29.
5. The Economic Times, "Economic Survey 2011: Allow pashed opening of FDI in multi-brand retail", 25 February, 2011.
6. The Hindu, "Allow FDI in multi-brand retail in phased manner : survey", March 45,2012

Corporate Governance Framework in India

Deepa Mittal
Asst. Prof.
IITTM, India, Email: deepa_shrivastav2000@yahoo.com

Abstract

The concept of good corporate governance has gained importance internationally after a string of high profile corporate scandals. Corporate Governance consists of procedures and processes according to which an organisation is directed and controlled. The Corporate governance structure specifies the distribution of rights and responsibilities among the different participants in the organisation such as the board, managers, shareholders and other stakeholders and lays down the rules and procedures for decision-making.

Corporate Governance is concerned with holding the balance between economic and social goals and between individual and communal goals. The corporate governance framework is there to encourage the efficient use of resources and equally to require accountability for the stewardship of those resources. The aim is to align as nearly as possible the interests of individuals, corporations and society. After Enron, WorldCom, and other corporate governance catastrophes, SEBI felt that there was a need to improve further the level of corporate governance standards in India and constituted various committees for a right code on corporate governance. Although in India's company's act 1956 along with its several amendments has provisions related to corporate governance. Further, CII in 1998 and SEBI in year 2000 had also come with some code on corporate governance. Presently there are some mandatory and non-mandatory provisions for corporate governance practices.

Keywords: Corporate Governance; Agency Cost; Stakeholders Interest; Firm value; Disclosure Practices.

Introduction

The concept of good corporate governance has gained importance internationally after a string of high profile corporate scandals. Corporate Governance consists of procedures and processes according to which an organisation is directed and controlled. The Corporate governance structure specifies the distribution of rights and responsibilities among the different participants in the organisation such as the board, managers, shareholders and other stakeholders and lays down the rules and procedures for decision-making (OECD, 1999).

A company is a congregation of various stakeholders, namely, customers, employees, investors, vendors, government and society. A corporation should be fair and transparent to its stakeholders in all its transactions. This has become imperative in today's globalized business world where corporations/ companies/firms need to access global pools of capital, need to attract and retain the best human capital from various parts of the world, need to partner with vendors on mega collaborations and need to live in harmony with the community. Unless a corporation embraces and demonstrates ethical conduct, it will not be able to succeed. Corporate governance is about ethical conduct in business. Ethics is concerned with the code of values and principles that enables a person to choose between right and wrong, and therefore, select from alternative courses of action. Further, ethical dilemmas arise from conflicting interests of the parties involved. In this regard, managers make decisions based on a set of principles influenced by the values, context and culture of the organization. Ethical leadership is good for business as the organization is seen to conduct its business in line with the expectations of all stakeholders.

Corporate governance is the acceptance by management of the inalienable rights of shareholders as the true owners of the corporation and of their own role as trustees on behalf of the shareholders. It is about commitment to values, about ethical business conduct and about making a distinction between personal and corporate funds in the management of a company. (Report of SEBI on CG, 2003) Corporate governance is beyond the realm of law. It stems from the culture and mindset of management, and cannot be regulated by legislation alone. Corporate governance deals with conducting the affairs of a company such that there is fairness to all stakeholders and that its actions benefit the greatest number of stakeholders. It is about openness, integrity and accountability.

Perhaps the simplest and most common definition of this sort is that provided by the Cadbury Report (U.K.),: "Corporate governance is the system by which businesses are directed and controlled."

The definition in the preamble of the OECD Principles is also all encompassing? "Corporate governance . . . involves a set of relationships between a company's management, its board, its shareholders and other stakeholders. Corporate governance also provides the structure through which the objectives of the company are set, and the means of attaining those objectives and monitoring performance are determined."

International Corporate Governance Background

The first corporate governance code of the modern era - that was instituted in the UK by the Bank of England and London

Stock Exchange in 1992, and chaired by Sir Adrian Cadbury. Some of those codes are the Bosch Report, Australia (1995), the Cardon Report, Belgium (1998), the Dey Report, Canada (1994), the Vienot Report, France (1999), the King Report, South Africa (1994), the Peters Committee, Netherlands (1997), the Corporate. Governance Forum of Japan, (1998), the Governance of Spanish Companies, (1998), the Swedish Academy Report, (1994), the Mexico also adopted Corporate governance practices in 1999 with the publication of the Code of Best Corporate Practices by the Mexican Stock Exchange, the German Panel on Corporate Governance, (2000), the Sarbanes- Oxley Report, US (2002), etc. Studies of corporate governance practices across several countries conducted by the Asian Development Bank (2000), International Monetary Fund (1999), Organization for Economic Cooperation and Development (OECD) (1999) and the World Bank (1999) reveal that there is no single model of good corporate governance. This is recognized by the OECD Code. The OECD Code also recognizes that different legal systems, institutional frameworks and traditions across countries have led to the development of a range of different approaches to corporate governance. Common to all good corporate governance regimes, however, is a high degree of priority placed on the interests of shareholders, who place their trust in corporations to use their investment funds wisely and effectively.

Which System is the Best? Corporate governance mechanisms vary a great deal around the world. Firms in the United States and the United Kingdom substantially rely on legal protection of investors. Large investors are less prevalent, except that ownership is concentrated sporadically in the takeover process. In much of Continental Europe as well as in Japan, there is less reliance on elaborate legal protections, and more reliance on large investors and banks. Finally, in the rest of the world, ownership is typically heavily concentrated in families, with a few large outside investors and banks. Legal protection of investors is considerably weaker than in Japan and Germany, let alone in

Britain and the United States. This diversity of systems raises the obvious question: what arrangement is the best from the viewpoint of attracting external funds to firms? Legal protection and large investors are complementary in an effective corporate governance system. Indeed, the successful corporate governance systems, such as those of the United States, Germany, and Japan, rely on some combination of concentrated ownership and legal protection of investors. In the United States; both small and large shareholders are protected through an extensive system of rules that protects minority rights, allows for easy transfer of shares, keeps elections of directors relatively uninhibited by managers, and gives shareholders extensive powers to sue directors for violations of fiduciary duty, including through class-action suits. Because of extensive bankruptcy protection of companies, however, creditors in the United States have relatively fewer rights than do creditors in Germany and Japan. These legal rules support a system of active public participation in the stock market, concentration of ownership through takeovers, but little governance by banks.

Evolution of Corporate Governance framework in India

There has been a lot of interest in corporate governance in India post liberlisation of 1991. On the one hand various advantages of good corporate governance practices such as raising capital from international markets motivated firms to adopt good corporate governance practices whereas on the another hand corporate frauds by some big firms brought the concept to popular business lexicon. Exposed malpractices in 2008 at Satyam Computer Services Limited (SCL), the fourth largest software company from India, again brought the spotlight on corporate governance.

The corporate/company form has existed for centuries. The East India Company, for example, was chartered by Elizabeth I in 1600 AD. One might imagine, given this long history, that the issue of how corporations should be governed would have been settled some time ago. Yet, for nearly as long as corporations have existed, there have been complaints about corporate governance and agitation to improve it. Negligence and profusion, therefore, must always prevail, more or less, in the management of the affairs of such companies. Moreover, these complaints and agitation have had real effects: Over the centuries, they have led to various changes in corporate law and regulation.

Companies Act, 1956 provides for basic framework for regulation of all the companies. Certain provisions were incorporated in the Act itself to provide for checks and balances over the powers of Board viz.:

- Loan to directors or relatives or associated entities (need CG permission) (Sec 295)
- Interested contract needs Board resolution and to be entered in register (Sec 297)
- Interested directors not to participate or vote (Sec 300)
- Appointment of director or relatives for office or place of profit needs approval by shareholders. If the remuneration exceeds prescribed limit , CG approval required (Sec 314)
- Audit Committee for Public companies having paid-up capital of Rs. 5 Crores (Sec 292A)
- Shareholders holding 10% can appeal to Court in case of oppression or mismanagement (397/398).

Further, SEBI is empowered under Section 11 and Section 11A of SEBI Act to prescribe conditions for listing. However, Section 32 of the SEBI Act, 1992 states that the provisions of the SEBI Act, 1992 shall be in addition to, and not in derogation of, the provisions of any other law for the time being in force.

Special efforts for corporate governance initiatives in India began in 1998 with the "Desirable Code of Corporate Governance" a voluntary code published by the CII, and the first formal regulatory framework for listed companies specifically for corporate governance, established by the SEBI. The latter was made in February 2000, following the recommendations of the Kumarmangalam Birla Committee Report. SEBI's Board, in its meeting held on January 25, 2000, considered the recommendations of the Committee and decided to make the amendments to the listing agreement on February 21, 2000 for incorporating the recommendations of the committee by inserting a new clause in the Equity Listing Agreement – i.e. Clause 49.

Subsequently, after Enron, WorldCom, and other corporate governance catastrophes, SEBI felt that there was a need to improve further the level of corporate governance standards in India and constituted a second corporate governance committee chaired by Mr. Narayana Murthy, of Infosys Technologies Limited. Based on the recommendations of the aforesaid Committee, SEBI issued a circular on August 26, 2003 revising Clause 49 of the Listing Agreement. Based on the public comments received thereon and the revised recommendations of the Committee, certain provisions of the regulatory framework for corporate governance were modified and relevant amendments were made to Clause 49 of the Listing Agreement.

The revised clause 49 superseded all the earlier circulars on the subject and became effective for listed companies from January 01, 2006. It is applicable to the entities seeking listing for the first time and for existing listed entities having a paid up share capital of Rs. 3 crores and above or net worth of Rs. 25 crores or more at any time in the history of the company. In December 2009, Ministry of Corporate Affairs specified Voluntary Guidelines on Corporate Governance. In March 2012, Ministry of Corporate Affairs constituted a committee under the Chairmanship of Mr. Adi Godrej, Chairman, Godrej Industries Limited, to formulate policy document on Corporate Governance. In September, 2012 the Committee submitted its document, specifying seventeen guiding principles on corporate governance. The areas covered include, among others, size, composition, charter, responsibilities and meetings of the board of directors; tenure of directors; age limit for appointment as directors; liability of directors; accountability to shareholders and stakeholders; access to information; nominee directors and their remuneration; committee on grievances of shareholders; executive vs non-executive chairman of the board; audit committee; remuneration committee; nomination committee; board procedures; accounting standards and financial reporting; disclosure and transparency; auditor independence; responsibilities of individual and institutional shareholders; and matters relating to implementation of the canons of corporate governance.

Gist of Clause 49

Clause 49 of the Equity Listing Agreement consists of mandatory as well as non-mandatory

Provisions:

- Mandatory provisions comprises of the following:
    - Composition of Board and its procedure - frequency of meeting, number of independent directors, code of conduct for Board of directors and senior management
    - Audit Committee, its composition, and role
    - Provision relating to Subsidiary Companies
    - Disclosure to Audit committee, Board and the Shareholders
    - CEO/CFO certification
    - Quarterly report on Corporate Governance
    - Annual compliance certificate
- Non-mandatory provisions consist of the following:
    - Constitution of Remuneration Committee
    - Dispatch of Half-yearly results
    - Training of Board members
    - Peer evaluation of Board members
    - Whistle Blower policy

As per Clause 49 of the Listing Agreement, there should be a separate section on Corporate Governance in the Annual Reports of listed companies, with detailed compliance report on Corporate Governance. The companies should also submit a quarterly compliance report to the stock exchanges within 15 days from the close of quarter as per the prescribed format. The report shall be signed either by the Compliance Officer or the Chief Executive Officer of the company.

Rating Companies on Corporate Governance

There are few international rating agencies/firms which give rating to the companies on the basis of compliance of corporate governance norms. Three of them are discussed in brief here with the help of which, we can identify the standard parameters used for corporate governance disclosure practices world wide.

ISS, founded in 1985, provides research and proxy advisory services to institutional investors. In 2002, ISS introduced its corporate governance ratings (called the Corporate Governance Quotient, CGQO) that aim to "measure, the strengths, deficiencies and overall quality of a company's corporate governance practices and board of directors." ISS considers the following factors: board of directors (structure, size, attendance, chairman/CEO separation, etc.), audit committees, board, and committee independence, and the presence of a financial expert, charter and bylaw provisions, antitakeover provisions, executive and director compensation, qualitative factors, such as board performance reviews, meetings of outside directors, CEO succession plan, director and executive ownership, and director education. CGQs range from 0 to 100 and measure the quality of governance relative to other firms in the company's primary stock market index.

Another firm for rating on Corporate governance GMI was founded in 2000 to provide the tools that make it possible for its clients to monitor firms' corporate governance. Similar to

TCL and ISS, GMI considers various aspects of governance, such as board accountability, financial disclosure and internal controls, shareholder rights, executive compensation, market for control and ownership base, and corporate behavior. Companies are scored on a scale of 1 (lowest) to 10 (highest). GMI global ratings measure the strength of corporate governance relative to all other companies in the GMI universe. GMI also gives companies a home market rating that reflects the strength of each one's governance mechanisms relative to others in their home country. However, these ratings are not available from Bloomberg (our main data source), which provides data only on overall global rating.

The third company is TCL Sub-Ratings, TCL Sub-Rating Description Board composition Covers board independence, director age and tenure, overcommitted directors, active and former CEOs on board, and whether the past CEO is the chairman. CEO compensation Covers pay-for-performance sensitivity, stock awards and stock ownership, restricted stock, perquisite payments, fixed and variable components of the CEO pay, and several red flags such as base salaries in excess of $1 million, bonuses greater than twice the annual salary, high tax or leisure expense payments, a declining number of CEO shares held, and excessive option compensation. Shareholder reflects a board's history in responding to shareholder proposals that receive responsiveness majority of the votes. A board's failure to accept a shareholder proposal that receives majority indicates the degree to which the board acts in the best interest of management rather than shareholders. It includes a regulatory evaluation of the amount of disclosure of current or potential liability problems exposure and the existence of repeated regulatory infractions or fines. Firms with more "shareholder-friendly" takeover defense configurations get higher ratings. Accounting compares current quarter reports against prior four quarters for indicators of potential earnings management to identify firms that favor accounting methods that emphasize and enhance current period earnings but may also lead to poor long-term (three- to five-year) market performance. Also accounts for other accounting concerns such as SEC or IRS enforcement actions. Strategic decision Focuses on board approval of mergers and acquisitions with lower ratings making assigned to approvals of mergers resulting in significant loss of shareholder value.

Fourth corporate governance rating agency is CRISIL, it gives rating to the listed companies in India on various parameters of corporate governance as per SEBI Code on corporate governance (Mandatory and non-Mandatory provisions of Corporate Governance), IFRS, Indian Accounting Standards and OECD norms on it.

The current Scenario of Corporate Governance in India Overall scenario in top 100 companies in India (Pillania, 2013)

It is seen that ninety-seven out of the one hundred firms studied have taken up corporate governance compliance and guidelines and for the rest data was insufficient. Eighty percent of the companies strictly follow clause 49 measures as stipulated by SEBI and seventeen percent of the companies are interested in doing more than the mandatory requirements of SEBI. Though the reasons are varied, e.g. compliance to SEBI guidelines, Companies' Act, etc., what is seen is that most companies are also providing a separate corporate governance report within their annual report and are also mentioning it in their management discussion and analysis. Most companies studied have been following corporate governance guidelines provided by the Ministry of Corporate Affairs. Corporate governance guidelines have been issued by the Ministry of Corporate Affairs. There are certain mandatory requirements as well as certain non-mandatory requirements. Most companies studied are displaying an inclination towards complying to the non-mandatory requirements as well. There is a green initiative by the Ministry of Corporate Affairs which most companies studied are trying to comply with. It has also been observed that quite a few companies studied like Dabur had been following corporate governance before it became mandatory. As has been observed, the Tata Group of Companies have a "Tatas Code of Conduct" and the Reliance Group of Companies has a "Reliance Group Code of Conduct". This reflects the fact that these companies are already aware of the importance of corporate governance in meeting the goals of their stakeholders and have been implementing measures to achieve them.

There are certain companies which have even won awards for the best practices in the area of corporate governance. Some of the examples are:

- Bharti Airtel: CRISIL has assigned CRISIL GVC Level 1 to the company.
- L&T: The Company was awarded the "National Award for Excellence in Corporate Governance-2010", by the Institute of Company Secretaries of India.
- Wipro: The Company has been awarded the National award for excellence in Corporate Governance from Institute of Company Secretaries of India during the year 2004.
- M&M: Given highest level rating by CRISIL for governance and value creation.
- HDFC Bank Ltd.: Rating of GVC Level 1 by CRISIL in Governance and Value Creation.
- Union Bank: Award for Excellence in Corporate governance was given at the 10th ICSI National Award for Excellence in Corporate Governance 2010.

Conclusion

It is widely believed that good corporate governance in different industries can contribute to stability and sustainable growth. One important element in the nexus of good corporate governance is more competition in financial markets, since it becomes imperative on management and ownership to perfect their relationships so as to better perform and withstand the competition.

The importance of corporate governance can be easily identified from the statement of Sir Adrian Cadbury in 'Global Corporate Governance Forum', World Bank, 2000, "Corporate Governance is concerned with holding the balance between economic and social goals and between individual and communal goals. The corporate governance framework is there to encourage the efficient use of resources and equally to require accountability for the stewardship of those resources. The aim is to align as nearly as possible the interests of individuals, corporations and society." Source: http://www.corpgov.net/library/library.html-December 2008, website surfed on July 20, 2013.

The literature identifies several avenues through which corporate governance might affect growth and firm performance: 1. Increased access to external financing by firms, which can lead to greater investment, higher growth, and more employment creation; 2. Lower cost of capital and the associated higher firm valuation, which makes investment more attractive and again furthers growth and employment; 3. Better operational performance, through better allocation of resources and better management, which creates and adds to wealth; 4. Reduction in the risk of financial crises and - just as important - in the large economic and social costs that they usually entail; 5. Better relationships with all stakeholders, which help improve social and labor relationships and deals more favorably with issues such as environmental protection, etc. Apart from the above channels, an important feature that enhances good corporate governance and furthers its favorable growth implications is a more competitive market.

There are several reasons to support this essential connection. First among them is the fact that incumbent firms in monopolistic markets earn excess profits that render needless any improvement in corporate governance to better perform and use resources more efficiently. Also, the deep pockets engendered by excess profits reduce the need of incumbent firms to rely on securities markets where external financiers often demand transparency and accountability of corporate insiders. Perhaps most interesting is the reason that existing corporate elites can use their influence to resist policy reforms, and in consequence entrench the position of the limited number of existing firms and the interests of their management and corporate insiders. Not surprisingly, countries that have more competitive and regulated markets have proven to have better corporate governance practices and more developed financial markets.

References

Banerjee, Chandrajit and Tandon, Amit (2012) Institutional Investors-Driving Force for Good Governance, A Survey by CII and IIAS, http://www.nfcgindia.org/research.htm surfed on July 22, 2013, Pp. 1-20.

Kadam, Sunil (2013) Consultative Paper on Review of Corporate Governance Norms in India, Corporate Finance Department, Division of Issues and Listing, SEBI, January 2013.

KPMG (2012) ASX Corporate Governance Principles and Recommendations on Diversity: ASX Diversity Report: Analysis of 31 December 2011 year end disclosures, www.asxgroup.com.au/media/asx_diversity_report.pdf, surfed on July 22, 2013.

OECD. (1999) Principles of Corporate Governance. OECD. Paris.

Pillania, Rajesh K. (2013) Practice of Corporate Strategy in India: A Research Book presenting Learnings from Successful Companies, LAP LAMBERT Academic Publishing, Germany, year 2013, Pages 216.

Report of SEBI (2003) Report of SEBI Committee on Corporate Governance Chaired by N.R. Narayana Murthy, February 8, 2003.

Indian Journey to Generally Accepted Accounting Principles (GAAPS)

Dr. Manoj Sharma
Assistant Professor, Department of Commerce,
Himachal Pradesh University Regional Centre Dharamshala,
Mob. No.: 09418626127
Email: manojhpu@gmail.com

A strong financial reporting system supported by good governance, high quality standards and firm regulatory framework is the key for any economic development. In other words, sound financial reporting standards underline the trust that investors place in financial reporting information and thus play an important role in contributing to the economic development of a country. As the world continues to globalize, a number of multi-national companies are establishing their businesses in various countries with emerging economies and vice versa. More and more Indian companies are also being listed on overseas stock exchanges. Therefore, Sound financial reporting structure is imperative for economic well-being and effective functioning of capital Markets.

In view of the above, the Generally Accepted Accounting Principles (GAAPs), issued by the Accounting Standards Board (ASB) of the Institute of Chartered Accountants of India (ICAI) in consultation with National Advisory Committee on Accounting Standards (NACAS) and notified by Ministry of Corporate Affairs (MCA) are widely used and accepted by the entities as notifies by the MCA. This paper is an attempt to highlight the Indian journey of accounting reforms in the form of Accounting Standards (ASs).

Generally accepted Accounting Principles (GAAPs) commonly known as Accounting Standards are written documents, policy documents issued by expert accounting body or by Government or other regulatories body covering the aspects of recognition, measurement, treatment, presentation and disclosure of accounting transactions in the financial statement. Accounting Standards in India are issued by the Institute of Chartered Accountant of India (ICAI) set up under an act of parliament in 1949.

Accounting Standards Board:

Recognising the need for international harmonisation of accounting standards, in 1973, the International Accounting Standards Committee (IASC) was established. It may be mentioned here that the IASC has been reconstituted as the International Accounting Standards Board (IASB) in April 01, 2001. The objectives of IASC included promotion of the International Accounting Standards for worldwide acceptance and observance so that the accounting standards in different countries are harmonised. In recent years, need for international harmonisation of Accounting Standards followed in different countries has grown considerably as the cross-border transfers of capital are becoming increasingly common.

The Institute of Chartered Accountants of India (ICAI) being a member body of the IASC, constituted the Accounting Standards Board (ASB) on 21st April, 1977, with a view to harmonise the diverse accounting policies and practices in use in India. After the avowed adoption of liberalisation and globalisation as the corner stones of Indian economic policies in early '90s, and the growing concern about the need of effective corporate governance of late, the Accounting Standards have increasingly assumed importance. While formulating accounting standards, the ASB takes into consideration the applicable laws, customs, usages and business environment prevailing in the country. The ASB also gives due consideration to International Financial Reporting Standards (IFRSs)/ International Accounting Standards (IASs) issued by IASB and tries to integrate them, to the extent possible, in the light of conditions and practices prevailing in India.

Composition of the Accounting Standards Board

The composition of the ASB is fairly broad-based and ensures participation of all interest-groups in the standard-setting process. Apart from the elected members of the Council of the ICAI nominated on the ASB, the following are represented on the ASB:

- Nominee of the Central Government representing the Department of Company Affairs on the Council of the ICAI
- Nominee of the Central Government representing the Office of the Comptroller and Auditor General of India on the Council of the ICAI
- Nominee of the Central Government representing the Central Board of Direct Taxes on the Council of the ICAI
- Representative of the ICWAI, ICSI

Representatives of Industry Associations (1 from Associated Chambers of Commerce and Industry (ASSOCHAM), 1 from Confederation of Indian Industry (CII) and 1 from Federation of Indian Chambers of Commerce and Industry (FICCI)

- Representative of Reserve Bank of India
- Representative of Securities and Exchange Board of India
- Representative of Controller General of Accounts
- Representative of Central Board of Excise and Customs
- Representative of Financial Institutions
- Representatives of Academic Institutions (1 from

Universities and 1 from Indian Institutes of Management)

- Eminent professionals co-opted by the ICAI (they may be in practice or in industry, government, education, etc.)
- Chairman of the Research Committee and the Chairman of the Expert Advisory Committee of the ICAI, if they are not otherwise members of the Accounting Standards Board
- Representative(s) of any other body, as considered appropriate by the ICAI

Functions/Objectives of Accounting Standards Board

- To conceive of and suggest areas in which Accounting Standards need to be developed.
- To formulate Accounting Standards with a view to assisting the Council of the ICAI in evolving and establishing Accounting Standards in India.
- To examine how far the relevant International Accounting Standard/International Financial Reporting Standard can be adapted while formulating the Accounting Standard and to adapt the same.
- To review, at regular intervals, the Accounting Standards from the point of view of acceptance or changed conditions, and, if necessary, revise the same.
- To provide, from time to time, interpretations and guidance on Accounting Standards.

To carry out such other functions relating to Accounting Standards

The accounting standard setting process

The accounting standard setting, by its very nature, involves reaching an optimal balance of the requirements of financial information for various interest-groups having a stake in financial reporting. With a view to reach consensus, to the extent possible, as to the requirements of the relevant interest-groups and thereby bringing about general acceptance of the Accounting Standards among such groups, considerable research, consultations and discussions with the representatives of the relevant interest-groups at different stages of standard formulation becomes necessary. The standard-setting procedure of the ASB, as briefly outlined below, is designed in such a way so as to ensure such consultation and discussions:

- Identification of the broad areas by the ASB for formulating the Accounting Standards.
- Constitution of the study groups by the ASB for preparing the preliminary drafts of the proposed Accounting Standards.
- Consideration of the preliminary draft prepared by the study group by the ASB and revision, if any, of the draft on the basis of deliberations at the ASB.
- Circulation of the draft, so revised, among the Council members of the ICAI and 12 specified outside bodies such as Standing Conference of Public Enterprises (SCOPE), Indian Banks' Association, Confederation of Indian Industry (CII), Securities and Exchange Board of India (SEBI), Comptroller and Auditor General of India (C& AG), and Department of Company Affairs, for comments.
- Meeting with the representatives of specified outside bodies to ascertain their views on the draft of the proposed Accounting Standard.
- Finalisation of the Exposure Draft of the proposed Accounting Standard on the basis of comments received and discussion with the representatives of specified outside bodies.
- Issuance of the Exposure Draft inviting public comments.
- Consideration of the comments received on the Exposure Draft and finalisation of the draft Accounting Standard by the ASB for submission to the Council of the ICAI for its

consideration and approval for issuance.

- Consideration of the draft Accounting Standard by the Council of the Institute, and if found necessary, modification of the draft in consultation with the ASB.

The Accounting Standard, so finalised, is issued under the authority of the Council.

Finalization of Accounting Standards

The Accounting Standards finalized by ASB of ICAI are considered by National Advisory Committee on Accounting Standards (NACAS) which is a body set up under section 210A of the Companies Act, 1956 by the Govt. of India. It Advises the Central Government i.e. Ministry of Corporate Affairs (MCA) on the formulation and laying down of accounting policies and accounting standards for adoption by companies. The advisory committee shall consist of the following members, namely:

1. A chairperson who shall be a person of eminence well versed in accountancy, finance, business administration, business law, economics or similar Discipline;
2. One member each nominated by the chartered accountants of India constituted under the chartered Accountants Act, 1949, The Institute of Cost and Work Accountants Act, 1959 and The Institute of Company Secretaries of India constituted under the Company secretaries Act 1980.
3. One representative each of the Central government , Reserve Bank of India, Comptroller & Auditor general of India to be nominated by it.
4. A person who holds or has held the office of professor in Accountancy , Finance or Business Management in any University or deemed university;
5. The Chairman of the Central Board of Direct Tax(India) constituted under the Central Board of Revenue Act, 1963. (India) or his nominee;

6. Two members to represent the chambers of commerce and industry to be nominated by The Central Government of India; and
7. One representative of the Security and Exchange Board of India to be nominated by it.

Applicability of Accounting Standards

For the purpose of applicability of accounting standards, enterprises are classified into three categories-

- Level -I enterprise
- Level-II enterprise
- Level-III enterprise

Level –I enterprise- Enterprises which fall in any one or more of the following categories, at any time during the accounting period, are classified as Level-I enterprises:

- Enterprise whose equity or debt securities are listed whether in India or outside India.
- Enterprises, which are in the process of listing their equity or debt securities as evidenced by the board of directors' resolution in this regard.
- Banks including co-operative banks.
- Financial institutions.
- Enterprises carrying on insurance business
- All commercial, industrial and business reporting enterprises, whose turnover for the immediately preceding accounting period on the basis of audited financial statements exceeds Rs. 50 crores. Turnover does not include 'other income'.
- All commercial, industrial and business reporting enterprise having borrowings, including public deposits, in excess of Rs. 10 crores at any time during the accounting period.
- Holding and subsidiary enterprise of any one of the above at any time during the accounting period.

Level-II Enterprise- Enterprises, which are not Level-I enterprises but fall in any one or more of the following categories, are classified as Level-II enterprises:

- All commercial, industrial and business reporting enterprises, whose turnover for the immediately preceding accounting period on the basis of audited financial statements exceeds Rs. 40 lakhs but does not exceed Rs. 50 crores. Turnover does not include 'other income'.
- All commercial, industrial and business reporting enterprises having borrowings, including public deposits, in excess of Rs. 1 crore but not in excess of Rs. 10 crores at any time during the accounting period.

Level-III enterprise- Enterprises, which are not covered under Level-I and Level- II, are considered as Level-III enterprises.

- Applicability of Accounting Standard to Level I- All the 29 Accounting standards are fully applicable to Level-I enterprises.
- Applicability of Accounting Standard to Level II and III enterprises (SMEs) - For the purpose of applicability of accounting standard to Level-II enterprises, the case can be divided into three categories:
- Accounting standards fully applicable
- Accounting standards applicable but relaxation from certain disclosure requirements.
- Accounting standards not applicable

Accounting Standards fully applicable

AS-1, AS-2, AS-4, AS-5, AS-6, AS-7, AS-8, AS-9, AS-10, AS-11, AS-12, AS-13, AS-14, AS-15, AS-16, AS-22, AS-26 and AS-28.

AS-28, "Impairment of Assets" is applicable

- For Level-I enterprises w.e.f. 1.4.2004
- For Level-II enterprises w.e.f. 1.4.2006 and,
- For Level-III enterprises w.e.f. 1.4.2008.

Accounting Standards applicable but relaxation from certain disclosure requirements

As prescribed in AS-19, AS-20, and AS-29.

Accounting Standards not applicable

AS-3, AS-17, AS-18, AS-24, AS-21, AS-23, AS-25 and AS-27 are not applicable because of existing regulation in India.

List of Existing Accounting Standards

AS 1 Disclosure of Accounting Policies

AS 2 Valuation of Inventories

AS 3 Cash Flow Statements

AS 4 Contingencies and Events Occurring After the Balance Sheet Date

AS 5 Net Profit or Loss for the Period, Prior Period Items and Changes in Accounting Policies

AS 6 Depreciation Accounting

AS 7 Construction Contracts

AS 9 Revenue Recognition

AS 10 Accounting for Fixed Assets

AS 11 The Effects of Changes in Foreign Exchange Rates

AS 12 Accounting for Government Grants

AS 13 Accounting for Investments

AS 14 Accounting for Amalgamations

AS 15 Employee Benefits

AS 16 Borrowing Costs

AS 17 Segment Reporting

AS 18 Related Party Disclosures

AS 19 Leases

AS 20 Earnings per Share

AS 21 Consolidated Financial Statements

AS 22 Accounting for Taxes on Income

AS 23 Accounting for Investments in Associates in Consolidated Financial Statements

AS 24 Discontinuing Operations

AS 25 Interim Financial Reporting

AS 26 Intangible Assets

AS 27 Financial Reporting of Interests in Joint Ventures

AS 28 Impairment of Assets

AS 29 Provisions, Contingent Liabilities and Contingent Assets

AS 30 Financial Instruments: Recognition and Measurement*

AS 31 Financial Instruments: Presentation*

AS 32 Financial Instruments: Disclosures*

* AS 30, AS 31 and AS 32 are nor mandatory in nature and only encouraged to follow.

References

1. Ghosh T.P., (2010), "IFRSs", taxmann allied services pvt. Ltd.
2. Shukla M.C., Grewal T.S. & Gupta S.C., (2010), "Advanced Accounts", S. Chand Company ltd.
3. Rawat D.S., (2011), "Accounting Standards", Taxman publishers.
4. Vinayakam N. & Charumati B., (2010), "Financial Accouning", S. Chand Company ltd.
5. Chandra Krishna (2002), "Accounting for managerial control", Saruf and sons, New Delhi. Gupta S.K. & Sharma S.K., (2010), "Financial Accounting", Kalyani Pub.

Emerging Technological Trends in Digital Marketing: An Indian Perspective

Dr. Richa Rana
Assistant Professor
Himachal Pradesh University, Regional Center, Dharamshala
Email: ranaricha@hotmail.com

Abstract

This paper highlights, emerging mobile device technologies in the field of digital marketing. The paper reviews and evaluates extensive literature and cases on the use of new age applications, which have been utilized in developed regions. Special emphasis has been placed on marketing strategies, which involve mobile devices. A view on location based digital marketing and its effectiveness has also been results of this evaluation have been detailed in the form of utility framework for digital marketing in context for running a campaign. The paper also details the adoption of these technologies from the perspective of running campaign. This may involve both complementary digital and traditional marketing strategies. The pros and cons of using emerging technologies have been highlighted, with the authors making recommendations for the scope of future research in this area.

Keywords: Digital marketing, mobile applications, location based services, customer engagement, conversations

Purpose of Research:

To explore the applicability of new emerging technologies like Augmented Reality(AR), Quick Response Codes(QRC) and Near Field Communications(NFC) in the field of digital marketing from an Indian context.

Augmented Reality (AR) is a real time view of the environment whose elements are augmented/supplemented by intelligent and application based information and communication technology that enhances and adds value to the real time view of the customer. A Quick Response Code (QRC)is attached to an item that records information related to that item, this code is readable by any imaging device such as a camera and can be processed further for identification of that item. Near field Communication (NFC) is a set of standards for smart phones and similar devices to establish radio communication with each other by bringing them into close proximity for data exchange.

Research Method:

Content analysis was the method adopted. Under this, various examples and research papers pertaining to emerging digital technologies like augmented reality, quick response codes and near field communications were studied and cases relevant to the topic were found.

The cases were then studied and the applications of these technologies in different industries and different facets of business advantages were analyzed. The current status of the Indian consumer adoption of such technologies was researched through published papers.

A model/framework to make these technologies work to the business advantage for the benefits of buyers/customers as well as sellers/firms is proposed in this paper. Examples and excerpts are quoted to highlight the relevance of these emerging digital technologies.

Major Results:

The international companies have made use of this technology to their advantage. They are mentioned in brief below.

- Food Industry- McDonalds the fast food chains tackled their erosion of brand image through a global transparency drive by launching the application "Track My Macca's" on the I-phone, which is an augmented reality application. Customer's scanned QR code (mobile barcode) on the side of a burger's container and got the entire view of the company's supply-chain data based on the user's location through animated augmented reality. The users could also connect and chat with real farmers, bakers and fishermen who supply the ingredients. So customers were not only engaged but also were driven to have a conversation. This kind of campaigns let the customers discover themselves about you rather than you telling them and marketing yourself. This creates factual credibility and customers believe and trust you and builds Brand Equity.
- Retail (on-line super market) - Tesco faced a challenge of having fewer numbers of stores as compared

to many of No .l player E-mart in South Korea. They expanded their online sales through mobile shopping rather than spending a lot of money opening new shops, as South Korea has more than 10 million smart phone users in a population of less than 50 million. The consumer behaviour of the South Korean also revealed that they were hardworking people and shopping once a week used to take a toll on their on them and eat away their rest and leisure time. Tescotargeted on commuters waiting for their train. To get the same experience as shopping mall they plastered the glass walls of subway stations with pictures of their products, they laid it out in the same fashion as they would be in a traditional shop. The 'shelves' featured QR codes which they scanned and the product automatically landed in their on-line cart.

- Online-Retail: eBay has launched an application called 'sunglass finder'. The customers can upload their photograph and try wearing the sunglasses as you do in the real world at an eye-wear store and choose the one which suits you and then purchase the product. This is the most popular application and has overcome the barrier of on-line shopping and has enabled on-line and mobile shopping to become more interactive and easy for the customers.
- Brand Positioning: Unilever, clear Shampoo campaign in Thailand- Clear shampoo positioned itself as the Shampoo that will give you a healthy scalp. They desired that the customer should perceive them product benefit as 'Healthy Scalp'; they created a campaign with the help of a Hair stylist and an IT Engineer. A hairstyle with the QR code was designed, that means that the hair was cropped in a fashion which will show the QR code design. The idea was to communicate that you can have this type of hairstyle only if you have a healthy scalp. A troop of guerilla troop was sent across the city so that people will pay attention to their hairstyle. The brand was also endorsed by a TV celebrity and he had the same hairstyle of the QR code. All that the customers needed to do was to take a picture or scan the hairstyle, which copied the QR code and it directed the customers to the healthy scalp website., This PR exercise was talked about by people created a huge buzz and was written about in the magazines. It resulted in a huge inflow of traffic to the website (by 400%) and the result was that they gained the mind share of the people and could differentiate themselves from the competitors.
- Tourism: NFC at London of Museum- They help their visitors to learn more through providing information about their exhibits, all that the visitors/customers have to do is bring their close to a sensitive tag and receive more information about that exhibit. It works as a detailed Guide who can give you as much information as you would like

to know and store it with you for your future use. It also provides as an access voucher for the Museum's shop and café's. You can also book tickets for special show at the museum.

- BTL (Below the line)marketing: NFC Smart Poster: Unlike the traditional poster which has the only the visual impact, Smart poster has the enhanced ability to connect the physical world with the virtual world. Traditional poster gives a call for action by specifying the 'Offer', 'Phone No' or Web address', here the customer needs to take an effort to remember the offer and then go to the physical store to avail it, customer has to physically key-in the phone number and note down the website address to know more about the product and the offer. In all these scenarios it is very likely that the all this effort might not really convert into a prospect into your customer, again in today's competitive world the customer is bombarded every-moment with different offers and customer have no time for all this. So the need of the hour is to make it simple for the customer to act on these- offers on the move. Smart poster do this by enabling someone just to take a picture of the offer or scan the QR code, the customer is directly diverted to the details of the offer and NFC makes it possible to make a purchase smooth andcomplete the transactions. Thus can be used for anything from creating awareness about a product and know more, to view the product attributes in details, to reward the customer for repeat purchase, to run a loyalty program, to run a contest which would enhance the brand association with some acti or game played through such campaigns.
- Product Promotion: Swarovski AR Instagram contest: promoted 'Style yourself with jewelry' mobile application. Users can use the AR application and virtually try on the jewelry and upload their image on Istangram. This application is integrated with social media platform which has photo sharing like the Facebook and all your friends can view and comment on this.

- Operational efficiency: Ticketing System for Public transport- In Germany, Frankfurt the regional transit authority has merged its 'tap-in' payment system with the national railway operator to allow commuters to access travel information and schedules.
  - o Hotels- keyless entry into hotel suite doors through NFC
  - o Security clearance or authorized access- Into Laboratories, Garages or Conferences though NFC
- Induce trial: In Sydney University campus Unilever promoted their Lipton Ice Tea product by allowing users to 'like' it via Facebook and offered them coupons.

There are many applications in Construction industry, Industrial design, Medical, Military, Navigation, Sports and entertainment and Tourism.

This literature review on understanding the behavior of the Indian customers towards adoption of these technologies and thus the factors that influence their use of mobile banking reveal that Perceived risk majorly impact the customers intention towards using mobile banking services, followed by Perceived image of the service, perceived usefulness and perceived ease of use.

It is found that all 3 technologies i.e. Augmented Reality, Quick Response Codes and Near Field Communications are used to establish and sustain customer or consumer engagement. The digital marketing field is all about creating conversations, which aid engagement with the brand.

The digital World Wide Web where products and services are marketed online is restricted with its sensory inputs to the viewer. A marketer where in all marketing messages have to be supplied to the user can use only visual and auditory stimulus. The touch and feel stimulus which is critical to making a buying decision is missing. Augmented reality bridges the gap between the lacks of sensory inputs of touch in the digital world. It compensates the lack of touch by providing an interactive engagement experience with the viewer. This is done by augmenting basic product or service information with linkages to deeper information on product composition, dynamic rate display and on the fly customization.

Quick response (QR) codes originally meant for tracking inventory, marketers in developed nations have ingeniously used it to good effect in their campaigns. As QR codes are 2 dimensional, they have the ability to store more information than a conventional 1-dimension bar code. Marketing campaigns have utilized QR codes effectively using gamefication or by making a play on the intrinsic quality of curiosity of human beings and the need for discovery.

This works since the very nature of a QR code is cryptic and can just about lock in any information such as a web unique resource locator or a discount coupon code.

For QR codes to be effective in a distinct market like India, first awareness about this technology has to be created among consumers. Telecom service providers and cell phone manufacturers have to buy-in to the concept and incorporate QR code reader applications in mobile devices prior to sale of the device. We find that while QR codes are being used by organizations in India on their products they have not found acceptability with the Indian consumer.

While, Augmented Reality and QR codes are tools in engagement and aid in the creation of conversations, Near Field Communications (NFC) which a hardware driver solution on a mobile provides a call to action to the customer/consumer. Our research has found NFC is primarily being used for contactless secure payments, it is slowly picking up pace as engagement tool in developed nations. For such a technology to be successful in an Indian context, more messages in mobile security have to be conveyed to the Indian populace, as security is a huge concern in this region.

Implications of Research:

Marketing communication agencies can now design entire campaigns around creating conversations between customer/ consumer and the depth of information can be provided at multiple levels using augmented reality. richer experience can also be created with a new concept call articulated naturality web which forms scope for further research in this direction. [1]

There are numerous indigenous brands in India that lack visibility can incorporate QR codes on their product to run contests, campaigns and establish interactivity with their customers/ consumers. Studies and tools can designed in measuring QR code analytics, this will help marketers to find out the 'Return on Investment' or I effectiveness of their marketing campaign and this can also increase their marketing effectiveness. All of this subject to mainstream adoption and acceptance of the technology. Further studies into the mindset of the Indian consumer regarding QR codes are needed in this regard. '

Commercial establishments like the hospitality industry can be leading drivers in using NFC in India. NFC can as a call to action tool by marketers to drive users in making seamless payments. NFC enabled posters its affiliates in a non-digital setting can be utilized to engage with potential customer/consumers. Additional in this area is required in relation to digital contactless payments and its perception in an Indian setting.

Key References:

1. Speiginer, G. (2012, January 17). Articulated Naturality Web I Mixed Reality Design. Retrieved December 12, 2013, from http://ael.gatech.edu/mrdesignclass/tag/articulated-naturality-web/
2. http://www.telegraph.co.uk/technology/mobile-phones/8601147/Tesco-builds-virtual-shops-for¬Korean-commuters.html
3. http://www.telegraph.co.uk/technology/mobile-phones/8601147/Tesco-builds-virtual-shops-for¬Korean-

commuters.html. Mohammad Umair Yaqub, Umair Ahmad Shaik; Near Field Communication- Its Applications and Implementation in K.S.A; King Fand University of Petroleum & Minerals

4. Dasgupta, Siddhartha Paul, Rik; Fuloria, Sanjay; Factors Affecting Behavioral Intentions towards Mobile Banking Usage: Empirical Evidence from India Romanian Journal of Marketing 1 (Jan-Mar 2011): 6-28.
5. Kumar, Reji G; Rejikumar, G; Ravindran, D Sudharani; AN EMPIRICAL STUDY ON SERVICE QUALITY PERCEPTIONS AND CONTINUANCE INTENTION IN MOBILE BANKING CONTEXT IN INDIA; Journal of Internet Banking and Commerce 17.1 (Apr 2012): 1-22.
6. http://www.nfcworld.com/category/applications/
7. http:/ /en.wikipedia.org/wild/Near field communication
8. http://en.wikipedia.org/wild/Augmented reality
9. http://en.wildpedia.org/wild/QR code
10. Scalped: QR Code haircuts reach 10 million in Thailand
11. McDonald's Track My Maccas - YouTube
12. Tesco QR Code Subway Store - YouTube
13. http://computer. financialexpres s. com/20120315/coverstory01. shtnil
14. http: / / s ands tormdigital.com /2012 /10(03 /near-field-communication-nfc-3-case-stdies /
15. http: / /www. lux urydaily.com / swarovski-boosts-ecommerce

Marketing Strategies of Housing Finance Companies in Himachal Pradesh

Inderjit Singh

Ph.D. Research Scholar, (NET JRF, SET Qualified), Department of Commerce, H.P.University Shimla.

Prof. Kulwant Singh Pathania

Former Director UGC-ASC and Presently Senior Professor, Faculty of Commerce and Management Studies, H.P.University Shimla.

Abstract

Housing institutions have traditionally operated within a highly stable environment. In the last twenty years, dramatic changes have impacted on the competitive environment of the housing services industry, including institutions specialized in house loan. These changes have required providers of house loan services to re-think their marketing and distribution strategies. The era of consumerism has arrived as an immediate benefit of liberalization in India. The House loan Industry has developed immensely and with its growth came superior schemes coupled with higher competition as an implication to manage the service oriented marketing strategies for serving the customers better. This present study investigates the contributing factors which have an impact on customer experience management for house loan. This paper intends to study the structure of the newly liberalised housing finance market of India and analyse its effect on the Indian housing market. The paper has analysed the relationship between Housing finance variables such as House disbursements and Interest rates and Housing demand variables such as Housing sales in Himachal Pradesh. The methodology used in the study consisted of a survey among 60 people who have shown their awareness about the presence of banks dealing housing loans and the findings are fully analysed. Furthermore, some recommendations are proposed to assist house loan providers to better manage customer experiences in the housing sector. Hence, the present study would serve as an initial and invaluable research work for house loan providers to understand the underlying motives of customers and their perceptions on customer experiences while they are dealing with housing loan.

Keywords: Housing Loan, Consumer, Marketing Strategies, Companies.

Introduction

Housing which means next to food and clothing amongst basic human needs, has always had and continues to have important socio-economic implications. Housing is one of the basic requirements for human survival. For a normal citizen-owning a house provides significant economic- security and dignity in society. It is found that housing remained a problem, not from last few years but from 30-50 years back also. Problem not confined only to ABNORMALS who live in tents, hired houses or in vacant spaces in jungles, on the land of agriculturists. But to middle and EFFLUENTS sections of society too. Why problem for housing has arisen? It is because of increasing explosion of population on earth. Governments lands and forests, land owned by residents, getting reduced day by day, year-by- year, decade by decade. In the facet of vast increasing explosion of population which is a Non-Fixed variable, but land is a fixed variable which can't be increased.

Earlier banks did not lend for housing, which was non-priority advance, middle and poor sections of society could only dream about good houses. With concerned efforts of parliament and state governments, housing boards and co-operatives came into existence. Housing for public requires well planned housing policies from Himachal Pradesh state government, because housing is a state government subject. Central Development Institutions have been developed under the act of parliament, i.e. RBI, LIC and NABARD. They are re-financing institutions to banks. Housing finance institutions provide housing re-finance to banks and HFCs. When government declared finance as priority for housing the bank for having maximum share of economy attracted towards lending house loaning.

Himachal Pradesh is not a very rich state, whose people can afford to develop very good standard houses from their pockets, except few ones. Study involves easily making housing finance available to needy persons, making them aware of facilitators and suppliers of raw material of housing units, make them aware about different housing products, coupled with different add-ons, different insurance policies. The purpose of the study is to fulfil the housing needs of different segments of society in Himachal Pradesh. The paper lays stress on implementation of policies as set out by Government of India, Reserve Bank of India and monitoring of progress of banks and HFCs operating in Himachal Pradesh under the jurisdiction of controlling regional offices. Implementation and monitoring has to be done by controlling offices about achievements/performance vis-à-vis targets set for housing advances. Banks and HFCs have to implement the different schemes as formulated by Government of India and H.P.

Marketing Strategies of Housing Finance Companies: Marketing of any product is in four phases- product, price, policy, promotion and perfect performance.

- Product: Product is housing to whom to be sold which groups to be talked, Types of housing, Renovation/improvement of houses and Interior/Exterior decorations.

- Pricing: Price of house is entirely determined between buyer and seller. If it be one's own land/plot, it is the loan amount determined by bank based on data supplied by proposed borrower to bank regarding salary slip, service age, margin money, take home salary, repayment time etc.
- Policy: Policies of banks are already approved by corporate office of banks. Policy regarding simple mortgage of house or equitable mortgage of sale deed of house/plot of land kept as collateral security for loan. Repayment methods and recovery methods, all are mentioned in approved policies.
- Promotional Methods: In marketing, promotional methods play an important role. The promotional methods are- Good contacts with house builders, contacts through depositors/ influential persons, by signing an MOU with government departments, universities, Panchayati raj institutions offices. Common promotional methods are publicity, advertising, media, and road shows.
- Perfect Performance: Last and most important step of marketing strategies is perfect performance. Making of any product, fixing prices, framing suitable policies and developing good methods for promotion of housing product by housing companies and banks is not sufficient in itself until and unless perfect performance strategies are not adopted to all things remain written on papers/books if not implemented and working persons are not given targets and they are not made to contact persons to whom housing products are to be sold. If officers are adequately trained, work with open-eyes, good performance leads their institutions to bigger heights.

Objectives of The Study

1. To study the existing marketing strategies of banks involved in housing finance.
2. To analyze the status of banks involved in housing finance in

the state of Himachal Pradesh

3. To examine the reasons and purposes of availing housing finance.
4. To know the views of respondents about the banks engaged in housing finance.
5. To identify the problems faced by the stakeholders and recommend suggestions to strengthen the existing system of housing finance.

Research Methodology

The study is based on primary data as well as secondary data. The secondary data was collected from Books, Journals, Internet, magazines, and newspaper reports. Primary data was collecting through questionnaires, personal interview and by observation from Respondents of Shimla Cites the State Capital of Himachal Pradesh at different places regarding housing strategies. Questions are framed to study the status and awareness of housing finance. The data was gathered from lead bank offices and from officers working in few selected banks and quantities analysis is including interviews of different officers working with few selected banks, site visits, discussions with sample group and through questionnaire replies. While selecting the sample an utmost care has been taken to ensure that the respondents of different age, religion, educational background and family income, etc. are included. Consistent to the study objectives, different techniques like simple random sampling, percentage methods and averages have been used to analyze the data. In case of certain hypothesis, an advanced statistical technique such as Chi square test has been used. Interpretation of data is based on rigorous exercises aiming at the achievement of study objectives.

Data Analysis and Discussion

Status of Banks Involved in Housing Finance: The comparative chart of banks operating in Himachal Pradesh shows the total branches of banks in H.P. is 725 , total deposits is Rs. 27824 crore, total advances is Rs. 11707 crore during the period of 31 March 2012 are shown in table-1 mentioned below. To analyze the status of banks involved in housing finance in the state of Himachal Pradesh PNB is the largest bank with 264 Branches and total deposit of PNB is Rs. 11326 crore and Bank of India with 15 branches and total deposit of Bank of India is Rs.338 crore has a least financial contribution for Himachal Pradesh. But SBI is on the top with Rs. 4259 crore in the field of total advances. With the Capital Adequacy Ratio ICICI is the largest bank with 18.50 percent and Bank of India by means of 11.57 percent is on the bottom.

Table –1 Profile of Banks Involved in House Finances in H.P.

Bank	Total Branches in H.P.	Total Deposit (in crores)	Total Advances (in crores)	CD-Ratio (%)	Capital Adequacy Ratio (%)
PNB	264	11326	3423	30.22	12.63
Bank of India	15	338	287	85.91	11.57
Canara Bank	21	715	320	44.75	13.76
Union Bank of India	19	594	235	39.56	11.85
HDFC Bank	24	562	172	30.60	16.52
ICICI	18	414	1056	25.50	18.50
SBI	203	9380	4259	45.70	13.86
Bank of Baroda	17	517	358	69.24	14.67
UCO Bank	144	3978	1597	40.06	12.35
Total	725	27824	11707		

Source: Primary data from field survey

Reasons of Availing Housing Loans: In Table -2, 60 people are taken, 12 persons replied that housing loans provides economics security, 30 persons replied for social status/prestige. 8 persons estimate them as future security for children, 8 persons replied to fulfil their dream to have their house in life. The calculated chi-square value of below table is 20.53 and table value is 7.82

at 5% significance level. Since calculated chi-square value is more than table value, therefore null hypothesis is rejected and advantages of housing finance are significant.

Table – 2

	Factors	People	%
a)	Because home loans provide economic security	12	20
b)	Social Status/Prestige	30	50
c)	Future security for children	10	17
d)	Dream to have their own house in life to live in than to live in rented house	08	13
	Total	60	100

Note: Value of Chi-Square is 20.53

Source: Primary data from field survey

Purpose of Availing Housing Loan: A survey of 60 persons have replied that 30 persons are aware of first category in home loans, 15 persons are aware of purchasing flats, only 5 persons are aware of purchasing Big Bungalows' and 10 persons replied about home improvement. Different banks have named housing loans differently but almost tabled kinds are common in all banks. Calculated chi-square value of above table is 23.33 where at 5% significance level, critical value given is 7.80.

Table - 3

	Factors	People	%
a)	Home loans individuals to purchase ready built houses	30	50
b)	Purchase of Flats in Multi-Stored buildings	15	25
c)	Purchase of Big bungalows'	05	08
d)	Home improvement/Home loan extension	10	17
	Total	60	100

Note: Value of Chi-Square is 23.33.

Source: Primary data from field survey.

Banks involved in Housing Finance: Perception of Respondents

Mainly housing loans are given for the purchasing of ready-made-built houses, purchasing of land with construction, purchasing of flats in multi- structured buildings and renovation/improvement of houses. Table-4 shows that out of 60 person's awareness of Union Bank of India is 18%, UCO Bank 20%, PNB 21% and SBI 41%. Chi-square value of above table calculated value is 9.20 and at a 3 degrees of freedom, and at 5% significance table given value is 7.82. Awareness of UCO Bank is 20% and State Bank of India is 41% with reason that SBI has highest density in H.P. as compared to UCO Bank branches. Both banks are spread everywhere in H.P. and have deep rooted relations with customers.

Table – 4 Awareness Levels of People towards Banks Involved in Housing Finance

Banks	Awareness of People	In % Terms
Union Bank of India	10	18
UCO Bank	12	20
PNB	13	21
SBI	25	41
	60	100

Conclusion and Suggestions

Every individual has different types of housing requirements. These needs have been fulfilled by companies/banks, awareness of housing finance companies/banks that are providing housing finance in H.P. The study has shown that capital adequacy ratio is not full proof that bank is strong enough. It shows only the maintenance of deposits and advances ratio. It is only the requirement of the RBI, who enables the banks or forces the banks to lend money to people who are in need of finance to run their business/productive activities. Ultimately, a flexible policy environment that takes into account the reality of housing conditions will produce better results than strict enforcement of high minimum standards. Rigid housing and financing laws that establish high minimum standards that are unachievable for the poor will reduce rather than increase the quality and volume of available housing. Instituting regulations that reflect how the poor building can encourage lenders to develop innovative products to improve the quality of the guarantees taken by these institutions and allow the poor to improve their living conditions. Some suggestions to make the study more result oriented are:

- Customers should have full knowledge of banks-players in providing housing finance in H.P.
- Customers should have knowledge of different products housing loan segments.
- Customers should contact different banks for better rates of interest on housing loans, their housing products.
- Housing loans availed, value of houses availed, and houses situated in good localities after 25 to 30 years, values grow to skies. Customers should obtain such information from banks and customer friends.
- Customers should have information · from banks like innovative methods of recovery, Flip repayment method.

References

1. Brar, J.K. and Pasricha J.S. 2005. Housing Loans- A Comparative Study of Institutions. Indian Journal of Commerce, Vol. 58, No. 2, April – June, pp. 71-79.
2. Devlin, J.F. 2002. An Analysis of Choice Criteria in the Home Loan Market. International Journal of Bank Marketing, 20/5, pp. 212-226
3. Gilmore, A. Response Book, Service Marketing and Management.
4. Gonit, C. 2008. Customer services: A paradigm shift. Journal of Housing Finance, Vol.1, Issue 1, pp.63-64.
5. Pathak, V. K. 2009. Presentation on Land as a Resource for Financing Urban Infrastructure during Workshop on Alternate Sources of Financing Urban Infrastructure NIUA. New Delhi March 26.
6. Singh F. and Sharma R. 2006. Housing Finance in India: A Case Study of LIC Housing Finance Limited. ICFAI Journal of Financial Economics, Vol. 4, No. 4. December, pp.63-4.

7. Vaidya, C. and Vaidya, H. 2008. Creative Financing of Urban Infrastructure in India through Market-based Financing and Public-Private Partnership Options. In Metropolis Congress, Sydney. Verma, V.K. Marketing and Business Strategy for Retail loans

Corporate Governance: A Conceptual and Legal Framework Analysis

Kamal Singh
Assistant professor in commerce govt. college Indora

Abstract

The word "Governance" is a current buzzword not only in management but also in public administration and public life. It is considerably a new phenomenon in the corporate world. It was in late 1980's that for the first time there was a going awareness and a serious concern in the trade and business community in the UK that all was not well with the system of corporate management. A formal set of rules and recommendation was made available on recommendations of Cadbury committee only in 1992. In India 1st attempt was made by CII in 1999 by forming a committee under chairmanship of Rahul Bajaj. Since then a numbers of committees were formed by different organization, governments, and societies at national and international level. All these committees have provided their own set of rules and recommendations but the purpose is still not achieved. As per the words of president of SEBI, in next few days SEBI is coming up with new and tight set of norms for Indian companies as there are still many scams and irregularities like Sahara, Kingfisher and many more. The present paper is an attempt to examine the conceptual and legal framework of corporate governance of past, present and to assess the direction may be taken in the coming years.

Introduction

Corporate Governance may be defined as "A set of systems, processes and principles which ensure that a company is governed in the best interest of all stakeholders." It ensures Commitment to values and ethical conduct of business, Transparency in business transactions, Statutory and legal compliance, adequate disclosures and Effective decision making to achieve corporate objectives. In other words, Corporate Governance is about promoting corporate fairness, transparency and accountability. Good Corporate Governance is simply Good Business. The Corporate Governance structure specifies the distribution of rights and responsibilities amongst the different participants in the organization such as the board, managers, shareholders and other stakeholders and lays down the rules and procedures for decision-making and operation. In a narrow sense, corporate governance involves a set of relationships amongst the Company's management, its board of directors, its shareholders, its auditors and other stakeholders. These relationships, which involve various rules and incentives, provide the structure through which the objectives of the company are set, and the means of attaining these objectives as well as monitoring performance are determined. Thus, the key aspects of good corporate governance include transparency of corporate structures and operations, the accountability of managers and the boards to the shareholders and corporate responsibilities toward all other stakeholders. 'Corporate governance is concerned with ways of bringing the interests of investors and manager into line and ensuring that firms are run for the benefit of investors'.1[1] In a broader sense, good corporate governance is the extent to which companies are

1 F. Mayer (1997), 'Corporate governance, competition, and performance', In Enterprise and Community: New Directions in Corporate Governance, S. Deakin and A. Hughes (Eds), Blackwell Publishers: Oxford.

run in a transparent and honest manner. This is important for overall market confidence, the efficiency of capital allocation, the growth and development of economy, industrial bases, and ultimately the nation's overall wealth and welfare. Corporate governance includes 'the structures, processes, cultures and systems that engender the successful operation of organizations'2[2]

The need for regulation:

A natural question arises, why do we need to impose particular governance regulations through stock exchanges, legislatures, courts or supervisory authorities? If it is in the interest of firms to provide adequate protection to shareholders, why mandate rules, which may be counter productive? There are certain reasons for regulatory intervention.

1. If the founder of the company was allowed to design and implement a corporate charter he likes, he may not clearly address the issues faced by other shareholders.
2. Corporate collapses of giants in India and world like satyam computers, lehman bros. One Corporate failure or scandal can potentially erode shareholders trust in the whole of the corporate sector and thus negatively affect the businesses of honest firms as well.
3. A few instances of fraud destroy the faith of investors in the entire corporate sector and thus hurt the larger interest of the economy.
4. Shareholders may favour the increase in the value of their shares even if there is great losses for unprotected creditors or employees.
5. Small share holders are not collective hence go unheard.

---

2 K. Keasey, S. Thompson and M. Wright (1997), 'Introduction: The corporate governance problem -competing diagnoses and solutions,' In K. Keasey, S. Thompson and M. Wright, Corporate Governance: Economic, Management, and Financial Issues. Oxford University Press

6. Concentration of wealth and power.
7. No high level executives prosecuted in connection with fraud and financial crises
8. Independent directors are used as a political tool.
9. Lack of proper check on the work of auditors and their firms.
10. Corporate social responsibilities are not defined.

Corporate governance on international perspectives:

"A code of corporate governance cannot be imported from outside, it has to be developed based on the country's experience. There cannot be any compulsion on the corporate sector to follow a particular code. Equilibrium should be struck so that corporate governance is not achieved at the cost of the growth of the corporate sector" -Sir Adian Cadbury

The real genesis of the corporate governance lies in the business scams and failures. The Junk Bond Fiasco in USA and the failure of Maxwell, and Polypeck in UK Resulted in the Treadway Committee in USA and the Cadbury Committee in UK on corporate governance. A number of committees were set up to look into various aspects of corporate governance throughout the world.

International scenario: at a glance		
year	Name of committee/body	Area/Aspects covered
1992	Sir Adrian Cadbury Committee, UK	Financial Aspects of Corporate Governance
1994	Mervyn E. Kings Committee, South Africa	Corporate Governance
1995	Greenbury Committee UK	Directors' Remuneration
1998	Hampel Committee,UK	Combine Code of Best Practices
1999	Blue Ribbon Committee, Us	Improving the Effectiveness of Corporate Audit Committees

1999	OECD (Organization for Economic Cooperation and Development)	Principles of Corporate Governance
1999	CACG	Principles for Corporate Governance in Commonwealth
2003	Derek Higgs Committee, Uk	Review of role of effectiveness of Non-executive Directors
2003	2003 ASX Corporate Governance Council, Australia	Principles of Good Corporate Governance and Best Practice Recommendations.
2010	OECD	White paper on corporate governance

Source: Economic India info services, cited from the regulatory norms of corporate governance in India'

Corporate governance initiatives in India.

There are various committees formed with a view to reform the Corporate Governance in India since 1990s. Some of the committees and their recommendations are highlighted below.

1. Confederation of Indian Industries (CII) set up a task force in 1995 under the chairmanship of Rahul Bajaj, chairman Bajaj group. Committee submitted its report in 1997. In 1998, the CII released the code called "Desirable Corporate Governance". It looked into various aspects of Corporate Governance and was first to criticize nominee directors and suggested dilution of government stake in companies.
2. SEBI had set up a Commission under the chairmanship of Kumarmanlagam Birla in1999. This committee covered the issues like protection of investor interest, promotion of transparency, building international standards in terms of disclosure of information.
3. In 1999, Department of Corporate Affairs (DCA) modified the Companies Act, 1956. This amendment introduced the provisions relating to nomination facilities for shareholders, buyback of shares and formation of Investor education and protection fund.

4. In 2002, Department of Corporate Affairs constituted Naresh Chandra Committee. The committee covered the statuary auditor-company relationship, rotation of statutory audit firms/partners, procedure for appointment of auditors and determination of audit fees, true and fair statement of financial affairs of companies.
5. In response to rapidly evolving international standards and corporate collapses in US and elsewhere, the Securities and Exchange Board of India (SEBI) constituted a new committee in late 2002 to "evaluate the adequacy of existing corporate governance practices and further improve these practices". Chaired by Shri N.R Narayana Murthy, Chairman and Chief Mentor of Infosys, the committee examined a range of issues relating to audit committees and their reports, independent directors, related party transactions, risk management, director compensation, codes of conduct and financial disclosure. It then made a series of recommendations that aimed to encourage the companies to follow the substance, not just the form, of good governance. The committee's report was released on February 8, 2003.
6. In December, 2004, the Ministry of Company Affairs set up the Expert Committee headed by Dr. J. J. Irani, Director, Tata Sons, to advise the Government on proposed revisions to the Companies Act, 1956.
7. In November, 2009 CII Task Force on Corporate governance issued Recommendations for voluntary adoption on Corporate governance norms. The report is structured according to the different elements of corporate governance i.e. Non-executive and independent directors, Committees of the board, Significant related party transaction, Independence of Auditors, rotation of audit partners, Legal and regulatory standards, Effective and credible enforcement, Institutional investors and media.
8. In March 2012, the Ministry of Corporate Affairs constituted a committee under the Chairmanship of Mr. Adi Godrej,

Chairman, Godrej Industries Limited, to formulate policy document on Corporate Governance. In September, 2012 the Committee submitted its document, specifying seventeen guiding principles on corporate governance.

9. It may be noted that the Lok Sabha has passed Companies Bill, 2012. Though SEBI suggested that SEBI should be given jurisdiction to prescribe matters relating to corporate governance for listed companies. But the Ministry of Corporate Affairs decided that the core governing principles of corporate governance may be provided in the bill itself. Thus, in the Companies Bill 2012, various new provisions have been included (which were not provided in Companies Act, 1956) for better governance of the companies. Some of those new provisions are:
   - Requirement to constitute Remuneration and nomination committee and stakeholders grievances committee.
   - Granting more powers to Audit Committee.
   - Specific clause pertaining to duties of directors.
   - Mode of appointment of Independent Directors and their tenure.
   - Code of Conduct for Independent Directors.
   - Rotation of Auditors and restriction on Auditors for providing non-audit services.
   - Enhancement of liability of Auditors.
   - Disclosure and approval of RPTs.
   - Mandatory Auditing Standards.
   - Enabling Shareholders Associations/Group of Shareholders for taking class action

     Suits and reimbursement of the expenses out of Investor Education and Protection Fund.
   - Constitution of National Financial Reporting Authority, an independent body to take action against the Auditors in case of professional mis-conduct

- Requirement to spend on CSR activities.

Clause 49 of listing agreement of SEBI: One of the significant developments in the field of corporate governance in India was Clause 49 of the Listing Agreement which derived mainly from the S&O Act in USA. The SEBI issued Clause 49 in Feb. 2000 and was amended in October 2004 and it comes into force with effect from January 1, 2006. and further amended in April, 2008. It contains a number of norms some of which are compulsory and rests are desirable for listing a company in any stock exchange.

Indian scenario at a glance		
year	Committee/body	Areas / Aspects Covered
1998	Confederation of Indian Industry (CII) Desirable Corporate Governance – A Code	Protection of Investor Interest, Promotion of transparency, Building International standards in terms of disclosure of information
May 1999	May 1999 Report of the Committee (Kumar Manglam Birla) on Corporate Governance Governance (SEBI, May 7, 1999)	Responsibilities and Obligations of the board and the management in Instituting the systems for good corporate governance. Disclosures to be made mandatory and to be published in the annual report.
November 2000	Report of the task force on Corporate Excellence through Governance Corporate Governance in India: A status report	Best Practices in Corporate Governance: An Indian and International Position Review. Corporate Citizenship and Social Responsiveness Legislation, Regulation and Voluntary Initiatives, Recommendations relating to Corporate Governance matters, Proposal for setting up a Centre for Corporate Excellence.
March 2001	RBI – Report of the advisory group on Corporate Governance: Standing Committee on International Financial Standards and Code.	The comparison of the status of corporate governance in India vis a vis the internationally recognized best standards.
April 2002	RBI Report of the consultative Group of Directors of Banks/ Financial Institutions	Supervisory Role of Board of Banks and Financial Institutions. Feedback on the functioning of the boards, compliance, transparency, disclosures, audit committee etc.

December 2002	Report of the committee (Naresh Chandra) on Corporate Audit and Governance Committee	The statuary auditor company relationship, rotation of statutory audit firms/partners, procedure for appointment of auditors and determination of audit fees, true and fair statement of financial affairs of companies.
February 2003	N. R. Narayan Murthy – SEBI report on Corporate Governance	Audit Committees, Audit Reports, Independent Directors, Risk Management. Directorships and Financial Disclosures.
July 2003	Naresh Chandra Committee II:	Report of the committee on regulation of private companies and partnerships.
2009 November	Recommendations for voluntary adoption, Report of the CII Task force.	The report is structured according to the different elements of corporate governance: Non-executive and independent directors, Committees of the board, Significant related party transactions, Independence of Auditors, Rotation of Audit Partners, Legal and regulatory standards, Effective and credible enforcement, Institutional investors, Media
December 2009	CG Voluntary Guidelines Ministry of Corporate Affairs, Government of India.	The report is structured according to the different elements of corporate governance: Responsibilities of the Board, Audit Committee, Secretarial Audit, Institutional mechanism for Whistle Blowing.
March 2012	Ministry of Corporate Affairs constituted a committee under the Chairmanship of Mr. Adi Godrej	Grievances Committee, Granting of more powers to Audit Committee, Specific clause pertaining to duties of directors, Mode of appointment of Independent Directors and their tenure. Code of Conduct for Independent Directors, Rotation of Auditors and restriction on Auditor's for providing non-audit services, Enhancement of liability of Auditors, Disclosure and approval of RPTs, Mandatory Auditing Standards etc.

Expected future direction of corporate governance movement:

The SEBI chief has pointed out that of the listed companies, more than 1,100 are non-compliant of clause 40A of the Listing Agreement and over 900 firms don't follow clause 49. This is the situation after 10 years of continuous and rigorous efforts done by different govt. and non- govt. organization. As per World Bank report our rank in global business index is still miserable. Our govt. and SEBI are committed to protect the shareholders and nations wealth. The government has passed company bill 2012 with strict rules and same is expected from SEBI. According to SEBI sources it has already placed the documents for consolidation and ready with new norms. In last few years things have changed socially and politically and similarly in the business world. People have become more aware about their rights. Now corporations can not ignore this movement. The corporate governance movement is now market driven movement and in future only those will survive who follow the corporate governance norms and fulfill corporate social responsibilities otherwise they have to meet the same fate as of kingfisher and others. In future the role of company secretary is going to be very crucial; he may be called as the governance officer of the company.

Referances:

1. Sir Adrian Cadbury, "Developments in Corporate Governance, The Company Secretary, The Institute of Chartered Secretary of India, New Delhi, May 97, p. 497.
2. CII (1998), Desirable Corporate Governance A Code, http://www.CII.com
3. Joshi, V. (2004) Corporate Governance: The Indian Scenario. Foundation Books.
4. (OECD): Principles of Corporate Governance, Paris, May 1999.
5. Reports on Corporate Governance, (2004), Economica India Info Services. Academic Foundation.

6. Rajesh Chakrabarti, Corporate Governance in India Evolution and Challenges, undated
7. Gopinath, Shyamala., Corporate Governance towards Best Practices, RBI, Dec, 2004,

Web Links References:

http://www.sebi.gov.in/ Securities and Exchange Board of India

http://www.bseindia.com/ Bombay Stock Exchange Limited

http://www.nfcgindia.org/library_int.htm National Foundation for Corporate Governance

http://www.ita.doc.gov/goodgovernance/ International Trade Administration

http://www.oecd.org/ Organization for Economic Cooperation and Development

http://www.corpgov.net/ Corporate governance network

CSR: A Competetive Advantage

Lipika Bhardwaj
Research Scholar, Punjab Technical Panjab University, Jalandhar
E-mail: lipika_b@yahoo.com

Abstract

CSR talk about the different ways the companies can contribute to the society they are working with. Corporate social responsibility is a concept and a movement that relates to positive actions that go over and above the legal and financial duties of a company. Proponents of corporate social responsibility (CSR) argue that CSR activities allow firms to improve relationships with key stakeholder groups and gain a sustainable competitive advantage over industry rivals. This study examines how corporate social responsibility is capable of enhancing corporate reputation and some of the main strategic decisions which are faced by various business organizations in their efforts to improve or enhance their performance. Barney (1991) analyzed competitive advantages from point of view of resources: Valuable, Rare, Imperfectly Imitable and Non-Substitutable.

Introduction

Corporate social responsibility is a concept whereby organizations consider the interests of society by taking responsibility for the impact of their activities on customers, suppliers, employees, shareholders, communities and other stakeholders, as well as the environment. This obligation is seen to extend beyond the statutory obligation to comply with legislation and sees organizations voluntarily taking further steps to improve the quality of life for employees and their families as well as for the local community and society at large. Corporate Social Responsibility means the way in which business firms integrate environmental, economic and social concerns into their culture, values, strategy, decision making and operations in an accountable and transparent manner and, therefore, leading to better creation of wealth and improved society. According to European Union's definition of corporate social responsibility, one of the key goal is to "identify, prevent and mitigate possible adverse impacts which enterprises may have on society (www.europa.eu).

According to the article by the Harvard Law School on Financial Regulation and Corporate governance, it was ascertained that activities, which were related, to Corporate Social Responsibility had a greater potential in the creation of various forms of value which were distinct to the customers. It was through the perception of customers towards this value that can mediate the relationship between a company's CSR activities and its subsequent performance in finance.

It is also through this article that it can be established that CSR increases a business firms' profitability due to increased loyalty of the clients, lower risks in reputation during crisis and willingness of paying the premium prices (Chandler, 2010, p.48-50; Carroll and Shabana, 2010).

The CRS has shifted to "new world of CSR", focuses on financial success (Jackson, 2004; Lazlo, 2003; Waddok, 2002).

The strategic position can range from CSR as cost of charitable donations or good works (Asongu, 2007) to the emerging concept of "For Benefit Corporation" as a type of business that integrates social and environmental aims with business approaches (Stephanie Strom, 2007 and International Finance Corporation, 2007

Strategic Alliance and CSR

Corporate social responsibility (CSR) can be a source of sustainable competitive advantage for a firm. It is commonly acknowledged that many companies' do not reap the maximum benefit from their efforts to improve the social and environmental consequences of their activities because they fail to approach CSR activities as a source of the advantage in their strategy (Porter & Kramer, 2006; Collis & Rukstad, 2008). CSR, when thought of as part of strategy can lead to opportunities that benefit both society and the business (Grayson & Hodges, 2004). Today, business cannot afford to ignore CSR, society through consumer activists should be the last thing to force a firm to behave in a socially responsible manner. Kentucky Fried Chicken (KFC) has been called Kentucky Fried Forests because of its non-environmentally friendly sourcing of packing material from unprotected forests (National Public Radio report, April 14, 2009), ExxonMobil has been embroiled in a costly legal battle to fend off fines for the Exxon-Valdez oil spill (on march 24, 1989 in Alaska) and Nike had a costly public relations disaster when reports surfaced of sweat shops in Asia. How far should a firm invest in CSR and be rewarded for doing so, is a question that must be answered with the strategic alignment of the firm's resources and gaining advantage over its competition in mind. It is clear that no business can survive in a failing society and as such CSR should be considered as investment and not a cost (Porter and Kramer). The tremendous amount of resources, expertise and insights that businesses command can be used to meet shareholder expectations for profit and in a manner that yields social progress.

In terms of Porter and Kramer "a company must integrate a social perspective into the core frameworks it already uses to understand competition and guide its business strategies." They argue that companies should stop thinking of "corporate social responsibility" and start thinking in terms of "corporate social integration". This thought is supported by Porter and Kramer conclude that, "When a well-run business applies its vast resources, expertise, and management talent to problems that it understands and in which it has a stake, it can have a greater impact on social good than any other institution on philanthropic organization." So, companies can achieve much good and it should fit within their strengths. The highest and best use of a company's CSR efforts is to have them closely aligned with the strengths of an organization.

Therefore, it should be considered as a form of strategic investment. Even when it is not directly tied to a product feature or production process, CSR can be viewed as a form of reputation building or maintenance. A second strategic implication is that it is possible to generate a set of predictions regarding patterns of investment in CSR across firms and industries. For example, we expect to observe a positive correlation between CSR and R&D and advertising (Siegel, 2000). The propensity of firms to engage in strategic CSR depends on two factors: the intensity of competition in the market and the extent to which consumers are willing to pay a premium for social responsibility. There is an inverse relation between intensity of competition and provision of CSR. That is, in more competitive markets, less of the public good will be provided through strategic CSR. Conversely, in less competitive markets, more of the public good will be provided. This is easy to understand, since more competition results in lower margins and, therefore less ability to provide additional (social) attributes or activity. Conversely, less competition leads to the potential for higher margins and more ability to provide additional attributes or activity.

Why CSR?

The classical aim of the firm, to make profit for its shareholders or the profit motive of the firm (Garrigues, 1971, Jensen, 1976), has evolved over several decades to include meeting expectation for its stakeholders. Stakeholder theory is a broad concept that combines economic, social and environmental objectives to meet expectations of society, environment, employees, customers, suppliers and other entities in affected by the corporation (Calafell et. al, Jensen, 1976). Companies are in fact corporate citizens that exist in society and must consider the effect of their activities on the broader society. Blake notes that "the private sector has a duty to contribute to the evolution of equitable and sustainable communities and societies" (2006). The debate is no longer whether corporate managers have an obligation to consider the needs of society, rather to what extent should these needs be relevant (Blake, 2006; Wilson, 2003).

Competitive Advantage

Competitive advantage is generally believed that the company holds the trumps in resources, capacity, and value created for customers, profit levels and market share and so on. Barney (1991) said a firm is said to have a competitive advantage when it is implementing a value creating strategy not simultaneously being implemented by any current or potential competitors. The basis of a competitive advantage comprises low costs for raw materials and energy, efficient production technologies and locational advantages. (Bernd Hansjurgens,2005). The opportunities for competitive advantages derive from the following implications: regulation and information.(A. B. Jaffe, R. G. Newell, R. N. Stavins,2001)

The Relationship of CSR & CA

Porte (1995) identifies the objectives of environmental improvements and enhanced competitiveness can be combined in a win-win situation. There is no consensus that the relationship of Corporate Social Responsibility and Competitive Advantage. In this paper, the relationship between CSR & stakeholders is analyzed. CSR is divided into the main stakeholders - investors, employees, consumers, business partners, natural environment, community and government responsibility, using the description of corporate social responsibility and stakeholder theory framework. The competitive advantage has three dimensions: strategic resources, enterprise core competencies and business environment according to the comprehensive theory of competitive advantage.

Harrison, Bosse and Phillips (2007) expand on the definition of competitive advantage arguing that organizations must do more than create a competitive advantage that is appealing to customers. In order to create a true competitive advantage, Harrison and coworkers assert that: "Competitive advantage implies more than merely creating value. Rather, the key is to create more value than competitors are able to create. A firm is said to have a competitive advantage if it creates and appropriates more value than the least efficient rival capable of breaking even. Simply extending the prior logic, this occurs when the firm drives a wedge between the willingness to pay it generates among buyers and the costs it incurs and then collects returns in excess of its own opportunity costs".

In an effort to provide a link between CSR and CA, Porter and Kramer (2006) argue that over the course of the last two decades, there have been a number of incidents that have shaped how organizations respond to social issues and larger relationships with external stakeholders. For instance, Nike was boycotted after it was revealed that the company had been engaged into abusive labor practices. As a consequence many organizations soon came to realize that in order to ensure that they could preserve their image and maintain a positive relationship with customers, these social issues had to be addressed in the context of business practices that would improve operations in the organization and allow actions based on ethical business practices.

According to Porter and Kramer (2006) organizations developed four unique frameworks for conceptualizing and applying corporate social responsibility programs. These include:

Moral Appeals: Many organizations adopted CSR programs because they believed that it was simply the right thing to do.

Sustainability: Some organizations chose to adopt CSR as a principle means to ensure the sustainability of operations over the long-term.

License to Operate: Organizations adopting this approach recognized the interconnectedness of business operations and larger external regulation set by governments, communities and stakeholders.

Reputation: Organizations came to realize that CSR initiatives could be justified on the grounds that they could improve the image of the organization, its brands and its stock.

Based on these specific paradigms, Porter and Kramer (2006) go on to report that organizations began developing corporate social responsibility programs that would provide them with a competitive advantage. While social good can result from the application of these programs, the most notable advantage is that these programs will produce gains for the organization's bottom line.

Corporate Social Responsibility as Strategy

Society is becoming less tolerant of companies that fail to address their social responsibilities (Asongu,2007). Many academics agree that CSR should be viewed much more than a cost, a constraint or charitable deed and that it can be a source of opportunity, innovation and competitive advantage (Porter, Asongu). In defining strategy, researchers have identified the three parts to strategy as objective, scope and advantage. Companies tend to think of CSR in ways that are disconnected from the strategy of business and as a result miss out on opportunities that both benefit the society and the organization. CSR can become a source of competitive advantage through either differentiation or cost leadership (Porter). Du Pont's corporate vision is "to be the world's most dynamic science company, creating sustainable solutions essential to a better, safer and healthier life for people everywhere" (Asongu, 2008). According to Asongu, the company, through its CSR programs, has gained 67 percent reduction in green house emissions since 1990 while at the same time increased production efficiency by 35 percent, achieved $2 billion in energy savings and its home insulation product, Tyvek is the market leader in the construction industry. The company has successfully imbedded CSR into its strategic management. This case contrasts with observations where many companies' green initiatives are framed in terms of risk reduction, reengineering or cost cutting and not in terms of strategy, revenue growth or technological developments (Hart, 1997). Jones and Mourrasse (2003) report that "companies that improve their environmental performance over their peers are likely to achieve superior financial returns and competitive positioning over the mid to long term". Porter advises companies to integrate a social perspective into its frameworks used to understand its competition and manage its strategy.

CSR initiatives can be aligned with the corporate values system. Lenovo has effectively integrated its image with CSR activities in building awareness and value for a new global brand (Ladousse, 2009). The company took over the personal computer business from IBM and was faced with challenges of a name and brand little known elsewhere except in China and the need to seek growth in consumer markets which used not to be a focus for IBM. Ladousse writes that the company decided to sponsor two major global sports that rely computing for mission critical tasks; Formula1 racing and Olympic Games. Ladausse further notes that the focus on technology and innovation is aimed not only to achieve visibility but also to associate the brand with the values closest to the company; performance, engineering excellence, reliability and global reach.

CSR: Way to Sustainable Competitive Advantage (Case Studies Discussion)

CSR should be seen as a tool to help secure a sustainable competitive advantage by integrating social and business goals. The business landscape is changing fast with the rapid globalization. Support of local communities has become crucial for sustainable development of firm. CSR should not be seen from a short sighted viewpoint of philanthropy or charity. Under the growing pressure from customers, investors, public, local communities, media and civil society organizations, companies can remain sustainable if CSR is used as a strategic tool by absorbing it in the business philosophy and integrating it to the core of the business.

Monetary donations and aid based CSR approach creates a dependence syndrome amongst the recipients of the aid. This form of CSR seriously impacts the long term sustainable development of the recipients. Corporate world needs to collaborate with communities, civil society organizations and government for business needs such as educated and skilled workforce, sustainable resources and social infrastructure. Progressive organizations have learnt that what is good for community and environment is also good for business. We have numerous examples of such organizations such as Tata, ITC, Wal-Mart, Pepsi etc. Pepsi Refresh and ITC e-Chaupal are some of the examples of socially responsible growth model.

Selected Case Studies: Global Outlook			
S no	Company	Csr Initiative	Award
1	E-Chaupal	e-Chaupal is an initiative of ITC Limited, recipient of Golden Peacock Award for CSR and one of India's most admired companies, to empower small and medium farmers in India. This was an initiative to avoid the hefty profit earned by middlemen in wholesale market at the cost of small farmers. With the help of e-Chaupal internet kiosks in villages, farmers can access the rates in free market and negotiate the sale of their produce. By direct purchasing from farmers, ITC could eliminate non value added activities in supply chain resulting lower cost of procurement and better quality products. E-Chaupal provides information to farmers about best farming practices, seeds, fertilizers etc which helps farmers improve productivity and quality of their products and hence helps them in obtaining higher income.	Golden Peacock Award
2.	GE	GE used its "Ecomagination" efforts with respect to innovative household appliances to alternative energy sources to safer, cleaner jet engines. GE has repositioned itself so that consumers see constructive and innovate environmental efforts as part and parcel of the GE brand.	Prime Minister's CSR Award 2011(Malaysia)
3.	COCO COLA	One example of a corporate pursuing this approach is Coca-Cola. The most important ingredient in Coca-Cola is water. The company is working on making clean water available to the communities it serves through partnerships with organizations such as the WWF, US Agency for International Development and the Gates Foundation	Golden Peacock Award third year in a row for CSR

Selected Case Studies: Global Outlook			
S no	Company	Csr Initiative	Award
4.	DU PONT	DuPont is saving money by preserving the environment are DuPont that has saved over $ 2 billion from reductions in energy use since 1990	(AMCHAM) 2012 Corporate Social Responsibility (CSR) Excellence Recognition Award.
5.	MAC-DON-ALD	MacDonald's reduced solid waste by 30% by changing the material used to wrap their food.	2011 Maclean's/ Jantzi-Sustainal-ytics list of the 50 Most Responsible Corporations in Canada
6.	IBM	An example in the hi-tech industry is IBM. The computer giant links its business model and do-good efforts by its promised "to build a smarter planet." IBM demonstrates its use of technology as the linch-pin for solutions for smart traffic, smart food and health care to smart energy and infrastructure.	2012 CSR award from Global Views Monthly
7.	NESTLE	In 1962, Nestle was expanding in India and they got a permission from the government to build a dairy in Moga. Nestle built refrigerated dairy which was the collection point for milk from the farmers in town and trucks were sent from these dairies to the veterinarians, ergono-mists to test the quality of the milk. The farmers were also trained and the sick animals were taken care off. This improved the productivity of the cows and also improved the working conditions in the area for the farmers. Initially when the company expanded in the area there were only 180 farmers supplying milk but today there are almost 75000 farmers involved with around 650 dairies in the region and the milk production has increased 50 times. Nestlé's working with the small workers gives them an advantage of saving the costs that they would have to incur if they had middlemen.	CSR Online Awards 'Glob-al Leaders' 2010 Nestlé ranks second as global leader. & the Best Corporate Citizen 2011 for CSR
8.	AMUL	Amul has pioneered inclusive growth through work with dairy farm-ers at grass –root level which change their lives, enhanced income & empowered women .	
9.	PAK MARU-TI SUZUKI MOTOR COM-PANY	Pak Suzuki is committed to act responsibly, create value for it's Stake-holders and to contribute to economic development of Pakistan. Whilst enhancing the quality of life of our employees, we also believe in positively contributing to local communities and society at large.	CSR Business Excellence Award 2012
10.	JOHN-SON & JOHN-SON	Impacting the lives of more than a billion people each day through its healthcare products and services, Johnson & Johnson takes sus-tainability very seriously. A global leader in sustainability initiatives for decades, the company announced its new five-year sustainability plan in 2011, "Healthy Future 2015", which goes beyond environ-mental issues to include a broader focus on transparency and social responsibility. The company established a new, proprietary process for developing and marketing greener products through lifecycle analysis, and expanded the number of products covered by the initiative to 30, bringing it closer to its 2015 goal of 60 products. It also acquired the company Sterilmed, which helps hospitals reduce waste by extending the useful life of medical devices and hospital equipment. This year, Johnson & Johnson was recognized for leadership in green health care. The award recognizes businesses that successfully improved their en-vironmental performance and helped their healthcare facility clients do the same.	CSR AWARD-"Cham-pion of Change" Awards at the 2012 CleanMed Con-ference.(for lead-ership in green)

Selected Case Studies: Global Outlook			
S no	Company	Csr Initiative	Award
11.	Smart Communications Inc. (Smart)	SMART's "Alternative Power for Cell Sites" program uses renewable energy sources to power cell sites in "off-grid locations" or areas where setting up and operating a cell site is not normally feasible. To date, Smart has about 68 cell sites in different areas across the Philippines powered by renewable energy. Of this figure, 41 are run by wind energy while 27 are hybrid – using both wind and solar energy. Benefits of the program include reduced operational costs due to lower diesel consumption, reduced oil spills and carbon emissions, better community relations and seamless data/ voice service in off-grid areas. The successful deployment of alternative energy-powered cell sites has also encouraged the company to pursue other pro-environment alternative energy solutions.	Under CSR "Green Mobile Award" in 2009 given by the GSMA
12.	Ultratech Cement Limited (India)	Ultratech Cement Limited utilizes its core competence for economic development. One example of this is their innovative use of Birla White cement applicators, which have generated small businesses as a result of the company's investment in skills development and training. Ultratech collaborates with different organizations to implement their projects, placing a special focus on women empowerment and improving the overall quality of life.	"Governance and Society"-Asian CSR Awards 2013
13.	Pt Unilever Indonesia (Indonesia)	PT Unilever Indonesia's CSR programs begin with a strategic vision: to double the business by 2020, at the same time reduce environmental impact and improve livelihood. Each business function implements the principles of care for people, economic improvement, and environmental protection throughout the value chain. Unilever engaged with more than 24,000 farmers who produce black soya bean and coconut sugars, implementing sustainable agriculture practices. It has also worked with over 1,500 women farmers, engaging them in post-harvest processes and creating a home industry for additional family income. Its manufacturing operations have been recognized by Indonesia's Ministry of Environment for its adherence to environmental and safety standards. To lessen environmental impact, emissions and water consumption were reduced by 30-40% and efforts to reduce post-consumer wastes from packaging were put in place. Unilever started educating households on the segregation of domestic waste. They have also developed a communal waste bank, where communities create cooperatives to collect and manage dry waste. More than 2,000 communal waste banks have been created throughout Indonesia.	Intel-AIM Corporate Responsibility Award 2013
14.	APPLE INC.	Over the past year, Apple has increased sustainability efforts as consumers have become more aware of the beloved brand's impact globally and across its supply chain. Apple focuses on optimal product engineering and design to reduce GHG emissions, and touts itself as the only company in its industry whose entire product line not only meets but also exceeds the strict energy guidelines of the Energy Star specifications. The company has announced plans to build a 20-megawatt solar power facility to support the operations of their new data center in North Carolina, which also earned the coveted LEED Platinum certification in 2011. The company's new headquarters in California are expected to house approximately 13,000 employees, but will be totally self-sufficient in terms of energy use, with the national power grid serving only as a backup.	Best Global Green Brand 2012

The key components of CSR should include workplace and labor relations, supply chain, customers, environment and community. Companies need to formulate a strategy for CSR in above fields which should result in sustainable competitive advantage. In last few years, many global companies have come up with their sustainability reports which reflect firm's strategy for getting benefit from CSR.

However to get the benefit of the concept 'CSR as competitive advantage', companies need to be inward looking. They must analyze their business processes and identify the right opportunity for creation of competitive advantage.

Activities, which were related, to Corporate Social Responsibility had a greater potential in the creation of various forms of value which were distinct to the customers. It was through the perception of customers towards this value that can mediate the relationship between a company's CSR activities and its subsequent performance in finance. It is also through this article that it can be established that CSR increases a business firms' profitability due to increased loyalty of the clients, lower risks in reputation during crisis and willingness of paying the premium prices. The adoption of Corporate Social Responsibility by business organizations is beneficial because it leads to improved financial performance by the company, increased customer loyalty and sales, reduced regulatory oversight, workforce diversity, decreased liability, access to capital and product safety, more ability in attraction and retention of employees by the company, lower operational costs, greater quality and productivity and enhanced brand reputation and brand image among others (Joyner and Pyane,2002, p. 297-311).

CSR& Corporate Reputation

Corporate reputation might be extended to a large range of product brands. Corporate reputation finally is able to bring competitive advantage for enterprises and it is an important strategic resource. Corporate reputation comes from stakeholders; therefore, companies must be responsible to its stakeholders. That means CSR could affect corporate reputation, thus affecting the competitive advantage. Conversely, good reputation will also help companies to promote corporate social responsibility. Since the reputation determines attitude of the public and generates more favorable effect. Some multinational companies with high reputation, such as Wal-Mart, Starbucks, Nike and McDonald's fulfilled corporate social responsibility in brand-building to rebuild corporate reputation, image and corporate culture, thus enhanced the influence of brand. From a long-term perspective, corporate social responsibility is more conducive to enhance the long-term development and public image.

HRM AND CSR

From the point of human resources, human capital is the basis for competitiveness. Staffs including employees and employers are makers, implementers, innovators and evaluators of core competitiveness of enterprises. Barbara and Parker (2008, p.434) state that CSR assist companies to hire and retain the employees whom they want. The Echo study (2003, cited in Barbara and Parker, 2008, p.434) also claims that business managers believe CSR leads to attracting, retaining and drive their employee. In addition, a US study showed that in companies that contribute to their communities in some way, the employees have higher motivation to work (Lewin and Sabater, 1996, cited in Barbara and Parker, 2008, p.434). It seems likely that employee's motivations have a direct connection to how companies work well, which get companies managers to think about taking CSR as a part of their business management.

Business survival and development depends on initiative and creativity of staff. Staff is the driving force for the development. Staff is a powerful competitive advantage to obtain protection. An enterprise survival depends on staff. Therefore, how to retain staff and how to develop staff's contribution of core competitiveness is the core issue. Companies must not only provide employees with reasonable salary and benefits, but also need to create equality, non-discrimination, safety and health, continuing training, working environment. All these are responsibility that enterprises must bear to employees. Staff loyalty and satisfaction result in competitively in the market. The enterprises fulfill their social responsibilities to their staff, such as attracting staff, retaining staff and stimulating creativity, which would have a positive impact.

Transformation and Influence between CSR & CA

CSR can be transformed into competitive advantages.

1) Corporate social responsibility is good for optimizing the living environment. Corporate social responsibility can help corporations avoid condemnation, punishment and restrictions from government, community and the public so that decision-making and management are flexibility and autonomy. Maybe they enjoy preferential policies and incentives by government.
2) Enterprises carry out their social responsibility to improve the public image, advance enterprise's visibility, reputation, enhance social harmony, to attract consumers. All these can create a broader market and better development.
3) Corporate social responsibility can cross international barriers. At present, corporate social responsibility has become accepted indicators of "high standards and strict requirements". In an increasing economic globalization, corporate social responsibility would help enterprises to international markets, reduce the impact of social responsibility and enhance and upgrade competitiveness in the international market.
4) Corporate social responsibility will help to attract talent. Corporations regularly involved in social responsibility are more well-known to easily recruit and retain talent.
5) Corporate social responsibility will help improve financial performance, because Investors are always interested in responsible corporation.

Conclusion

It is important for the companies to understand that if the prevailing approach to CSR is changed and more emphasis is given on the importance of social responsibility like other core competencies of a firm, it can be discovered that CSR is more than just a cost, constraint or a charitable deed; it is a source of innovation, opportunity and competitive advantage (Porter & Kramer, 2006).

Milton Friedman believes, "the only social responsibility of a business is to increase its profit" (Porter & Kramer, 2002, p. 6). According to Freidman the only aim of an organization is to achieve profit on the other hand Freeman argues that a firm has responsibility towards the internal or external stakeholders of the firm which should be taken into account (Galbreath, 2009). Freeman's Stakeholder theory basically describes what a firm should do or should not do in terms of their societal responsibilities and is more inclined towards CSR.

CSR can be used to gain economic benefits for the company by also creating a social impact. Social and economic benefits are often seen as two distinct objectives but companies need to find out where these two objectives converge for their organization. Therefore it's hard to say whether CSR leads to competitive advantage directly but it most definitely supports the other core competences of a firm, indirectly giving a competitive advantage. Gaining a competitive advantage by only introducing Triple Bottom Line is difficult, instead a company should focus on developing an innovative model of Triple Bottom Line. Adoption of CSR also gives the company an opportunity to premium price its product also helping in the promotions of the product and attracting consumers which impacts positively on the company's financial performance (Mason & Simmons, 2011).So, CSR is now considered as investment, part of corporate strategic management and a source of innovation rather than an expense.

References

Adam B. Jaffe ,Richard G. Newell ,Robert N. Stavins October 2001"Technological Change and the Environment"

Asongu,J.J. (2007a).Sustainable Development as a Business Responsibility. Journal of Business and Public Policy. Volume 1 Number 1 Winter 2007.

Asongu, J. J. (2007b), Strategic Corporate Social Responsibility in Practice, Greenview Publishing Company, Georgia

Asongu, J.J. (2007c). The history of corporate social responsibility. Journal of Business and Public Policy, 1(2), 1-18.

Bernd Hansjurgens; Dirk Heinrichs, Helmholtz Centre for Environmental Research – "Risk Habitat Megacity"- Strategies for Sustainable Development in Megacities and Urban Agglomerations.

Carroll A. B. and Shabana, K. M. (2010). The Business Case for Corporate Social Responsibility: A Review of Concepts, Research and Practice. International Journal of Management Reviews Volume 12, Issue 1, pages 85–105, March 2010

Catherine J. Morrison-Paul & Donald S. Siegel, 2006. "Corporate Social Responsibility and Economic Performance," Rensselaer Working Papers in Economics 0605, Rensselaer Polytechnic Institute, Department of Economics.

Catherine Ladousse- Executive Director of Communication EMEA at Lenovo

Chandler, Daniel (2010) 'Advertising'. In Glen Creeber (Ed) The Television Genre Book (2nd Edn). London: Palgrave Macmillan/ BFI, pp. 178–180

Coca Cola, (2012). Corporate responsibility & Sustainability summary 2011/2012 Coca Cola, Inc

David J. Collis and Michael G. Rukstad "Can You Say What Your Strategy Is?" Harvard Business Review

Grayson, D. and A. Hodges, Corporate Social Opportunity: Seven Steps to Make Corporate Social Responsibility Work for Your Business (Greenleaf Publishing, Sheffield, 2004).

Hart S. L.: 1997, 'Beyond Greening: Strategies for a Sustainable World', Harvard Business Review 75

Harrison, J.S., Bosse, D. & Phillips, R.A. (2007) Stakeholder theory and competitive advantage, Academy of Management Proceedings, p. 5.

IFC (2007). Available at
http://www.ifc.org/wps/wcm/connect/554e8d80488658e4b76af76a6515bb18/Final%2B-%2BGeneral%2BEHS%2BGuidelines.pdf?MOD=AJPERES.
Accessed on 3 December 2013.

Jackson, K.T., 2004. Building Reputational Capital: Strategies for Integrity and Fair Play that Improve the Bottom-Line. Oxford: Oxford University Press.

Jensen, Michael. "Reflections on the State of Accounting Research and the Regulation of Accounting." In Conflicts and Compromises in Financial Reporting, edited by John C. Burton.Stanford Lectures in Accounting. Palo Alto, CA: Stanford Graduate School of Business, 1976.

Jensen, Michael C. and Meckling, William H., Theory of the Firm: Managerial Behavior, Agency Costs and Ownership Structure (July 1, 1976).

Jeremy Galbreath, (2009) "Building corporate social responsibility into strategy",European Business Review, Vol. 21 Iss: 2, pp.109 – 127

Joyner,B. E.,& Payne,D. (2002). Evolution and implementation:A study of values,businessethics,and corporate social responsibility. Journal of Business Ethics,41(4)

Laszlo, C., 2003. The Sustainable Company: How to Create lasting Value through Social and Environmental Performance. Washington: Island Press.

National Public Radio report, April 14, 2009-available at-http://www.npr.org/templates/story/story.php?storyId=103119167

Porter, M., & Kramer, M. (2002, December). Corporate philanthropy. Harvard Business Review.

Strom, Stephanie (2007-12-13). "Foundation testing potential of philanthropy via Internet". The New York Times. Retrieved 2010-04-28.

Waddock, S., 2004. Parallel universe: Companies, academies, and the progress of corporate citizenship. Business and Society Review, 109 (1): 5-62

Problems & Challenges in First Time Adoption of IFRS

MadhuBala Sharma
Dr. Prateek Gupta

Abstract

The International Financial Reporting Standards (IFRS) aims to make international financial reporting comparisons as easy as possible because each country has its own set of accounting rules. In India, GAAP is being used to prepare financial statements of entities. Now, as the world globalizes IFRS has been designed and introduced by IASB (International Accounting Standard Board) & it has been adopted by more than 100 countries including India. In India theInstitute of Chartered Accountants of India (ICAI) is playing key role in implementation of IFRS in three phase manner. This paper deals with the problems &Challenges faced by Indian corporates in first time adoption of IFRS & measures taken to address the challenges.

Keywords: GAAP, IFRS, IASB & Challenges in first time adoption.

Themes: Accounting, Global Accountancy

Introduction

IFRS refers to International Financial Reporting Standards. IFRS has been developed & issued by the IASB (International

Accounting Standard Board), an independent organization based in London, UK. IFRS can be defined as "A single set of high quality, understandable and enforceable global accounting standards thatrequire high quality, transparent and comparable information in financial statements and other financialreporting to help participants in the world's capital markets and other users make economic decisions".In India theInstitute of Chartered Accountants ofIndia (ICAI) is playing key role in implementation of IFRS & decide to implemented it in three phases.

Phase-1: 1st April 2011 for the:

(i) Companies which are part of NSE, Nifty 50

(ii) Companies which are part of BSE-Sensex 30

(iii) Companies whose shares or other securities are listed in stock exchanges outside India.

(iv) Companies whether listed or not which have a net worth in excess of Rs. 1000 crores.

Phase -2: 1st April 2013:

(i) The companies whether listed are not having a net worth exceeding Rs. 500 crores but not exceeding Rs. 1000 crores.

Phase-3:1st April 2014

(i) Listed companies which fall in the following categories, will not be required to follow the notified accounting standards which are converged with IFRS (Though they may voluntarily opt to do so)

However, India have been not succeeded to resolve its issues relating to conversion with IFRS such as taxation. Corporate Affairs Minister Salman Khurshid said on the sidelines of an Assocham seminar on International Financial Reporting Standards (IFRS) here "We are still working on fair value concepts and other issues like depreciation, but I can assure you that we will stick to the roadmap laid for convergence of Indian standards with theIFRS".After enactment of Companies Act 2013 the ministry of corporate affairs has focus to implementIFRS from April 1 2011. According to the draft plan the ministry announce to implement IFRS in the companies having turnover over Rs. 1000 crore from April 1, 2015 and from April 1, 2016 for those whose turnover is between Rs. 500 crore to Rs. 1000 crore but the professionals are still having difference on how to get fair value of assets and liabilities.

First Time Adoption

Adoption of IFRS has become a vital issue of discussion and debate due to the variation in Indian GAAP &IFRS . Adopting IFRS in India is going to be very challenging by Indian Corporates but at the same time Indian Corporates are likely to obtain significant benefits from adopting IFRS. IFRS 1 specifically deals with how to apply IFRS for the first time. Full retrospective application of IFRSs effective at the reporting date for an entity's first IFRS financial statements with certain optional exemptions and mandatory exceptions. An entity shall explain how the transition from previous GAAP to IFRSs affected its reported financial position, financial performance and cash flow.

IFRS Adoption Procedure in India

Three steps process was laid down by the accounting professionals in India which are summarized as follows:

Step 1 – IFRS Impact Assessment: In this step the firm will assess the impact of IFRS adoption on Accounting and Reporting issues, on procedures and systems, and on core business of the entities.

Step 2 – Preparations for IFRS Implementation: This process will carry out such activities required for IFRS implementation like: analyzing the firm internal reporting systems and processes and also deals with the first time adoption and implementation process of IFRS.

Step 3 – Implementation: In this last step IFRS will implement according to plan. The initial phase of this step is to prepare an opening Balance Sheet at the date of transition to IFRS.

To understand the actual impact of the transition from the Indian Accounting Standards to IFRS is to be developed. This will follow the full application of IFRS as and when it is required. At the initial stage of implementation of IFRS requires lot of training and various technical difficulties may be experienced. The smooth implementation of the transition from Indian Accounting Standards to IFRS, regular training to personals and identify the problems while carrying out the implementation.

Objectives of The Study

To study the Problems and Challenges faced by Indian Companies in first time adoption of IFRS and Measures taken to address the Challenges.

Methodology

For the purpose of present study, mainly secondary data has been used. The required secondary data was collected from the authorized Annual Reports and Official Website of ICAI and IFRS, various Journals and Research Papers, diagnostic study reports, newspapers, articles & other online research papers have been surveyed in making this study.

Problems and Challenges:

Despite several benefits as may be looked out by the different people, there will be several challenges that will be faced on the way of IFRS convergence.

I. Difference in Indian GAAP &IFRS: Adoption of IFRS means that the entire set of financial statements will be required to undergo a drastic change. The differences are many & it is a challenge to bring about awareness of IFRS and its impact among the users of financial statements.

II. Issue of GAAP Reconciliation: The Securities Exchange Commission(SEC) laid out two options in its proposal-one calling for the traditional IFRS first-time adoption reconciliation, the other requiring that step plus an on-going unaudited reconciliation of the financial statements from IFRS to U.S. GAAP which is clearly more costly approach for companies and for investors.

III. Professional Training :-Professional Accountants are looked upon to ensure successful implementation of IFRS. Along with these Accountants, Government Officials, Chief Executive Officers, Chief Information Officers are also responsible for a smooth adaptation process. India lacks to provide training facilities to train such a large group. It has been observed that India does not have enough number of fully trained professionals to carry out this task of adoption of IFRS in India.

IV. Need of Amendments In the Existing Laws :-

In India, accounting practices are governed mainly by Companies Act, 1956 and Indian Generally AcceptedAccounting Principles (GAAP). Existing laws such as Securities Exchange Board of India (SEBI) regulations, Indian Banking Laws & Regulations, Foreign Exchange Management Act (FEMA) also provide some guidelines on preparation of Financial Statements in India. IFRS does not recognize the presence of these laws and the accountants will have to follow the IFRS completely with no overriding provisions from these laws. Indian lawmakers will have to make necessary amendments to ensure a smooth transition to IFRS.

IFRS adaptation will affect most of the items in the Financial Statements and consequently, the tax liabilities would also undergo a change. Currently, Indian Tax Laws do not recognize the Accounting Standards. A complete change of Tax laws is the major challenge faced by the Accounting Principles (GAAP). Existing laws such as Securities Exchange Board of India (SEBI) regulations, Indian Banking Laws & Regulations, Foreign Exchange Management Act (FEMA) also provide some guidelines on preparation of Financial Statements in India. IFRS does not recognize the presence of these laws and the accountants will have to follow the IFRS completely with no overriding provisions from these laws. Indian lawmakers will have to make necessary amendments to ensure a smooth transition to IFRS. IFRS adaptation will affect most of the items in the Financial Statements and consequently, the tax liabilities would also undergo a change. Currently, Indian Tax Laws do not recognize the Accounting Standards. A complete change of Tax laws is the major challenge faced by the Indian Law Makers immediately. Enough changes are to be made in Tax Laws to ensure that tax authorities recognize IFRS-Compliant financial statements otherwise it will duplicate the administrative work for the Firms.

V. Fair Value basis to value Financial Statements:-IFRS uses fair value to measure majority items in financial statements. The use of Fair Value Accounting can bring a lot of volatility and subjectivity to the financial statements. Adjustments to fair value result in gains or losses which are reflected in the Income Statements and valuation is reflected in Balance Sheet. Indian Corporate World which has been preparing its Financial Statements on Historical Cost Basis will have tough time while shifting to Fair Value Accounting.

VI. Review of existing Financial Reporting System: -IFRS provide complete set of reporting system for companies to make their Financial Statements. In India, various laws and acts provide the financial reporting system but not as comprehensive as provided by the IFRS. Indian Firms will have to ensure that existing business reporting model is amended to suit the requirements of IFRS. The amended reporting system will take care of various new requirements of IFRS. Enough control systems have to be put in place to ensure the minimum business disruption at the time of transition.

Measures Taken to Address The Challenges

1) For changes required in rules and regulations of various regulatory bodies, draft recommendations

   Have been placed before Accounting Standard Board.

2) The ICAI issued 30 interpretations of accounting standards, with a view to resolve various intricate Interpretational issues arising in the implementation of new accounting standards.
3) Guidance notes have been issued by ICAI for providing immediate guidance on accounting issues.
4) To facilitate discussions at seminar, workshops, etc. ICAI has issued background material on newly issued accounting standards.
5) For the purpose of assisting its members, the ICAI council has formed an expert advisory committee to answer queries from its members. Moreover to face the challenges we need to take more effective steps like we should build adequate IFRS skills professionals by investing in training processes for Indian accounting professionals to manage the conversion projects for Indian corporate. This can be done by research on effect of IFRSc on version in different countries and brief knowledge of IFRS should be added into the studies for professional courses with worldwide latest examples.

Conclusion

It is very much clear that conversion from Indian GAAP to IFRS will face many difficulties but at the same time looking at the advantages that this adoption will confer, the convergence with IFRS is strongly recommended because the measures taken by ICAI and the other regulatory bodies to facilitate the smooth convergence to IFRS are creditable and give the positive idea that the country is ready for convergence. Corporates need to gear themselves for constant updation and not only for the first time adoption.

References

1. IFRS: A quick reference Guide by Robert Krik.
2. Sujatha B Accounting Standards in India: Towards convergence published by ICFAI.

3. Mahender K. Sharma, IFRS & India – its problems and challenges, International Multidisciplinary. Journal of Applied Research Vol: 1/Issue: 4/ July 2013/ ISSN 2320 - 7620.
4. Poria, Saxena, Vandana, 2009, IFRS Implementation and Challenges in India, MEDC Monthly EconomicDigest. Retrieved on Dec 12,2013.
5. Sunita Ajay Kumar Rai, IFRS- Problems and Challenges in First Time Adoption, International Indexed & Referred Research Journal, Vol. I /Issue-1/April/2012/ISSN- 2250-2556
6. http://articles.economictimes.indiatimes.com/2011-07-27/news/29820849_1_implementation-indiancompanies-accounting-advisory-services
7. http://economictimes.indiatimes.com/opinion/view-point/ifrs-the-impact-on-indian-corporates/articleshow/3204158.cms.
8. http://www.indianexpress.com/news/indian-companies-likely-to-shift-to-ifrs-from-april-2015/1184894/Research
9. http://www.article base.com/accounting-articles/working towards a global convergence of accounting standars-1379167.html
10. http:// online library.wiley.com/doi/10.1002/jcaf.20406/abstract
11. http://icai.org/resoucre
12. International Multidisciplinary Research Journal Vol I Issue VII Jan 2014 ISSN No: 2321-5488
13. http://www.pwc.com/en-GX/gx/ifrs-reportingservices/pdf/viewpoint_convergence.pdf
14. www.zenithresearch.org.in317

A Study Of Corporate Social Responsibility Practice in India

Dr. Satish K. Mittal,

Asst. Professor, School of Management, Gautam Buddha University, Greater Noida.

Abstract

CSR activities implemented by the companies are spread across many domains and tools of CSR, thereby showing the inclination of businesses to overall development of areas across education, health, environment and employment. There is a clear difference when it comes to focus on providing sustainable livelihood between Indian and foreign firms, showing than Indian firms are more sensitive to the cause of poverty and unemployment. Also, foreign firms show higher tendency to work on energy conservation, green management etc. showing that they are probably more sensitive to environmental impact. PSU focus their CSR action towards causes like education, employment, health and corporate citizenship, where as private firms largely focus on green management, energy conservation which serve the dual purpose of CSR as well as increasing bottom line.

Nearly all the companies we studied reported CSR activities in some form or the other except 4 firms who did not do any CSR and 3 firms who did not report any CSR activity. The percentage of the CSR practises is found to be higher for foreign firms. The CSR practises are more prominent among the private firms when compared with that of PSUs.

Keywords: Corporate Governance; Corporate Social Responsibility, Stakeholders Interest; Firm value; Disclosure Practices.

Introduction

Corporate sector is operating in an increasing complex and demanding international environment. On the one hand, the business is becoming more competitive whereas on the other hand, there is increasing pressure on corporate sector to be more socially responsible. The phenomenon of increasing environmental concerns, the anger against corporate greed, and the 24 by 7 active social and other media, has put increased pressures on companies to be more responsible, to be good corporate citizen. In this scenario, it makes sense for companies to be more socially responsible and to be good corporate citizen at least from two perspectives. One to minimize any potential damages caused by any irresponsible action and, second to use good CSR practices as a case for potential benefits. Differences in point of view and the issues addressed are shaping the various existing CSR concepts and the crucial problem inherent to many of them is the conflict between business interests, which are generally geared to profit generation, and the moral duties of business, which are reflected by potential stakeholder interests (Wuttke, 2011). A solution proposed by various scholars is the translation of CSR activities into business cases to generate win-win outcomes and thus in essence, CSR as a business case encompasses social and environmental activities that are planned and accomplished under investment aspects while considering their opportunities and advantages for the corporation (Wuttke, 2011).

With increasing demands for a more inclusive and sustainable global economy, UN launched the UN Global Compact (UNGC) in 2000, the first CSR initiative at global level (UNGC, 2012). Endorsed by chief executives, the Global Compact is a practical framework for the development, implementation, and disclosure of sustainability policies and practices, offering participants a wide spectrum of workstreams, management tools and resources — all designed to help advance sustainable business models and markets. This ever-increasing understanding is reflected in the Global Compact's rapid growth. With over 10,000 corporate participants and other stakeholders from over 130 countries, it is the largest voluntary corporate responsibility initiative in the world (UNGC, 2012). The Global Compact was launched in India at a high-level meeting of Business Leaders in Mumbai on 4 December, 2000 and over 100 leading organizations from India have joined the initiative to date (UNGC, 2012).

An ideal CSR has both ethical and philosophical dimensions, particularly in India where there exists a wide gap between sections of people in terms of income and standards as well as socio-economic status (Bajpai, 2001). Over the time four different models have emerged all of which can be found in India regarding corporate responsibility (Kumar et al.2001). This study concluded that the Indian companies placed emphasis on product improvements and development of human resources (Raman, 2006).

India's CSR approach continues to be largely externally oriented, i.e. traditional philanthropic commitment and various forms of community development dominate. In recent years, however, further steps to integrate CSR into a sustainable business strategy have been observed (Chahoud et al., 2006). According to the empirical survey, while traditional philanthropic approaches are still widespread, CSR activities in India have begun to conform to global trends, by integrating CSR into core business processes and assigning CSR responsibilities to corporate departments, for example. However, this reform is proceeding rather slowly and will take time (Chahoud et al., 2006). A lot of organizations today are trying to forge a strategic link between their business endeavors and their social responsibility and are trying to develop a model which will help them to serve the community at large, while still remaining profitable (Bansal and Srivastava, 2008).

This paper studies Corporate Social Responsibility in the biggest 100 firms in India. The paper is divided into seven sections including this introduction section. The second section explores the current state of CSR strategy in the firms. The third section identifies the major types of CSR strategy in the firms. The fourth section studies the reasons for CSR strategy in the firms. The fifth section enlists the impact on performance of CSR strategy in the firms. The sixth section identifies the future plan for CSR strategy in the firms. And the last part is the summary of the paper.

The current state of corporate social responsibility

Overall Scenario in 100 firms

Of the one hundred companies we studied ninety-three companies were involved in CSR, three were not doing it and for the other four no mention of their doing any CSR was found. There is voluntary reporting of CSR and there is a possibility that three companies might have chosen to not to report. There are a basic set of guidelines which were set by the Government of India with regard to environment and labour and companies who complied only with these basic guidelines were not considered to have done any CSR.

Across industries comparative analysis

Table 1 shows the industry comparison on presence of CSR in various industries. There are differences in firms across industries as well as within same industry in their approaches to CSR. No pattern was observed in the industry wise analysis but in every industry in the study, companies are making an effort to strive for a sustainable future. Only one firm each in Banking & Financial Services, Metals, Auto and Ancillaries, Chemicals & Fertilizers, Aviation, Food and Beverages and Textiles was not found to report any kind of CSR activities. The percentages are indicative of companies studied for that industry and should not be taken as average for the industry.

Table 1: Industry comparison on presence of CSR among firms

Industry	Presence of CSR
Banking & Financial Services	All the companies except one were doing it i.e. 95 % doing CSR
Metals	All the companies except one were doing it i.e. 90 % doing CSR
Auto & Auto Ancillaries	All the companies except one were doing it i.e. 88.88 % doing CSR
Oil & Gas	All the companies were doing CSR activities
Capital Goods	All the companies were doing CSR activities
IT & ITES	All the companies were doing CSR activities
Pharmaceutical & Healthcare	All the companies were doing CSR activities
Chemicals & Fertilizers	All industries except one were doing it i.e. 75 % doing CSR
FMCG	All the companies were doing CSR activities
Infrastructure, Construction & Real Estate	All the companies were doing CSR activities
Mining	All the companies were doing CSR activities
Telecom	All the companies were doing CSR activities
Aviation	All industries except one were doing it i.e. 66.66 % doing CSR
Food and Beverages	All industries except one were doing it i.e. 66.66 % doing CSR
Trading	All the companies were doing CSR activities
Power	All the companies were doing CSR activities
Shipping and Logistics	All the companies were doing CSR activities

Textiles	All industries except one were doing it i.e. 50 % doing CSR
Media	All the companies were doing CSR activities
Tourism	All the companies were doing CSR activities

Indian Vs foreign firms

All the eleven foreign firms selected for our study are found to be doing CSR. More than ninety-two percent of the eighty-nine Indian Firms selected for our study are found to be doing CSR. We couldn't find any evidence of the four Indian companies of their CSR activities reporting. Therefore we are not sure if these companies are doing CSR in any form or not. We have found sufficient evidence of the CSR practises followed by most (90%) of the Indian firms in the study. Also, the percentage of the CSR practises is found to be higher for foreign firms. Since the number of foreign firms selected for the study was much less than their Indian counterparts, we can't derive any comparative conclusion based on the above data.

Private sector Vs public sector firms

Out of the fifty-eight private sector firms selected for study (both Indian & foreign combined) almost ninety-five percent of them are found to be practicing CSR in any one form or many forms. Out of the rest forty-two public sector undertakings selected for our study ninety percent of the firms are practising CSR in one form or other. E.g. NABARD is doing it because its business model is defined by Government of India to do so. This is a mandate directed by Government of India to NABARD to facilitate smooth credit flow & economic development of rural areas.

Out of the total one hundred firms, one private and two PSUs were not found to report any CSR activity in their Annual reports

2009-10, 2010-11. Therefore we are not sure whether these companies are practising CSR in any form. The CSR practises are more prominent among the private firms when compared with that of PSUs.

Conclusion

- Nearly all the companies we studied reported CSR activities in some form or the other except four firms who did not do any CSR and three firms who did not report any CSR activity
- No pattern was observed in the industry wise analysis but we can say with confidence be it whatever industry companies come from in this study, they are making an effort to strive for a sustainable future
- We have found sufficient evidence of the CSR practises followed by most (90%) of the Indian firms as per our study. Also, the percentage of the CSR practises is found to be higher for foreign firms.
- The CSR practises are more prominent among the private firms when compared with that of PSUs.

The types of corporate social responsibility

Over scenario in the 100 firms

The top five types of implementing CSR in decreasing order are education; health; community services and infrastructure development; green management ; and, providing sustainable livelihood. Table 2 shows the top types of CSR among the one hundred firms.

Table 2: The top types of CSR in 100 firms

Rank	Top types
1	Education (15 %)
2	Health (13%)

Rank	Top types
3	Community Services (12%)
4	Green Management (9%)
5	Waste Management (8%)
6	Providing Sustainable Livelihood (8%)
7	Water Conservation (6%)
8	Energy Conservation (6%)
9	Partnership with Key Organizations (6%)
10	Other Ways (18%)

CSR activities implemented by the companies are evenly spread across most domains and tools of CSR, thereby showing the inclination of businesses to overall development of areas across education, health, environment and employment.

Some companies instead of focusing on particular ways to conduct CSR activities focus on geographical areas and conduct CSR activities using many types /tools presented in the table above. E.g. IDBI Bank Ltd adopted a village in the Leh region of Jammu & Kashmir. One such interesting example is:

Indian Vs foreign firms

There is a clear difference when it comes to focus on providing sustainable livelihood between Indian and foreign firms. Indian firms are more sensitive to the cause of poverty and unemployment. Also, foreign firms show higher tendency to work on energy conservation, green management etc showing that they are probably more sensitive to environmental impact.

Table 4: Top five types of CSR in Indian and foreign firms

Rank	Foreign firms	Indian firms
1	EDUCATION - Fostering self reliance	EDUCATION - Fostering self reliance
2	HEALTH - Improve living standards	HEALTH - Improve living standards

Rank	Foreign firms	Indian firms
3	Community Services/ Infrastructure Development	Community Services/ Infrastructure Development
4	Green Management - Reducing Carbon Footprint	Providing Sustainable Livelihood
5	Waste Management	Green Management - Reducing Carbon Footprint

Private sector Vs public sector firms

The top five types of CSR in private and public sector firms, in decreasing order are given in Table 5 .

Table 5: Top 5 types of CSR in private sector and public sector firms

Rank	Public sector firms	Private sector firms
1	EDUCATION - Fostering self reliance	EDUCATION - Fostering self reliance
2	Community Services/ Infrastructure Development	HEALTH - Improve living standards
3	HEALTH - Improve living standards	Community Services/ Infrastructure Development
4	Providing Sustainable Livelihood	Green Management - Reducing Carbon Footprint
5	Water Conservation	Waste Management

Conclusion

- CSR activities implemented by the companies are spread across many domains and tools of CSR, thereby showing the inclination of businesses to overall development of areas across education, health, environment and employment.
- Sectors like BFSI, Metals, manufacturing and infrastructure are using CSR tools more effectively and across the spread than other sectors. However, the primary focus area across all sectors remains on education, health and overall community service/infrastructure development.

- There is a clear difference when it comes to focus on providing sustainable livelihood between Indian and foreign firms, showing than Indian firms are more sensitive to the cause of poverty and unemployment. Also, foreign firms show higher tendency to work on energy conservation, green management etc. showing that they are probably more sensitive to environmental impact.
- PSU focus their CSR action towards causes like education, employment, health and corporate citizenship, where as private firms largely focus on green management, energy conservation which serve the dual purpose of CSR as well as increasing bottom line.

Summary

Nearly all the companies we studied reported CSR activities in some form or the other except 4 firms who did not do any CSR and 3 firms who did not report any CSR activity. The percentage of the CSR practises is found to be higher for foreign firms. The CSR practises are more prominent among the private firms when compared with that of PSUs.

CSR activities implemented by the companies are spread across many domains and tools of CSR, thereby showing the inclination of businesses to overall development of areas across education, health, environment and employment. There is a clear difference when it comes to focus on providing sustainable livelihood between Indian and foreign firms, showing than Indian firms are more sensitive to the cause of poverty and unemployment. Also, foreign firms show higher tendency to work on energy conservation, green management etc. showing that they are probably more sensitive to environmental impact. PSU focus their CSR action towards causes like education, employment, health and corporate citizenship, where as private firms largely focus on green management, energy conservation which serve the dual purpose of CSR as well as increasing bottom line.

Giving back to the society and Sustainability of Business are the two main reasons for the firms analysed and majority of the firms perform CSR activities for more than one reason. Foreign firms are much more efficiency and business sustainability concerned than their Indian counterparts. PSUs are more focussed towards giving back to the society than the private firms.

Ninety-one percent of the companies did not show any impact on performance and the reason can be either there is no impact or they are not portrayed as it is shown as a noble cause. Foreign companies have shown more impact than Indian firms and private companies have shown more impacts due to CSR than the public sector companies.

References:

Banerjee, Chandrajit and Tandon, Amit (2012) Institutional Investors-Driving Force for Good Governance, A Survey by CII and IIAS, http://www.nfcgindia.org/research.htm surfed on July 22, 2013, Pp. 1-20.

Kadam, Sunil (2013) Consultative Paper on Review of Corporate Governance Norms in India, Corporate Finance Department, Division of Issues and Listing, SEBI, January 2013.

KPMG (2012) ASX Corporate Governance Principles and Recommendations on Diversity: ASX Diversity Report: Analysis of 31 December 2011 year end disclosures, www.asxgroup.com.au/media/asx_diversity_report.pdf, surfed on July 22, 2013.

OECD. (1999) Principles of Corporate Governance. OECD. Paris.

Pillania, Rajesh K. (2013) Practice of Corporate Strategy in India: A Research Book presenting Learnings from Successful Companies, LAP LAMBERT Academic Publishing, Germany, year 2013, Pages 216.

Report of SEBI (2003) Report of SEBI Committee on Corporate Governance Chaired by N.R. Narayana Murthy, February 8, 2003.

HR Walking The CSR Talk

Richa Sinha

Asst. Professor

Govt. P.G. College, Dharamshala

'We must learn to judge a nation by how its poorest and most miserable human beings have fared' – Kaushik Basu, Sr.Vice President & Chief Economist,World Bank

Objectives :

1. To understand the concept of CSR
2. To explore the nexus between HR and CSR
3. To elaborate on the strategic role of HR in embedding CSR in corporate DNA.

Research Methodology:

Exhaustive literature survey regarding the topic and related concepts has been done. Secondary data collected from various sources including books, research papers, journals, newspapers, magazines, and websites is used for the purpose of study.

Introduction:

Long long ago, capitalism was born as Siamese twin to morality. However, with the advent of competitiveness, the twins got separated and as it happens in reality, the weaker twin got separated first. Morality could not find its voice among strong Machiavelli reprehensions and faded into oblivion while capitalism took in its giant form. After many years and in between several sporadic attempts, arrived the Mahatama Gandhi & infused the nation with his spiritual ethos and revived morality from its stagnation. The spirit of capitalism took cue and realized that the rules of the game have to change. Sustainability,the new dimension of growth, began to take roots and CSR took birth as corporate sins redemption, with an attempt to assuage the corporate conscience. CSR took birth as corporate social responsibility, finally establishing the resurgence of morality back into business and also a reunion of the Siamese twins.

CSR is about the way companies meet their wider obligations in society. A responsible organization realizes that it's activities have an impact on the society in which they operate. CSR is a commitment to improve community well being through discretionary business practices and contributions of corporate resources (Kotler). "Corporate Social Responsibility is the continuing commitment by business to behave ethically and contribute to economic development while improving the quality of life of the workforce and their families as well as of the local community and society at large".(World Business Council for Sustainable Development). Carroll(1991) describes CSR as a multi layered concept that can be differentiated into four interrelated aspects – economic, legal, ethical and philanthropic responsibilities. Carroll presents these different responsibilities as consecutive layers within a pyramid, such that "true" social responsibility requires the meeting of all four levels consecutively. This is probably the most accepted and established model.

Philanthropic
Ethical
Legal
Economic

While the definitions of CSR may differ, there is an emerging consensus on some common principles :

1. CSR is a business imperative: Whether pursued as a voluntary corporate initiative or for legal compliance .
2. CSR is a link to sustainable development: Businesses feel that there is a need to integrate social, economic and environmental impact in their operations .
3. CSR is a way to manage business: CSR is not an optional addition to business, but it is about the way in which businesses are managed.

In 1971, the Committee for Economic Development issued a report throwing light on different dimensions of responsibilities to be fulfilled by the corporate. The responsibilities of corporations are described consisting of three concentric circles. (a) Inner Circle: Clear cut, basic responsibilities for the efficient execution of the economic function, products, jobs and economic growth. (b) Intermediate Circle: Responsibility to exercise this economic function with a sensitive awareness of changing social values and priorities. (c) Outer Circle: Newly emerging and still nebulous responsibilities that business should assume to become more broadly involved in actively improving the social environment.

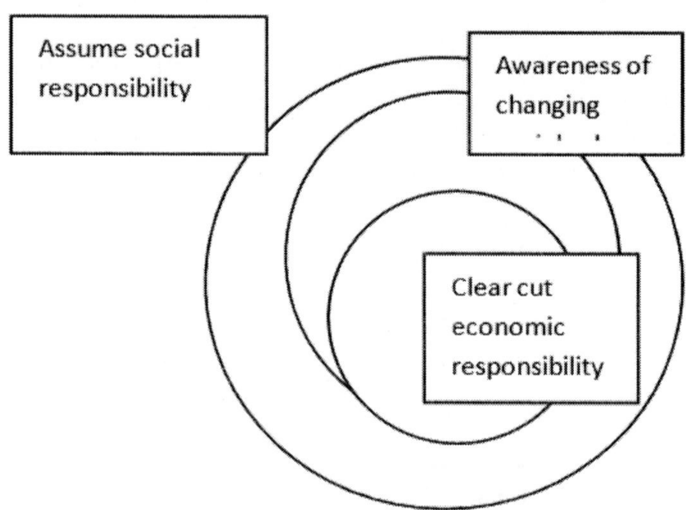

According to survey conducted by Tata Energy Research Institute(2001), evolution of CSR in India has followed a chronological evolution of 4 approaches:

Ethical or Trusteeship model – Businesses hold their entities as a trust in the interest of society.

Statist model – Driven by a mixed & socialist kind of economy.

Milton Friedman model – Businesses should earn profit & by paying taxes & other charitable actions are fulfilling social objectives.

Stakeholder model – Corporates should consider its different stakeholders, customers, employees, suppliers and perform according to 'Triple Bottom Line' approach.Triple Bottom Line(TBL)approach ie.Profit,People,Planet takes into account the social & environmental factors also besides the economic factors.

Ethical or Trusteeship model	Business is caretaker of wealth of society
Statist model	Driven by a mixed & socialist kind of economy
MiltonFriedman model	Purpose of business is generation of wealth
Stakeholder model	Business should follow triple bottom line approach

CSR works on the foundation principles of ethics, compliance, accountability, responsibility and transparency in business .It gives opportunities to business to enhance their reputation and sustainability. CSR is changing the way businesses develop strategy, engage and respond to customers, employees, communities etc. It addresses issues of climate change, carbon footprints, poverty, education, health, sanitation, malnutrition, women empowerment, energy conservation, community development etc. It is transforming organizations, their professional expertise and sentiments, required to tackle these issues. To have the desired impact, corporate social responsibility needs to be ingrained in a company's culture, be embedded in the corporate DNA. Traditionally, CSR has been a top management driven activity from policy conception to implementation stage. The other stakeholders have been conspicuously absent. Among the different stakeholders, the employees are the most strategic & their involvement and commitment is very essential to enliven CSR activities. Employees are always on the lookout for challenging, self actualizing roles and CSR would satisfy these needs. This can only be achieved by educating, engaging and empowering its employees. Human Resource professionals are very uniquely positioned to implement any CSR initiative. HR is the critical partner in making this happen.

Human Resource Management

HRM concerns with planning, organizing, directing & controlling of the procurement, development, compensation, integration, maintenance & separation of human resources to the end that individual, organizational and social objectives are accomplished(Flippo). Decenzo & Robbins state it to be concerning with the people dimension in an organisation. In short, HRM is an art of managing people at work so that they give their best to achieving organizational goals. This transactional and supportive function has given way to emergence of strategic human resource management(Inyang).Gupta(2010) notes that HR function has shifted focus from a narrow, reactive, maintenance oriented role to a broader canvas, integrating HR strategy with corporate strategy and empowering employees.

HRM-CSR Nexus

There is a definite nexus between HR and CSR, though the area is relatively unexplored. A survey by Tekin(2005), reveals that CSR promotes an organization attractively, to potential employees. During induction and orientation programs , training on CSR policies & initiatives, drives the nail deep down in the new recruits. CSR embedded in vision and mission statement of a business, becomes a mechanism for unlocking human capital (PR Leap) 2007.

Role of HR

1. Educate members on the value of CSR & provide action plans.
2. Communication & consultation
3. Positive psychological contract
4. Face & voice of employee
5. Help organization to develop responsible, sustainable & equitable employment practices .These are reflected through improved morale, increased engagement, higher productivity & better retention.
6. Help organisations achieve primary CSR standards of ethics, employment, community involvement that relate directly or indirectly with employees, customers & local community.
7. Help promote personal & professional employment, workforce diversity & empowerment.
8. Evolve HR practices considering employees as valued partners, fair labour practices, competitive wages, harassment free environment.
9. Work life balance
10. Encourage societal relations by implementing reward programs, charitable contributions, fund raising activities and community involvement practices.
11. Help in developing, monitoring & implementing triple bottom line activities.
12. Become employee champions(David Urwick)
13. Ensuring that company policies are effectively implemented
14. Helping to identify, measure and monitor application of corporate culture and values
15. Influencing management attitudes and skills through CSR competencies
16. Risk management

Walton & Weybridge (2006)

Thus HR needs to play a proactive, co-operative & collaborative role & logically so.

Strategic opportunities for HR

This is opportune time for HR to come to the forefront & demonstrate its competencies because companies,more than before need to show commitment to CSR.The credibility of CSR depends on ability to deliver & not rhetoric.HR is responsible for key systems and processes (recruitment, training, communications) underlying effective delivery & there is visible overlap between HR and CSR content and values. So HR is in a strategic position to readily align with CSR. It is apt time for HR to demonstrate boardroom and strategic impact & in doing so carve out new ,creative & significant image of its more relegated self. New profiles of Green Officer, CSR specialist,Corporate sustainability director etc can be created & in the process new avenues for professional growth charted out.

Organizations are large repositories of collective intelligence. HR needs to create intra organizational networks & channelize information & distil innovative ideas through facebook like platforms to foster cross cultural collaboration among employees such that they cut across hierarchies & eliminate core complexities that may exist in individuals. Seeding social innovation at the workplace, say Prithvi Shergill, Chief HR officer HCL technologies & NiharikaMohan,director(HR),Schneider Electric India.their companies have 'Meme' & has 'Spice' respectively for information collaboration & efficiency to help employees connect, learn and grow. This is helping in breaking shackles of traditional notions that act as barriers to free flow of thought. Companies are taking into account views expressed on such platforms to give shape to future policies. From the employees' perspective, such platforms are helping chart careers better. Career Connect , an application on Meme, enables employees to select the future roles they aspire for, seek referrals & then co-create their career development plan with their reporting managers or an expert of their choice. It acts as a mirror for employees to analyze their strengths & weaknesses & accordingly grasp opportunities. According to Tajinder Kumar, Head HR, Ratnakar Bank, the interaction among employees also helps the organization's customers get a brand aligned experience across geographies. All these policies help set the employment relationship right, which is a pre condition for effective relationship with external stakeholders(CIPD 2002).

Organizations are the foundation stones of future economies & the present generation owes it to the future generation to leave their share of resources intact & of value. To leave behind a legacy & as a reflection of responsible times, HR needs to co – create a CSR intergenerational fund similar to sovereign wealth funds(SWF) established by China(2007) & development funds by oil rich & other natural resources rich countries(IMF 2008). These saving funds intend to share wealth across generations by transferring non-renewable assets into a diversified portfolio of international financial instruments, to provide for future generations. A separate intergenerational fund would help in establishing transparency in pricing of our non-renewable resources etc. The Centre & States can have different such funds & these invested in safe instruments. These should be maintained separately, with complete transparency, responsibility & accountability to get safe returns for future generations. Similarly businesses can also set up a sustainability fund & work out the particulars. This is however open for corporate debate & HR needs to set the ball rolling.

Conclusion

There are definite organizational & academic implications arising from this exploratory study between CSR & HRM.

Organizational Implications

Businesses are realizing the strategic role of human resources in delivering sustainability. A survey by the World Business Forum reveals following benefits:

1. Cost savings
2. Risk reduction
3. Reputation enhancement
4. Innovation-innovative ideas can come from anywhere. If employees can link between issues that matter to them, their community, business & planet with a clear understanding of what this means in relevance to their own work, they would be motivated to address sustainability concerns.
5. Positive behavior changes in employees-Learning new skills, pursuing new goals
6. Attraction & retention of talent
7. Motivation & productivity-Employees are motivated when a business has a purpose. When they feel they are valued , are willing to go the extra mile,
8. Employer branding

(Adapted from Selfridges Performance Scorecard)

For academics

This is a wake up call for academicians to extend research to investigate the relatively unexplored nexus between CSR & HR

& clearly delineate role of HR professional in CSR activities. There is urgent need to undertake more empirical research & theoretical studies in this area & improve further understanding & knowledge in this global corporate phenomenon , which is not a fad but mainstream now. The findings would definitely help in proper embedding of CSR in the corporate DNA.

References

1. 'Year of governance reform in China' by Siddharth Peter de Souza The Tribune, pg 13, 26 Feb'2014
2. 'Being human' by Nonika Singh The SundayTribune Spectrum, pg 2,23 Feb'2014
3. 'Why HR needs CSR'-sneak peek preview by Elaine Cohen www.csrforhr.com
4. 'Why HR needs to take a leadership role in CSR http://www.forbes.com/sites/karenhigginbottom/2014/01/06/
5. 'Ethical Considerations In Human Resource Management' by Sandeep K. Bansal , CA(Dr.)Sanjeev K. Bansal and Rama Bansal Business Ethics And Corporate Governance, Kalyani Publishers.
6. Strategic Human Resource Management By Dr.S.S Khanka Human Resource Management (Text and Cases), S.Chand Publications
7. Leadership, Values and Corporate Social Responsibility By P.Jyothi , D.N. Venkatesh Human Resource Management, Oxford Publications
8. 'New dimensions of HR' by Prithvi Shergill-Guest column,The Tribune, Feb 26,2014
9. 'Different strokes for different folks' by Jayesh Pandey,Guest column,The Strategist-Business Standard,Monday Feb 17,2014
10. The Indian Economy-Rising to global challenges by Kaushik Basu Journal of Social and Economic Development,Vol.15 Special issue,2013
11. Nadkarni MV, Moral Responsibilities of Business , 2012 ,Journal of Social and Economic Development.
12. Ramachandran Venkataraman , The Dharma of business : Mahatma Gandhi
13. Inyang . Benjamin J,Awa Hart O, Enuoh Rebecca O. ,CSR-HRM Nexus : Defining the Role Engagement of the Human

Resources Professionals , The Special Issue on Contemporary Issues in Business and Economics , Centre for Promoting Ideas , USA.

14. Singh Charan , Pricing Natural Resources , The Tribune, Opinion , Jalandhar|Wednesday|5 March, 2014
15. Singh Namrata , Cos set up FB-like forums to tap ideas, the Times of India , TrendInc , Friday | 6 March ,2014
16. Corporate Social Responsibility – Towards a Sustainable Future , A White Paper , KPMG IN INDIA
17. Corporate Social Responsibility in India , Global CSR Summit 2013 An Agenda for Inclusive Growth , PHD Chamber.
18. The role of human resource management in corporate social responsibility , issue brief and roadmap , report for Industry Canada , Prepared By: Coro Strandberg Principal, Strandberg Consulting
19. Brown Duncan.Corporate social responsibility & HR's role: From Cindrella to Business impact,January 2006,CIPD Walton and Weybridge Branch